Defining Moments

Defining Moments

Stories of Character, Courage, and Leadership

Gordon Zacks

BEAUFORT BOOKS · NEW YORK

Library of Congress Cataloging-in-Publication Data is available.

ISBN-10: 0-8253-0541-1
ISBN-13: 978-0-8253-0541-2

Published in the United States by Beaufort Books, New York
www.beaufortbooks.com
Distributed by Midpoint Trade Books
www.midpointtradebooks.com

10 9 8 7 6 5 4 3 2

Printed in the United States of America

Dedicated to my late father, Aaron Zacks, and my mother, Florence Zacks Melton, who set the standards in my life for character, courage, and leadership. To my wife, Carol, and our children, Cathy and Kim, who permitted me to live the life that was the journey to this book. And to Edward and Elissa, our grandchildren, who face the challenge of making the future better than the past.

"If I am not for myself, then who will be for me? And, if I am only for myself, then what am I? And if not now, when? If not me, who?"
—Hillel the Elder, *Pirkei Avot* (Ethics of the Fathers)

Natan Sharansky's Prison Prayer

Blessed are You, Adonai, King of the Universe. Grant me the good fortune to live with my wife, my beloved Avital . . . in the Land of Israel. Grant my parents, my wife, and my whole family the strength to endure all hardships until we meet. Grant me the strength, the power, the intelligence, the good fortune, and the patience to leave this jail and to reach the land of Israel in an honest and worthy way.

CONTENTS

Preface

IN OCTOBER 1943, the Nazi SS occupying Denmark planned to deport the 8,000 Danish Jews to the death factories of East Europe. Non-Jewish Danes of every background and social class in the Resistance mobilized to prevent the deportation. Over a span of three weeks, about 7,500 Jews were smuggled to the Danish coast and evacuated to Sweden under the tarpaulins of small fishing boats. More than forty years later, I asked one of these courageous fishermen, "What made you do it? What made you risk your life to save Jews?" He scratched his head and said, "We just did what *anyone* would do." If only that were true! "Indifference to Evil is evil," as Elie Wiesel has so articulately stated. These heroes went a step further. They seized the moment and showed that resistance to Evil is good.

In *Defining Moments,* my goal has been to recount the experiences of heroic people such as these—people whom I have been privileged to know, work with, and learn from. It's my hope that these accounts will inspire, encourage, and guide leaders and aspiring leaders to be all that you can become, to have the courage to follow your passion, live your purpose, and make the world a better place. In philosophy and convictions, the people profiled in this book represent a wide range of beliefs. Yet, all of them share at least three traits: character, courage, and leadership. All of them have led purposeful lives. All of them have made the world a better place. But the pathways they followed are varied, because the pathways to the purposeful life are many.

Defining Moments is intended to be about others; not about me. These people helped inspire me and shaped my life, my values, my goals and my path. It is my hope that they will inspire you as well. They all represent the power of one person to make a difference—to make the world a better place. I am neither a historian nor a biographer. My goal is to capture the essence of the character and moral courage that gave these people the power to do the right thing at the right time in defining moments of their lives.

My own life has been charmed. Born free, Jewish, and healthy to loving and nurturing parents in the United States in 1933—the year Hitler came to power. I was old enough to become aware of the Holocaust as it was slowly revealed... and too young to do anything about it. The world I entered was indifferent, if not hostile to Jews. The Jews were dangerously unaware of the threats around them, and they were ineffectively organized to respond to those threats. Some six million men, women and children were slaughtered for the crime of being born with one-eighth or more Jewish blood. This atrocity was perpetrated by the highly "civilized," highly "cultured," highly "educated" country of Germany. I came to learn that morality has nothing to do with education, culture or civility. The Holocaust happened in my lifetime—this wasn't Christians being fed to the lions in ancient Rome. This occurred in the modern twentieth century, and there was hardly a blip on the conscience of the world.

The Holocaust and the indifference of the world to it helped shape my life. It is appalling that these events happened. But, they nonetheless helped crystallize what I was going to do with my life. By the age of fifteen, I knew that I would not move to Israel. It was clear to me that I would never be president of the United States. But, I was an organizer blessed with leadership skills and considerable self-confidence. At the age of fifteen, in 1948, when the state of Israel was born, I organized and ran a fund-raising drive for the United Jewish Appeal (UJA) at my high school. What else did I do? When Israel was born, I decided to write down what I hoped would be the centerpiece of my obituary:

> Gordon Zacks played a small role in a great cause. He partici-
> pated in the rebirth of the land and the redemption of the people
> of Israel.

The rebirth of the State of Israel was the defining moment of my life, and this statement documented what I intended to do about it. It was the declaration of a proud Jew. This crystallized my passion, defined my purpose, and has informed my life-choice decisions. Nearly sixty years later, I remain dedicated to making that obituary a reality.

Perhaps you recall the film version of Kazantzakis's novel *Zorba the Greek*. In it Zorba maintains that wise men and grocers can't be free because they weigh everything. It's the cord they can't cut, and it robs them of their freedom. The key to a purposeful life, I maintain, is to find your heart... and to have the courage to let it drive your life when those moments arise where you can make a difference.

In 1967 I went to Auschwitz. Not to study—I knew what had happened there—but to say Kaddish, and to simply be a living testament to the fact that although six million Jews died, Jews still live. The Holocaust has haunted me all my life. Israel was built out of the ashes of those six million. The conscience of the world was pricked and said let there be an Israel, and there was an Israel.

What a blossoming I have been blessed to witness and be a small part of in those sixty years since the seed of the state was planted! When founding father David Ben-Gurion died in 1973, Israel's land was hardly reclaimed. Its economy was centered on subsistence agriculture. And, it was fighting continuous wars to defend the survival of the state and its very existence. Today Israel has built a remarkable democratic, civil society. It is a democracy with a thriving cultural life, universal free education, and affordable health care for all of its citizens. Its economy is on the leading edge—a pioneer in nano- and biotechnology and advanced agricultural research. From nothingness to the very cutting edge of today's world. Israel did all this while absorbing three million immigrants speaking sixty different languages and coming from a hundred different countries. And, the nation did it while fighting six wars.

For the first eighteen years of my life, our family was not wealthy, but we were a very rich family: lots of love, and lots of deep, honest values that shape behavior. Starting my college education at Dartmouth, I completed it at Ohio State after I met Carol Sue, my wife of fifty years. In time, I learned the family business. When my father passed away suddenly in 1965, I took over the reins of the company. While the business grew steadily, I maintained my commitment to Israel and to the Jewish people.

My first years of involvement in Jewish causes were as a fundraiser. My philosophy? I wasn't asking my prospects to give money. Rather, I was giving *them* the opportunity to be part of something greater than themselves, the rebirth of the land and the redemption of the people of Israel.

My father Aaron's Uncle Morris was a great inspiration to me. He single-handedly brought his brothers and sisters—including my grandfather—out of Czarist Russia at the beginning of the twentieth century. One by one, Morris scraped together the money to pay for their passage. They came to America to seek a better life. For almost all of us in America, there is an "Uncle Morris" who seized the defining moment to rescue others. I would often ask both fund-raisers and prospects to reflect on who the Uncle Morris was in their personal history. That person or persons created an obligation to be paid back for the good fortune they brought us. As someone once told me, you can't pay back. You can only pay forward, and you do that by making the world a better place for someone else.

Fund-raising sharpened many skills for me. Commitment was not the least of them. One January, as a young leader, I remember accompanying Bill Rosenwald—son of Sears, Roebuck founder Julius Rosenwald and one of three co-founders of the United Jewish Appeal—on a solicitation in Miami Beach. Bill, who was about seventy five at the time, was mentoring me on this call. He flew in from Chicago, and I arrived from Columbus. Bill was a mild-mannered and humble person who shunned the spotlight. His commitment to Israel and Jewish causes was absolute and breathtakingly deep. Bill also, coincidentally, suffered from an illness that made him feel chronically cold, no matter what the climate or how warmly he was dressed. Bill and I found the prospect (whom I'll call "X") in his swimming trunks poolside at the Fontainebleau Hotel. Bill wore a heavy overcoat, a wool scarf, and a fedora hat. It was ninety-five degrees, and the entire crowd stared at us with total bewilderment.

Bill delivered his request in a soft-spoken voice asking for a $250,000 gift from a man who had given $10,000 the prior year. X was unmoved. Bill explained the reasons the money was needed. Still no answer. But it was plain to see that X wanted nothing more than to disappear. Well, extracting himself from the scene is exactly what he tried to do. Slowly but resolutely, he got up and walked toward the sand. Bill followed him, never missing a beat in his appeal. I was mystified—frozen in my tracks poolside. X moved toward the shoreline. So did Bill. Then X started *walking into the water*. So did the fully dressed Bill Rosenwald! With a steady rhythm, X was now wading out into the waves one step after another. In just a couple of minutes, both he and Bill were waist high, and the waves were splashing on top of Bill's fedora. Finally X turned to Bill and shouted: "All right, you win! I give up! I'll give the $250,000." That's commitment!

The United Jewish Appeal was a tremendous learning opportunity for me. It mentored me in so many skills. In particular, it taught me how to both raise money and get people involved for Israel's sake. In 1961, I was privileged to be involved as a founding member of the Young Leadership Cabinet for the UJA. Then I became a local chairman of that organization and later its national chairman. In those roles, I met key Jewish activists throughout the United States and the world. My network of fund-raising prospects included Jewish leaders in every profession and walk of life. These were demanding, discerning contributors, and I soon learned that these donors expected me to give them clear and credible answers as to how their money would be used.

During this time, I also met the leaders of the Israeli power structure and many of the most significant players in U.S. politics on both sides of the aisle. I was given scores of opportunities to acquire knowledge about Israel, the Middle East, and Israeli-American relations. During that time, I visited nearly a hundred countries, and I had the chance to learn about Jewish life in lands as disparate as China and Morocco. The experience taught me a great deal about how and where Jews live all over the world. It also taught me what their problems and aspirations were.

Then came another milestone. On Yom Kippur, Saturday, October 6, 1973, Israel was suddenly attacked—without the slightest provocation. The Soviet-supplied forces of Egypt, Syria, and Jordan swept down on an unsuspecting Israel and nearly annihilated the Zionist state. Without Richard Nixon's decision to resupply, the twenty-five-year-old refuge and homeland of modern Israel might have been destroyed. As a consequence, I studied the new reality of Israel's security needs. My evaluation: **You can't fly a dollar bill.** For Israel to survive, she needed the support of the U.S. for military equipment, financial aid, and political backing. That realization caused me to shift my focus from fund-raising to political activism.

For five years, between 1973 and 1978, I divided my volunteer time between fund-raising for the United Jewish Appeal and political activities in Washington. One of my proudest accomplishments was the groundwork I had the privilege to lay on behalf of the American Israel Public Affairs Committee (AIPAC). From 1973 to 1978, I worked in parallel with UJA and AIPAC. I got involved in Republican Party politics and advocacy—doing my best to engage the key leaders of national Jewish organizations in political activism. After my first trip to Egypt in 1976, I had the chance to brief then-Prime Minister Yitzhak Rabin and later his successor Menachem Begin. The latter seemed to value some information and impressions I shared with him. This background may have helped Prime Minister Begin as he weighed his options and charted a course that ultimately led to the Camp David Accords between Israel and Egypt.

In 1977, I was named general chairman designate for the United Jewish Appeal. Then fate intervened—in a way that it is prone to do in all of our lives—and compelled me to resign from that post in May 1978. My resignation was in protest to an effort by the UJA board of directors to whitewash mismanagement of the organization by its then-professional leadership. That mismanagement had just been discovered, but it was serious and embarrassing. Why did it happen? The UJA's board of directors had failed to provide adequate oversight. Over the next five years, these issues were ultimately addressed and corrected. An unintended consequence of my resignation was to free me to get more deeply involved in political activism.

It was increasingly apparent that the key zone of influence on Israel's behalf was steadily shifting to the political sphere. Where precisely would I channel my energies? I wasn't yet sure. In September 1978, came a phone call out of the blue asking if I'd be interested in helping to raise funds for George Herbert Walker Bush in his bid for the Republican presidential nomination in 1980. I didn't even know him.

When we met, I took an instant liking to George Bush. One-on-one, he is perhaps the most talented interpersonal communicator I have ever met. His moral compass permeates every viewpoint he takes and each decision he makes. Back in 1978, Bush was former everything— congressman, special envoy to China, U.S. ambassador to the U.N., Republican national committee chairman, and director of the C.I.A. In almost every respect, his credentials were stellar. But, in one crucial area, his knowledge and perspective fell short—Israel and the Middle East. Honest about this deficiency and eager to learn, he asked me to help educate him as a precondition for my becoming a member of his campaign. He was utterly absorbed by the briefings I arranged for him to receive, became an ardent and knowledgeable advocate of Israel, and showed great insight in his Middle East position paper developed for the campaign.

No longer the general chairman designate of the National UJA, I was free to pursue the political agenda without constraint. Then Ronald Reagan won the presidential nomination, and it appeared Bush was out. In a surprise move, Reagan picked George Bush as his running mate. In another defining moment in my life, I was suddenly presented with a great opportunity. During the Reagan administration, I turned down an ambassadorship, and during the Bush presidency, I declined a cabinet post. Neither position would have been germane to my central agenda. Accepting either offer would have made me a part of the administration and denied me the opportunity to be an informal advisor on policy matters affecting the Jewish agenda in a way that a friend and informal advisor can be. Several critical issues were on the table at the time, including Soviet Jewry and the Arab-Israeli and Arab-Palestinian peace processes. As a result of my remaining outside of government, I had the privilege of meeting regularly and privately first with Vice President and then President Bush over a period of twelve years. This gave me the chance to be involved with U.S.-Israeli relations at the highest level and during a period of intense and challenging geopolitical change.

These were my defining moments in experiencing the rebirth of Israel, in raising funds, and then in pursuing political action. Each involvement serendipitously, and unexpectedly, paved the way for the next step and helped reshape my purpose. Along this path, I have had the great good fortune to be guided by remarkable mentors like Bill Rosenwald, Herb Friedman, and Max Fisher. If I can take credit for any of my good fortune, it's that I have been thoughtful in choosing my mentors. From adolescence forward, finding mentors isn't a question of luck. Most people believe mentors choose you. I disagree. Choosing a mentor is a conscious choice and a personal responsibility that I urge everyone to exercise.

*   *   *

A note to those readers who are women, and I hope that there are many: The core experiences in this book happened in a different time. While most of the principles are timeless, one fortunate change has been underway and is destined to intensify: Growing, but not yet perfect equality for women. As the father of two talented and involved daughters, I am delighted to see the trend. Golda Meir was an early and exemplary role model for women of all faiths and cultures. But, even among Jewish feminists, the role of an at-home mother is a respected pathway. I have shunned creating a synthetic demographic balance in this book's profiles by writing about people I haven't known personally. That said, I think the principles and lessons outlined in *Defining Moments* are every bit as relevant for women as for men.

"If not now, when? If not me, who?" Hillel urges. When defining moments in life arise, one may well ask: Will I have the character to know and the courage to act? To display moral leadership at a crucial moment—as with the Danish fishermen—or over two presidential terms—as with Ronald Reagan—one must be prepared. The moral compass must be set in advance. One has to have the knowledge and the wisdom to *know* what to do . . . and the courage to *do* it. All the people profiled in this book inspired me, some mentored me, and all touched me. They helped make me more perceptive about what living a purposeful life really means. I hope their stories will have the same effect on you. My time for doing is over, my time for teaching is now. I need and want a new generation of doers to be more effective than my generation of doers. And this book is intended to help make that happen.

Everyone has defining moments—moments of opportunity to make the world a better place. The moments arise. The question is having the character and the courage to act upon them. If you are Jewish, you believe that if you have saved one life, it is as if you have saved the whole world. What is fulfillment in life all about? It's not about having fame, titles, celebrity, power, or wealth. It's about participating in something that's greater than you . . . in seizing the moment to serve that greater purpose. That's where it's at. How are character and courage translated into leadership at defining moments? I have learned from some amazing people how *they* got there. For decades, I have been sharing these stories with others. Let me share some of them with you.

FAMILY

It sometimes seems that intense desire creates not only its own opportunities, but its own talents.

—Eric Hoffer

The Romanian Widow

Before the Holocaust, there were about 700,000 Jews in Romania. Some were able to escape to Palestine by boat, but more than 300,000 were killed by the Nazis. By the end of World War II, there were 428,000 Jews in Romania. After the war, the freedom to emigrate was supported by the monarchy. A clamp-down resulted when the monarchy was abolished at the end of 1947, and the Communists staged their coup, which was directed and abetted by the Soviets. The 1950s were largely years of Romanian submission to Moscow. Throughout those years, emigration flowed and then stopped in intermittent waves, opening and closing abruptly.

In the early 1960s, Romania broke somewhat free of its Soviet harness and a new outflow began. Plain and simple, when the government of Romania needed cash, it "sold" Jews by collecting an "education tax" from international Jewish organizations to ransom their freedom. By 1961, Romania's Jewish population had dwindled to about 250,000. The Communist fascist regime in Bucharest was greedy for hard cash and eager to accept ransom. Once again, the window opened for Romanian Jews to leave. How long would it remain open? No one knew. The world Jewish community was determined to act and had started the process of buying Jews' freedom out of Romania once again.

Let me tell you about a defining moment along the Danube River in 1961. In that year, Rabbi Herb Friedman took a group of young American Jews to Israel. It was the first missionary trip of what was to become the Young Leadership Cabinet of the United Jewish Appeal. Our initial stop was Vienna, a city that had been one of the major transport hubs of Jews to the death camps. The city had been reunified in 1955, and at this time Austria was made a neutral country. Vienna had become a crossroads for contact between the East and the West. On this summer evening in 1961, we young Americans were at the railroad station in Vienna—a station with a horrific past—waiting for a trainload of Romanian Jews from Bucharest.

It was 11 P.M. when the train arrived. The occupants had been briefed en route and knew that members of our group would meet them in Vienna. By sheer happenstance, a woman with two heavy satchels got off the train right in front of me. She was slender and olive-complexioned, in her late thirties, and wearing a long dress with her hair wrapped in a rose-colored scarf. She suddenly dropped the satchels, grabbed my hands, and kissed them again and again. With her were three young children, between the ages of six and twelve. Each of them carried a piece of the family's humble luggage. The kids were scared and trembling despite the warm summer night. One could see easily that the family had packed every possession they could for this journey. Obviously, the woman had been crying. She had been briefed that we represented the American Jewish Joint Distribution Committee, which provides on-site relief for Jews throughout the world. Among the immigrants, we were known as "The Joint." Over and over again, she said, "Thank you, Joint!" Then she started to cry again, and told me her story in Yiddish.

The day before, the family had received a visa and were told they had twenty-four hours to leave Romania. The papers were valid *only* if every member of the family left together. The husband had tuberculosis, and doctors warned him against attempting the journey. Making it could cost him his life. Should the couple hope and wait for another visa opportunity later? Or, should they gamble on the health risk and leave now? The choice was agonizing. The man and his wife decided they would risk his life and leave while they had the chance so their children could be raised in freedom.

Once they were on the train, they had to pass through two border checkpoints to reach Vienna. Before they reached the first checkpoint, the husband died. The widow and her three children carried on imaginary conversations with their dead loved one to deceive the border guards ... not once, but *twice*. The last encounter happened only twenty brief minutes before the train's arrival in Vienna. As the woman—I will never know her name—cried, she told me, "Though my husband will not live in Israel, at least he will be buried in Israel ... and he died knowing that our children will be free. Thank you, thank you, Joint!"

Two things I learned from the Romanian Widow are:

Seize the moment!

This particular story is about family—the love of family and the care for its future. What went into this defining moment? The risk this couple underwent in sacrificing any certainty about their personal future for the sake of their children would be unthinkable for many of us. When presented with the ultimate choice, the Romanian father acted courageously. His action said he loved his children more than he loved life itself. Once the circumstances changed and the man died, the family did not let their grief get the better of them. Seizing the moment not only takes courage, but often presence of mind. The widow exhibited tremendous courage and absolute dedication to safeguard her family's escape to Israel. She refused to succumb to the grief that could have easily overwhelmed her. The children followed the mother's bold leadership example and exercised remarkable self-discipline. With tremendous courage, the family focused on the future for which the father had given his life.

Life is about the courage to seize defining moments.

It is about reaching out and touching someone and making some *one* life better. One person at a time. It's not enough to live life in the mind, it has to be lived in the heart. Lived with tears. Lived with joy. Lived with risk. Above all, lived with passion.

The parents had already been through the Holocaust during which 270,000 of Romania's 730,000 Jews had been murdered. They had been through hell twice, and were now living under the totalitarian oppression of the Soviet-backed regime in Romania. The couple's lives were totally dedicated to the dream of finding a way for their children to live in freedom, to realizing an age-old dream for a new generation. When the defining moment to seize the chance for freedom for their children came, they took it, even though it cost the father his life.

Avital Sharansky

On my first visit to the former Soviet Union in 1974, I met the 25-year-old Natan Sharansky in a sixth floor apartment on Moscow's Gorky Street. I was in the Soviet Union as a member of the Young Presidents' Organization (YPO). The Soviets had invited our YPO group as part of a charm offensive to try to overturn the Jackson-Vanik Amendment. This legislation linked repressive governmental campaigns against human rights within the Soviet Union to economic sanctions from the United States. Secretly, I also used my visit to four Soviet cities to meet with twenty-four Soviet refuseniks—Soviet Jews who were barred in their effort to emigrate to Israel. Natan was under surveillance by the KGB. He had been the press spokesman for Andrei Sakharov, the physicist who helped invent the Soviet H-bomb. Sakharov had abandoned the bomb and turned peace- and civil-rights activist. That put Natan squarely in the center of controversy in this repressive society.

On July 4, 1974, Natan married a young woman named Avital, and she left for Israel immediately. As I will explain, the Soviets gave the Sharanskys a "wedding present" of a visa to Israel but only for Avital and only if she exercised it in twenty-four hours. Suddenly, the Sharanskys were faced with a defining moment of choice.

At my first meeting with Natan in Moscow in 1974, he asked me to visit Avital on my next trip to Israel. "Tell her

I love her, and that I am well," he said. When I returned to the States, I telephoned Avital in Israel. At the time, she did not speak English. On my next trip to Jerusalem, I met her in person and communicated with her through an English-speaking friend of hers. In a matter of months after my visit to the Soviet Union, the KGB's harassment of Natan intensified.

In 1976, Avital was in Israel, and Natan was awaiting trial in the Soviet Union. On the second anniversary of their marriage on July 4, 1976, America celebrated its two hundredth birthday. On that same date, Israel rescued hostages from a hijacked Air France jetliner in Entebbe, Uganda. Avital and Natan felt that the liberation of the hostages was a good anniversary omen for them: If the hostages could be free to come to Israel, why wouldn't Natan be free to do so too?

Natan's pretrial persecution continued for three years until 1977, when he was unjustly charged and convicted of being a C.I.A. spy. On my first meeting with Avital in Israel, she had said to me through an interpreter, "I want to make a Jewish home with my husband."

That statement summed up what had become her sole purpose in life. Avital lived on that single hope and goal. She had no money. She had no family in Israel. One of the yeshivah in Jerusalem more or less adopted her, gave her a Jewish education, helped her to learn how to campaign for her cause, provided her with funds to travel, and made sure someone accompanied her. Her English improved, though it was still limited, but her travel was perpetual.

Not long after the Reagan-Bush ticket was elected in November 1980, Avital was in touch with me. Natan had been imprisoned for three years. She wanted to meet the political leadership in the U.S. In March 1981, I became her point person in Washington. Vice President Bush arranged for her to meet Secretary of State Alexander Haig. She met Mike Armacost, who was Undersecretary of Defense, and Lawrence Eagleburger, who was Undersecretary of State. In Congress, she met Senators Howard Baker, Rudy Boschwitz, Al D'Amato, and Bob Packwood—to name a few—and Congressman Jack Kemp. In the press, I introduced her to broadcast journalist Marvin Kalb and columnist George Will. Doorstep by doorstep, she became a signature figure for her husband and for the cause of Soviet Jewry.

I introduced George and Barbara Bush to Avital on their first trip to Israel on July 4, 1979, coincidentally, the Sharanskys' fifth wedding anniversary. The trip was in preparation for Bush's run for the 1980 Republican presidential nomination. In Jerusalem, Avital told her story as only she could. She concluded it with the words, "I . . . want . . . my . . . husband . . . back." Both George and Barbara had tears well up in their eyes. On that day in 1979, the Sharanskys celebrated their anniversary apart . . . once more. Avital in Jerusalem; Natan in Vladimir Prison in the Gulag.

The union of Avital and Natan is an unforgettable story of love and freedom . . . of defining moments and incredible courage, played against the backdrop of East versus West, good versus Evil, democracy versus tyranny. Here is how one woman seized the moment . . . and, ended up helping to change the course of human history.

The most important door to open was President Ronald Reagan's. I had no direct access to Reagan. Rather than approaching him through the vice president, I believed it would be best to build a base of support through Reagan's own staff. My closest friend among the president's aides was National Security Advisor Richard V. Allen. Avital and I visited with Dick, and he was deeply moved when he heard her story. At that session, I asked him if he could arrange for a meeting between Avital and the president. He said we should talk about it at a second meeting.

When I called Dick to arrange the second meeting, he said, "Gordy, stop by at 10 A.M. tomorrow and I may have a surprise for you." Security was particularly tight when Avital and I entered the White House. It was just three months after the attempted assassination of the president.

Dick Allen made good on his surprise. We *didn't* meet with Dick. Instead, shortly after ten, Dick ushered us into the Oval Office. It was May 28, 1981. Both the president and the vice president were there.

All eyes were riveted on Avital—a tall woman, dressed simply and modestly as she always is . . . not dressed in a way one would expect for a White House visit. Quiet descended on the office from the time Avital started telling her story. President Reagan and Vice President Bush absorbed what she had to say. They were totally engaged by her sincere, unpretentious appearance and words. Her manner made her message even stronger. She reached from her soul to connect with our souls—especially the president's. The depth of her love for her husband inspired awe and respect. She began:

Natan and I met outside of a synagogue in Moscow in the fall of 1973. We were in a class learning Hebrew together. Here in the U.S., you would call such a place a Jewish community center. My brother Mischa had just been arrested. He was part of a demonstration of Soviet Jews wanting to emigrate. Natan was one of the "regulars" rounded up by the KGB. I thought Natan could give me and our family helpful advice on what to expect. Natan and I fell in love . . . on the spot, you might say.

When we got married, it was with thirty-six-hours notice. We could only marry during one of those rare times between Natan's prison interrogations. I was just a twenty-three-year-old student. We ran around Moscow buying wedding bands. As best we could, we tried to follow the customs of our faith. I gave Natan a little copy of *The Book of Psalms* in Hebrew.

We got married on the fourth of July—American Independence Day. The next day, I left the Soviet Union...forever... without Natan.

Avital paused. The silence in the room was palpable. Avital was laying claim to her husband. To his liberation. This knock at the gate could not go unanswered. Not with a woman of such persistence and forthright integrity doing the knocking. The president leaned forward in his chair and nodded for Avital to continue.

On the day we were married, I got a visa to go to Israel. It was good for only twenty-four hours. It was issued in my name only. It said I had to leave the next day or the visa was invalid. Natan and I didn't know what to do. Should we wait and hope that we might get a joint visa later? Or, should I go and pray that Natan could join me some day? It was awful. Finally, we decided that I should leave. We hoped to be together again. It's seven years later. We are still apart.

Do I miss him? Of course, I miss him! But, I am worried sick about his health. He has been in prison for four years. Siberian work camps. Punishment cell. Solitary confinement. To stay sane, he reads *The Book of Psalms* I gave him or he plays chess games in his head.

His mother and his brother, Lenya, can visit him once a year. If they mention my name, the guard forces them to change the subject. He gets no care from a doctor. He has angina. The pain doesn't stop. I am so afraid he will die. He has rubbed a hole through his shirt at the spot where he tries to massage his heart.

I...want...my...husband...back.

She repeated these words with measured determination. Not loudly. But with invincible force. Not selfishly, but with compelling self-assurance. Drummed out with a cadence, as if each word were punctuated by a mailed fist pounding on a massive door. Relentless. Self-less. It was not just a plea for her husband. Avital also pleaded for intervention with the Soviets so that all Jews who wanted to leave the Soviet Union would be free to do so. "I . . . want . . . my . . . husband . . . back." Such a strong woman. Such a powerful declaration. Yet, as I heard it at the meeting, it could have been said a million times and more in Israel. "We . . . want . . . our . . . people . . . back." **Let our people go!** Avital's very personal struggle to free her husband was also a rallying cry for the 2.6 million Soviet Jews imprisoned to a life behind the Iron Curtain.

When the meeting began in the Oval Office on this day in May 1981, the president seemed tired. This was the four-month anniversary of his taking the oath of office. The tanned, glowing aura with which the seventy-year-old president dazzled Washington at his inauguration has waned. Ronald Reagan—the woodchopper and skilled horseman—had been out of the saddle for weeks because of the injuries from the assassination attempt. As Avital continued, the president was all ears for Avital's story. This was *his* kind of story. He had tears in his eyes. Sitting at the edge of his chair, he reached over for her hand. She extended it to him. This should not be overlooked. An Orthodox Jewish woman doesn't give her hand to any man but her husband. This was a spontaneous act of uncommon trust.

"Avital," the president told her, still grasping her hand, "I promise you that no meeting will take place between the Soviet Union and the United States on any topic, any place in the world in which the subjects of (1) the plight of Soviet Jewry generally, and (2) the specific issue of your husband's release will not be on the agenda. I will not rest until your husband is free."

In an instant, Natan had become a leading national priority for U.S. diplomacy. The president's pledge was not arrived at after consulting his staff. HE CONSULTED HIS GUT! His statement stunned and excited me, as much as it probably shocked most of the others in the Oval Office.

What happened at the White House on this day was not a political exchange. THIS WAS A MORAL ENCOUNTER: Good and Evil were being weighed in this room. And, a verdict was being called for.

Ronald Reagan kept his promise. Like saying grace before a meal, Soviet Jewry and Sharansky became the invocation. No matter if the session was about strategic arms limitations talks, grain sales, or Soviet submarines lost in the Baltic, Soviet Jewry and Sharansky were the preamble. Getting Natan out of the Gulag was now serious business and a policy priority for the United States.

In July 1983, Avital and I went to see my friend Max Kampelman. Max was then back in Washington for several days briefing and getting instructions in his assignment as the Ambassador to the Madrid Conference on Security and Cooperation in Europe. Max was sure he had all but negotiated the release of Natan with the Soviet delegate to this conference. Only one little catch. It required that Natan write a letter essentially saying:

> Dear President of the Soviet Presidium,
>   Because of reasons of health, I request an early commutation of my sentence.
>
> *Natan Sharansky*

Avital looked at the letter. She sighed deeply and said, "Natan will never sign it."

"Why?" Max asked.

"This letter would say Natan is guilty. He would never admit that. He's a victim. They're keeping him in prison illegally. He believes that. I believe that. He's not the guilty one," she answered.

"What if we called it a commuted sentence?" Max suggested.

Avital shook her head.

"Would *any* language work?" Max pressed on.

"Maybe something that said, 'I demand immediate release because I am very ill'" Avital offered as an option.

Indeed Natan refused to sign *any* letter.

Then came the Reagan/Gorbachev Summit in Geneva in November

1985, Avital planned to go to Geneva to demonstrate in front of the château where the Summit was to take place. Days before the Summit was to begin, she got a call from the U.S. State Department with essentially this message:

> We have reason to believe that your husband is going to be released soon. The Reagan/Gorbachev meeting is an important Summit for both the Americans and the Soviets. We are concerned that the consequences of your demonstrating in Geneva will be counterproductive. It will embarrass Gorbachev and could sour our negotiations. This may cause the Soviets to change their mind about Natan's release. We advise you not to go to Geneva.

Avital called me in Columbus from Jerusalem to inform me of the counsel she had received from the State Department and to ask for my advice. "Avital," I said, "the only reason Natan has a chance of getting out is because of all the noise you have made. Go to Geneva and make more noise, and *keep* making noise until he's out. Don't let your leverage disappear." She went to Geneva... and she made noise!

Reagan and Gorbachev met. Reagan gave Gorbachev (who had only been on the job eight months) the straight scoop about Avital. In his book *Fear No Evil,* Natan recounts Reagan's message:

> "You can say again and again that Sharansky's a spy, but the world believes this lady, and you won't be able to change your image until you let him go." I'd like to think that, the next time they meet, Western leaders will tell their Soviet counterparts, "You can say anything you want, but until you release all the Jews who want to emigrate, and all your political prisoners, you won't be able to change your image in the West."

It worked! Natan was released on February 11, 1986. Avital and Natan were reunited. The couple had two daughters, bringing to the world the family Avital so fervently wanted. There is much more to say about Natan, and I do so later in this book.

On several occasions before her visit with Ronald Reagan, Avital called on French president François Mitterrand. President Mitterrand later confessed to Natan that he wished he had done something to help Avital, but he never thought she would succeed. Mitterrand concluded that Avital's convictions were sound, and he had to admit he didn't size up the situation as perceptively as she did.

After Natan's release, an amazing thing happened to Avital. She vanished as a public person! Here was a woman who appeared on prime-time TV programs like Ted Koppel's *Nightline* and the *Today* show. Here was a woman who would be asked questions about Strategic Arms Limitation or détente and would refuse to be deflected. She would masterfully navigate back to her sound bite mantra of "I... want...my...husband...back." Once Natan was free, the *public* Avital evaporated. She took up her duties of being a Jewish wife and mother. Avital keeps a wonderful Kosher home in Jerusalem in which the children have been raised. She supports Natan's work and travel, but he must be home on Shabbat when she lights the candles. After awhile, the English language skills she so carefully groomed started to fade.

Avital was in love and she had integrity, tenacity, focus, and passion. She never lost faith or hope. She was never too tired to protest or to go to an interview. She was consumed by her absolute dedication to free her husband. She was completely committed to her mission. Her purpose was driven by her passion to free her husband so that they could live a Jewish life together. Once Natan was freed, her focus shifted immediately to building a Jewish family and home with her husband. Natan has created an organization to aid new immigrants to Israel from the former Soviet Union. As their daughters have become young adults, Avital now finds time to teach newcomers Hebrew, and to help mothers learn the ropes of the Israeli bureaucracy as well as teaching them about their Jewish heritage. She also works as a school counselor.

And, what of Soviet Jewry? On December 6, 1987, not long after his release, Natan masterminded one of the largest demonstrations in the history of the Washington Mall. On a freezing Sunday—Solidarity Sunday—I had the honor of introducing Vice President Bush to a rally of 250,000 people in support of Soviet Jewry's right to emigrate. When Avital had made her appeal: **"I … want … my … husband … back,"** she would also demand "Let … my … people … go." Reagan's promise to Avital was on both dimensions.

From 1989 to 2004, an estimated million and a half Jews left the Soviet Union, of which approximately a million went to Israel. All have gone from a land of oppression to lands of freedom. And, the land they have left is now embarked on a path to freedom itself.

SOME KEY THINGS I LEARNED
FROM AVITAL SHARANSKY ARE:

You don't need a title to lead—you need a passion.

Avital transformed herself from a humble Israeli immigrant to a world-recognized figure in order to gain Natan's release. Avital was a charismatic inspirational force. She was not a general in any army. She was not the head of any state, but her determination and conviction harnessed the most powerful political energy we know of on the planet— the president of the United States of America. When the goal of Natan's release was achieved, she returned to the realization of her dream—the making of a Jewish home and family. The only other person I have seen shed the mantle of public attention so easily was Ronald Reagan. Once his leadership role as president was completed, he was back on the ranch cutting brush, stringing fences, riding horses, and loving time spent with Nancy.

One person can make a difference.

Avital had the courage to engage the president as one human being to another. It took incredible character. In this defining moment, she took an unequivocal stand. It was an act of leadership in advancing her most precious cause—the safe return of her husband and the founding of a family. Responding to Avital was a very personal act for Reagan. In a defining moment for him as well, he reciprocated with a bold act of leadership. One-to-one: the deepest compassion of one very decent human being to the plight of another. This was classic Reagan. For him, Avital's plight epitomized the struggle between freedom and Evil. It was not until two years later that Reagan first used the term "Evil Empire" in a March 1983 speech. But, make no mistake about it, he had already identified the Soviets as the foe. In his *kischkes* (gut), he understood Natan's imprisonment as an injustice perpetrated by systematic Evil. Avital had declared: "I . . . want . . . my . . . husband . . . back." What if Reagan had said, "I want the State Department to study this matter and get back to me?" The topic would have receded into the bowels of the bureaucracy. It might never have been resurrected. Instead, Ronald Reagan demonstrated true leadership and gave Avital his hand as he uttered a bold two-point pledge. And, he honored it!

The true believer doesn't see the mountain.

Seizing the moment leads you to look for the path, not the mountain. Avital had no money, no access, no English language skills—yet she acquired everything she needed to perform the task before her. Nobody, but nobody, would undertake such a journey if they understood the mountain they had to climb. Yet, Avital climbed it without ever losing her breath. As they say, when you walk atop the mountain, you never see it. This Oval Office meeting was seven years in the making! And, no one ever knew when and where this defining moment in the rescue of Natan Sharansky would occur. This entire Oval Office session took no longer than fifteen minutes.

"It sometimes seems that intense desire creates not only its own opportunities, but its own talents," Eric Hoffer once wrote. Avital Sharansky is vivid proof of how powerful that truth can be. It *is* within the range of everyone's life to be a part of something great.

Defining moments are the doors and windows of opportunity that invite you to make the world a better place. Very few of us will be remembered a thousand years from now, but you can attach yourself to a great cause that helps improve the world. That's the secret to a fulfilling and purposeful life.

The Polish Survivors

Anna Yakobovitch & Simon Spiro

In 1966, my mother, my wife, and I visited Poland. We went to Auschwitz to reaffirm that the Jews still lived, and to pay our respects to the millions who were butchered there for the crime of being born Jewish. After paying our respects to the dead, we visited the surviving remnant of Jews in the once flourishing thriving Jewish community of Cracow. Earlier, more than 60,000 Jews lived in this city in southern Poland, which was a major center for Jewish scholarship and culture. In 1966, that number was decimated to around one thousand. They were mostly aged, orphaned, and broken survivors of the Holocaust. The Joint Committee operated a soup kitchen to give these people one hot meal a day. A family named Yakobovitch ran the soup kitchen.

Anna Yakobovitch and her husband both lost all of their first families in the concentration camps. Both were survivors who escaped the camps. They met in the Polish Resistance after the war. Rather than leave Poland, they felt an obligation to remain and care for this elderly, dying community. Akiva Kahane, the East European Regional Director of the American Jewish Joint Distribution Committee, accompanied us on this trip, and had let them know we were coming. Mrs. Yakobovitch stayed up all night to prepare a typical Jewish meal for us. She was fifty-four-years-old, but an old fifty-four. A soul that had seen much suffering, but still harbored and radiated inexhaustible love. She moved gracefully from table to table, cutting the food for these elderly people and helping to feed them. I wanted to express my gratitude to her.

"Mrs. Yakobovitch, your chopped liver is better than my grandmother's," I told her, and I meant it. Anna started to cry. "When I was a little girl," she mused, "my mother used to say more precious than diamonds and rubies is a Yiddishe momma. But, to be a Yiddishe momma, you must have Yiddishe *kinderlei*—children. Look around this room. These have been my children. Thank you—a young Jewish boy—for letting me be a true Yiddishe momma for a day." I was thirty-three at the time, but young enough to fill her passionate need to be a Yiddishe momma and she was moved enough to cry. The Yakobovitches had experienced unimaginable degradation and terror in the factories of death. But, it did not kill their capacity to love and to care and to give of themselves in helping to repair the world.

On the same trip, we went to visit a man named Simon Spiro at the only Jewish old-age home in Warsaw. He was a happy, energetic man, who was also a survivor. He must have been eighty-five or eighty-six at the time of our visit. He had his own little room. Spiro showed us pictures of his family, who had perished in the Holocaust. He had an exquisite oil painting on the wall of his room of a woman blessing the Shabbat candles.

Akiva Kahane said: "That's a beautiful painting. I'd love to own it. I'll give you $10,000 for it." Spiro looked at him and said, "Kahane, what would I do with $10,000? Could I pin it on my wall and look at it every morning when I wake up and get the joy of memory? Could it bring back the memory of the warmth of my mother and my family that we enjoyed on Shabbat? This painting is not for sale."

ONE KEY THING I LEARNED FROM THE POLISH SURVIVORS IS:

The treasure and power of memory help us to rediscover and harness the real values of life.

There are different paths to preserving tradition, even in defining the meaning of family. Caring for the needs of the elderly is God's work.

Being a leader doesn't necessarily mean commanding armies in a war room, rousing throngs of followers from a podium, or marshalling a cadre of PhDs to a scientific breakthrough. Leadership is also caring and taking responsibility for others, especially those whom the world has cast aside. Albert Schweitzer was a leader. So was Mother Teresa. Anna Yakobovitch was a leader too.

In a defining moment, both Anna Yakobovitch and her husband made the courageous choice to live in Cracow, within the shadow of Auschwitz, which is a mere thirty miles away. For me, this was an act of both care and defiance. When Anna escaped into the forest surrounding the death camp, she courageously fought with the Partisans— even though their trustworthiness in helping Jews was often suspect. Her compelling sense of responsibility to the Jewish community made her remain in Poland to minister to the needs of these elderly, orphaned people. "More valuable than diamonds and rubies," she became the matriarch of Jewish mommas to those she lovingly called her aging *kinderlei*. For Mr. Spiro, that portrait of the blessing of the Shabbat candles transfixed the warmest moment of humanity in his life and stood as a beacon of what is truly enduring. Humanity was alive! Hope had won! Decency had won!

Nation Building

*It's time for people of action to think ... and for people
of thought to act.*

—derived from Henri Bergson

David Ben-Gurion

David Ben-Gurion was born in Plonsk, Poland. He emigrated to Palestine when he was merely twenty in 1906, and nearly died of malaria. This was forty-two years before the formation of an Israeli state. Ben-Gurion wrote later: "Half the immigrants who came to Palestine in those early days took one look and caught the same ship home again." An ardent socialist, he formed Palestine's first Jewish trade union. At the time, Palestine was under Turkish control. During World War I, Ben-Gurion was expelled and went to the U.S. to raise money for the Jewish Legion. Later, during World War II, he fought against the Turks in Palestine. During the 1920s, he was the leading Jewish labor leader in Palestine. In 1930, he founded the Mapai (Labor) Party.

In advance of the creation of the state of Israel, David Ben-Gurion understood that a fledgling nation had to create facts on the ground. This came from a man who fervently believed in an Israel of Biblical proportions. He knew that the United Nations would establish Israel's borders based on where Jewish population existed. Before the state of Israel came into being, Ben-Gurion planned how settlements would be deployed. He erected tent cities. He did whatever he could to create realities that would support an Israel of the scope he envisioned.

Ben-Gurion became Israel's first prime minister in 1948. On May 14 of that year, Israel was born. The next day, a hundred million Arabs with their forces deployed in six armies declared war against roughly 600,000 ill-trained, poorly equipped Israelis. When they attacked, it was up to Ben-Gurion to save the imperiled infant state. His leadership made it possible. Ben-Gurion attempted retirement to the Negev Desert in 1953, but the Israeli people demanded his return for another term of service as prime minister between 1955 and 1963.

My first encounter with David Ben-Gurion took place in Israel in 1961. At this time, he was prime minister, but more importantly he was the George Washington of the State of Israel. Herb Friedman arranged the meeting for a group of young American Jews who were to become the founding members of the UJA Young Leadership Cabinet. Herb Friedman's purpose was to inspire them to get actively involved with the UJA raising people[1] and raising money for Jewish rescue and resettlement. Herb hoped we would provide future leadership for the UJA. Prime Minister Ben-Gurion came in to greet the group, "Welcome to Israel," he said. "We need you to move here. We don't need your money. We need *you.* We're trying to found a democratic state, but we don't have the experience you do, having grown up in a democracy. Come here and help us build democracy into our culture." A pall settled over the group—none of us were seriously considering moving to Israel. We thought raising money to support rescue and resettlement of Jews to Israel was a noble and important mission. This was very deflating.

Then someone asked the prime minister what he was worried about. "Color television," he answered without a pause. "Right now this country has black and white television. Already it's stealing time from the family, from reading, from writing, from people communicating

---

1 Raising people is a term often used by me and colleagues of mine in leadership development for Jewish causes. It means enlisting and helping to commit people to support a cause.

with each other. It's subverting our way of life. Our children aren't reading or studying. They're indulging themselves. Color television will be worse because it will be more attractive. If they have color television, they'll waste even more time doing in color, what they are already doing in black and white. This will undermine the moral fiber of the nation and the principle of sacrifice upon which the state has been built." That statement had more wisdom than we were prepared to admit at that time.

Menachem Begin and David Ben-Gurion were alive at the same time and you needed both to create the state. Ben-Gurion was a modern day prophet. So was Begin. Both were giants among giants. During the Israeli War of Independence, Menachem Begin headed the *Irgun*.[2] According to Howard Sachar in *A History of Israel,* Israel's Independence Day occurred May 14, 1948, when the British took down the Union Jack in the morning, and Ben-Gurion read the Declaration of Independence in the afternoon.

In June 1948, during the middle of the first ceasefire in the Arab invasion of Israel, desperately needed arms were being landed in Israel on an Irgun-chartered ship named the *Altalena.* The Irgun had demanded they be allowed to retain 20 percent of the weapons on the ship, which also transported Irgun crew and recruits. Rather than accept Begin's demands, Prime Minister Ben-Gurion ordered the ship sunk on June 21, 1948. The order was carried out by a Palmach unit led by a young Yitzhak Rabin. Sixteen Irgun crew and three members of the Israeli Defense Forces lost their lives. Ben-Gurion was determined to have a single Israeli military under one command—the *Hagana.* Even with the lives lost and the crucial weapons destroyed, Begin, as the leader of the Irgun, averted what could have easily become a civil war by refusing to retaliate and have Jews fight Jews. When the Arab armies violated the ceasefire and invaded Israel, the two Jewish factions fought side by side. The Irgun had been branded a terrorist organization by the British and it was not fully assimilated into the Israeli army until midyear 1948. What a statement of values by both

---

2 Also known by the Hebrew acronym Etzel.

Ben-Gurion and Begin! Ben-Gurion fervently believed that one nation could never have two rival armies and survive. Begin was passionately committed to a Jewish state and knew that no such state could endure the reality of Jews killing Jews.

In 1967, I was with David Ben-Gurion one month after Israel won the Six-Day War and captured all that territory. We were in the kitchen of his home in Jerusalem when I asked him for his thoughts about the war.

"Give it back!" he said forcefully, and I am sure he meant East Jerusalem, the West Bank, and Gaza in particular. "We will rue the day we took possession of the land and had to keep the people." That's the tragedy of Palestine. Everybody wants the land, and nobody wants the people. The tragedy of the Palestinian people is they lacked then, and now, leadership that was prepared to accept the existence of a sovereign Jewish State of Israel.

SOME KEY THINGS I LEARNED FROM DAVID BEN-GURION ARE:

There can only be one army in a sovereign state.

Otherwise the will of the state can be challenged by armed factions that disagree with the state's avowed purpose. The result will be chaos and anarchy as we witness today in Iraq, in Afghanistan, and among the Palestinians. The sinking of the *Altalena* was a defining moment both for Begin and for Ben-Gurion. Ben-Gurion needed to assert the imperative of a single army, and Begin had to muster the restraint to accept that fact. It takes great character and courage to confront these armed factions and to be willing to use lethal force against one's countrymen for the cause of building a nation. That demands exceptional leadership.

**A leader must both have a vision and be able to
translate that vision into practical realities.**

Prior to 1948, David Ben-Gurion was dedicated to establishing facts
on the ground—a presence on the land that could support the Jewish
claim to a particular piece of geography. He understood the linkage
between planning and reality, and he was knowledgeable and prepared enough to act in a way that would secure Israel the next advantage. He influenced the entire successor generation—especially
Dayan—to think in terms of facts on the ground.

**National leaders have a responsibility to
preserve the character of a nation and its people.**

Ben-Gurion's anxiety about color television may seem quaint, but it
had a pragmatic foundation. Ben-Gurion knew the power of a well-
read, disciplined mind. His focus was on values of service, duty, responsibility, and knowing your roots. He studied the Bible, not from
a religious perspective, but as a philosophical and historical foundation. Ben-Gurion was an avid reader and wanted Israel's youth to be
passionate learners. His vigilance was keen, and he didn't want to see
the strengths of Israeli youth squandered on pleasure, comfort, and
frivolous entertainment.

Golda Meir

Born in poverty in Kiev, Ukraine, in 1898, Golda Meir emigrated with her family to the United States in 1906. She became a teacher in Milwaukee, but in 1921 she and her husband moved to Palestine. In no time, she proved herself a formidable leader and was invaluable in coordinating Jewish interests between Palestine and the U.S. During the War of Independence. She was an exceptional fund-raiser in the States.

From 1945 to 1948, before the state was created, there was a Jewish Agency for Palestine. David Ben-Gurion was the chairman and Golda Meir was the equivalent of the foreign minister. At the time, there were illegal rescue operations to try to smuggle Jews into Palestine past the British blockade. The episode documented in Leon Uris's novel Exodus *was the most famous effort. After the war, a displaced person camp had also been set up on the site of the Bergen-Belsen concentration camp. A rescue operation attempted to move the children from that camp to Israel. The ship was intercepted by the British and the youngsters were taken to Cyprus, because of the strict British limitations on Jewish immigration to Palestine. Golda Meir went to Cyprus and assured the children that sooner or later they would come to Israel. The obstacles to immigration were enormous and in fact restricted as to the number of Jews who could enter Palestine in a given year, but these children were ultimately able to reach their new homeland.*

In 1948, Golda Meir was appointed Israel's ambassador
to the Soviet Union followed by a series of other posts un-
til she was named foreign minister in 1956. In 1969, Prime
Minister Levi Eshkol died suddenly in office, and Meir was
named Israel's first (and the world's third) female prime
minister. Golda Meir was seventy-one at the time. She gov-
erned Israel during the onslaught of the Yom Kippur War
and the country's triumphant response to it. Golda Meir
understood how critical the United States was to Israel.
She believed, "The only real friend [Israel has], and a very
powerful one" was America. Prime Minister Meir resigned
in 1974 because she felt the nation was ill-prepared for war
"during her watch." She died in 1978.

When asked what image Golda Meir brought to mind, Max Fisher, the most important Jewish leader in America, once responded: "An oak tree." Fisher thought a moment and then said, "No, two oak trees!" Golda's passion was to create a viable, secure, democratic Jewish state of Israel. She wanted to bring about this Jewish state to ensure a safe haven for Jews in need all across the world.

During 1969–1970, Egypt mounted the War of Attrition along the Sinai and Suez Canal. Their intent was to challenge Israel's resolve in holding on to the land it had occupied during the Six-Day War of 1967. I was chairing a United Jewish Appeal fund-raising campaign in the United States and flew to Israel for a briefing on how the war was faring. A group of us had dinner in the rose garden adjacent to the prime minister's home. Someone asked the prime minister if she hated the Arabs.

> I don't hate the Arabs, I hate that they make us kill. We are a people who love life and are taught to reach out and take responsibility for improving the world. It's not natural for us to kill, but the Arabs have given us no choice if we want to live.

When six million Jews perished in the camps, only a handful of nations reached out to help. There was no homeland to take those six million who were killed. In 1948, the world's sympathy and guilt moved them to partition Palestine. Although it was the second partition of land already promised in the Balfour Declaration, our Arab cousins didn't want to share the land. A hundred million Arabs went up against 600,000 Jews. Miracle of miracles, Israel won.

Now in 1970, the sympathy of the world is with us when we are bleeding. But, when we win, we defy the image of a defenseless, helpless Jew, and that sympathy evaporates. The price to hold the affection and support of the world—the blood of our children—is too dear. We fight for the chance to raise our children in peace. One day I hope both the Arabs and we can do that.

Golda Meir had an uncanny knack for summing up complex situations in powerful and clear thoughts. "We will have peace with the Arabs," she would say, "when they love their children more than they hate us."

I saw her every time she came to the States or I went to Israel. In November 1977, several years after her resignation, I attended a UJA national conference in New York. She was the keynote speaker. Shortly before this event, it was announced that Egyptian President Sadat would go to Jerusalem. When I saw Golda at the conference, I was excited and said to her that this was a great moment in Jewish history.

"Gordon please wait. Be patient," she cautioned me and was even a bit cynical. "Don't forget. This is the man who committed Pearl Harbor against Israel and the Jewish people. Let's see what he has to say. I don't trust him."

On Sunday, November 20, I attended Sadat's speech at the Knesset. In a very tough talk, he repeated the same message he had given publicly in Cairo many times. There was a letdown. Even though there was prolonged applause at the end of his speech, when Sadat proclaimed, "In all sincerity, I tell you that we welcome you among us with full security and safety... I declare to the whole world that we accept living with you in permanent peace based on justice." At a cocktail party in the Knesset that evening, I saw Golda once again.

"What did I tell you, Gordon?" she said. "A lot of fanfare. A circus. Not real."

The next day, Monday, November 21, Sadat had a meeting with the leaders of the Labor Party. Golda Meir and Anwar Sadat met with each other for several hours, sat next to each other, and exchanged presents for their grandchildren. I was invited to a lunch later in the day, where I saw Golda again. She said, "I believe Sadat is for real. I believe he wants peace. This is an historic opportunity." Despite all her past doubts, she seized the moment to express confidence in the future. In her meeting with Sadat, she looked him straight in the eye when they talked about their grandchildren. It was a defining moment for Golda. She now understood that there was a real opportunity for peace with Sadat. He left Jerusalem that evening. At that point, I still didn't know the essence of what had transpired during his visit or that Prime Minister Begin and President Sadat had engineered the framework for a bilateral peace agreement during the middle of the preceding night. That human rapport was essential for Golda. Her reappraisal of Egypt could never have happened with Sadat's predecessor Nasser. She once said of Nasser, "I have given instructions that I be informed every time one of our soldiers is killed, even if it is in the middle of the night. When President Nasser leaves instructions that he is to be awakened in the middle of the night if an Egyptian soldier is killed, there will be peace."

THREE KEY THINGS I LEARNED
FROM GOLDA MEIR ARE:

Leaders must ensure they get bad news in a timely way.

Prime Minister Golda Meir was ruthlessly objective. She retained the invincible optimism of a true leader even in the grimmest of situations. "We've been through worse, and will get through this," she would vow. But, while she inspired others, she remained tightly focused on the alternatives available to her and the state of Israel, and never shied from making and implementing tough decisions. She saw the situation as it was, not as she hoped it would be and as the situation changed, so would her assessment of it.

In the end, some contend that Golda Meir's only notable weakness as prime minister was that she wasn't vigilant enough. She was certainly willing to act on the hard realities when they were presented. But, did she press her generals to constantly deliver an accurate, complete picture of tactical facts in the field? Leaders must receive objective assessments of the situation—weaknesses and strengths, vulnerabilities and opportunities. Above all, leaders must ensure that they receive bad news in a timely way. Without it, you lose control of the moment. It is a testament to Golda's character and moral compass that she personally shouldered so much responsibility for the Yom Kippur War and then resigned.

Subordinate personal desires to the needs of a greater good.

Golda Meir's passion drove her purpose, which was to secure the state of Israel. To get that done, she paid a dear personal price. In her heart and mind, it was more important that she be grandmother to the nation and its head of state than to be grandmother of her own family. None of this ever turned her head about herself or made her posture for others.

Communicate in basic, human terms.

In my personal experience, only Ronald Reagan was Golda's match in crystallizing the great issues in simple human terms. She never read a speech. She never faltered in her spontaneity. She always made each person in the audience feel as though she were speaking directly to them, "We will have peace with the Arabs, when they love their children more than they hate us."

Moshe Dayan

Moshe Dayan was a dashing military Israeli hero and an archaeologist of international renown. Dayan was one of the founding members of the Hagana. *The British imprisoned him. He was released to serve in the British Army during World War II. He lost an eye during the war, which led to his wearing an eyepatch that became his visual signature. He served twice as defense minister and later as foreign minister under Menachem Begin. A practical secular centrist, Dayan was an early advocate of Palestinian autonomy. Dayan's writings included a work on bringing the Bible to life through examples from his formidable study of archaeology.*

In September 1970, Richard Nixon was the U.S. President. Prime Minister Golda Meir was the principal speaker at the major gifts dinner of the United Jewish Appeal. I was to introduce her. There was a civil war in Jordan, started by Yasser Arafat—a Palestinian uprising intending to overthrow King Hussein. The King was about to succeed in expelling the Palestine Liberation Organization (PLO) from Jordan into Syria. Golda had met with President Nixon and Secretary of State Kissinger the afternoon before this dinner. President Nixon had requested that the government of Israel not intervene in Jordan's civil war because Hussein appeared to be winning. Prime Minister Meir assured the president that Israel had no intention of intervening. She was pleased that King Hussein was succeeding and viewed the king as a potential partner for peace.

Golda Meir traveled from Washington to New York for the dinner event. During her speech, Simcha Dinitz, then political advisor to the Israeli prime minister, approached me on the dais with an urgent note: "Get Golda off the dais immediately. Kissinger must speak with her on the phone. It is an urgent national security matter."

I passed the note to the prime minister. She concluded her remarks briskly. We took her to a secure room, where she could call Kissinger. The former Soviet Union was urging their client state Syria to intervene in support of the PLO to overthrow King Hussein. Three hundred Syrian tanks were massing on Jordan's northern border. Nixon wanted Israel to come to the aid of Jordan and to defend Jordan against a Syrian invasion. In doing so, the U.S. wanted Israel to use *only* air power against the Syrians.

What a bizarre request! Israel was officially **at war** with Jordan. Nixon's goal was to prevent a Syrian threat to Saudi Arabia, which would have existed if Syria controlled Saudi Arabia's neighbor, Jordan. Prime Minister Meir said, "I'll get back to you, Henry." Most of her people were packed up and had already departed for JFK Airport. The prime minister wanted to call Moshe Dayan, the minister of defense. She asked Simcha to call Dayan, however, no one in what remained of her entourage had Dayan's unlisted number at home. Simcha phoned the operator at the Israeli Defense Ministry in Tel Aviv and identified himself as advisor to the prime minister of Israel. He explained that Prime Minister Meir needed to speak to the minister of defense immediately. The operator said, "Uh-huh. For all I know, sir, you're Mickey Mouse. I'm sorry, but nobody gets through to Moshe Dayan's unlisted number!"

The executive director of the UJA, Irving Bernstein, had an office across the street from the hotel. Irving rushed to his office, got Dayan's number, and Golda called Dayan. She directed him to meet with her as soon as her plane arrived back in Israel. Dayan convened his war cabinet. The only way to mobilize fast enough to support Hussein was to redeploy Israel's forces from the Suez Canal to their north-central command. This was a risky decision since the Egyptians were conducting the War of Attrition along the Suez.

When Prime Minister Meir arrived in Israel, Dayan recommended seven non-negotiable conditions the U.S. would have to accept in order for Israel to come to Jordan's assistance. To my recollection, the conditions were:

1. King Hussein would request Israel's assistance in writing.
2. The Israeli military would command the entire ground and air operation.
3. Israel alone would determine the type and level of firepower to be deployed.
4. The U.S. Sixth Fleet would coordinate their activities on this mission with the Israelis.
5. The Americans would agree that if Israel was condemned at the U.N., the Americans would veto any troublesome Security Council resolutions.
6. If Egypt took advantage of Israel because of the redeployment of troops away from the Egyptian border, and if Israel successfully fought in Jordan, Israel alone would determine when the fighting would stop with Egypt.
7. Israel would be resupplied by the United States.

President Nixon agreed to all these conditions. Dayan directed that the redeployment be done in a highly visible way. The Sixth Fleet leadership would meet with Dayan, and bring all intelligence about forces on the northern front of Jordan. The commanding admiral of the Sixth Fleet and his staff came to the Defense Ministry in Tel Aviv to share their intelligence on the Syrian positions. When Dayan reviewed the U.S. maps and intelligence reports, he was furious. "I can get better maps from the Triple A," he shouted at the Americans. "How can we operate with coordinates this big? How can I pinpoint a bomb at any of these targets with any accuracy? Our maps are much more detailed than these, and our intelligence is much better. We have the name of the captain of each tank, where he went to school, where he was trained, how long he has held a command post, his entire military history—even if he is inclined to deploy his tanks to the left or to the right!"

What happened? The Israelis redeployed. The Soviets assessed the redeployment and instructed the Syrians to withdraw immediately. The Syrians pulled back. As a result, Hussein won the civil war. The King drove the PLO out of Jordan in that month—known in the Palestinian history books as **"Black September."** Arafat and the PLO fled to Syria, which stabilized Jordan. Their stay in Syria was short lived. Syria expelled them and sent the PLO to Lebanon, which marked the beginning of the end of stability for Lebanon. And...oh, yes... from that point forward, U.S. intelligence and mapping techniques were radically improved to match the level of the Israelis.

Watching Prime Minister Meir's nimble handling of the Black September crisis left four indelible impressions on me. First, events can turn a current enemy into an ally if the circumstances of the moment demand it. Alliances should be flexible enough to shift decision making to the members with the best local knowledge. The U.S. dominated the U.S.–Israel alliance overall, but the Israelis had the convincing on-the-ground knowledge in this case. Second, potentially devastating confrontations can be solved without violence or destruction through skillful and pre-emptive shows of force. Peace through strength. Third, it pays to carry important phone numbers with you everywhere you go, especially if you happen to be an advisor to a prime minister!

Moshe Dayan was the most practical man I ever met and one of the most charismatic. He commanded respect by his aura. During his second term as defense minister in 1969–1974, there was a serious outbreak of Arab terrorist attacks against Israeli civilians. Under Dayan, Israel implemented a retaliatory measure: The Israeli Army went into the village that was the source of a particular attack. They located the home of the attacker, which was also the home of the attacker's parents and siblings. They gave the occupants notice to get out, and then they would blow up the house.

A group of Palestinian elders wanted a meeting with Dayan to discuss the fairness of doing this. I happened to be in Israel at the time, and he asked if I would like to come along. A translator accompanied us for my benefit. Dayan was born in Palestine, grew up with the Arabs, and spoke fluent Arabic. He understood their culture, their value structure, and their religion.

We entered a sprawling tent stitched together from countless goatskins. All the elders sat in a large circle. After the pleasantries and the coffee, the conversation began in earnest. "In the Bible," the senior elder said solemnly, "it is written: To visit the sins of the father upon the children is unfair. How then can you possibly justify visiting the sins of the son upon the parents of the child? We think this practice is unfair and un-Jewish, and it should cease immediately."

Dayan looked them straight in the eye, and said, "Gentlemen, let me be perfectly clear. I do not see your daughters whoring in Tel Aviv. If you can control the behavior of your daughters, you certainly can control the behavior of your sons. There will be no change in policy. I hold *you* accountable for assuring that terrorism stops." Dead silence. That was the end of the meeting. The elders knew that Dayan understood their culture and that he was right—there were no Arab prostitutes in Tel Aviv, only Jewish ones. With that Dayan rose, thanked the elders for the coffee, and left. The policy on terrorism articulated by Dayan remains in force to this day.

Not the architect of the 1967 war, Moshe Dayan was nonetheless the visible figure who rallied the nation and uplifted its confidence. Chief of Staff Yitzhak Rabin's health collapsed as a result of what is believed to be nicotine poisoning. Prime Minister Levi Eshkol made a radio address in which he stuttered. Both of these events unnerved national confidence. It was Moshe Dayan who conceptualized the situation almost instantly, and he stepped into the visible leadership vacuum that had been created. Public jubilation on Israel's gaining control of Jerusalem made him even more of a national hero.

However, memory is short. Although Israel was ultimately resupplied in 1973, and saved from total destruction, the scars of the Yom Kippur War ran very deep. An inquiry, known as the Agranat Commission, was launched to fix responsibility for Israel's vulnerability—the weakness that provoked the war in the first place. The Bar-Lev Line of fortifications on the east coast of the Suez Canal, for example, was quickly overrun because it was undermanned. Thousands of war veterans found that their leadership had been wanting and staged demonstrations, some of them violent. Dayan became the lightning rod for criticism. Forces in the Knesset pressed for his resignation and got it. Prime Minister Meir believed that a sense of responsibility obliged her to resign as well. That resignation paved the way for Yitzhak Rabin to become prime minister, but this proved an interim solution. The Israeli people wanted a much tougher stance on defense—policies that brought Likud and Menachem Begin to power.

SOME KEY THINGS I LEARNED FROM MOSHE DAYAN ARE:

Know your enemy... and that means REALLY know him.

Geography matters. Land matters. Dayan's mastery of archaeology helped him to know every inch of Israel—every tree, every rock and cliff, every wadi. Indeed, his encyclopedic awareness of the real world served to guide advanced military systems even more precisely. He set new standards for military intelligence—not only for Israel, but for the United States as well. But Dayan didn't stop with mastering geography. He also had an in-depth grasp of Arab language, culture, and values.

Be who you are.

Moshe Dayan once was asked by an American Jewish leader what the American Jewish Community could do to help Israel. Dayan replied, "Just be Jewish...Jews know what to do when Jews are in trouble." Dayan was an instinctive leader who radiated confidence. He knew how to reach down into his personality and call on the reserves of strength. In times of crisis, he could rally others by helping them call on the inner strengths within themselves.

Leaders rise to the occasion when a nation faces its defining moments.

Moshe Dayan stepped into the gap and filled a dire national need for visible leadership at the outbreak of the Six-Day War. He had the personal chemistry to face the situation with a commanding air that was both energizing and decisive. Certainly Dayan had a theatrical flair, but he was also thoroughly prepared to do the right thing. He had been a highly successful military chief of staff in the 1956 Suez War. Dayan's memorable presence in the Six-Day War may have a corollary in modern American history when New York Mayor Rudy Giuliani became such an inspiring symbol for American resilience after the 9/11 disaster in 2001.

Flexibility is the heart of pragmatism.

As an architect of the Camp David Accords negotiated by Prime Minister Begin, Dayan proposed dismantling the very settlements he fought to erect and had defended with young Israeli lives. Settlements up. Settlements down. Was it caprice? No! It was the clear recognition that history is organic, and methods must change constantly if you are to reach your ultimate goal. That's true leadership.

Menachem Begin

Menachem Begin was born in Brest Litovsk, Poland in 1913. Before attending Warsaw University as a law student, he was active in the Zionist youth movement Betar, *founded by Vladimir Jabotinsky. When World War II broke out in 1939, he went to Lithuania, where he was arrested by the Soviets in 1940. When Germany invaded the Soviet Union, Moscow concluded an agreement with the Free Polish Government in London. This enabled Poles incarcerated in Soviet prisons and labor camps to be released if they joined the Free Polish Army. As a volunteer in the Free Polish Army, the force Begin was part of moved to the Middle East via Iran and the Suez Canal.*

Begin and his associates arrived in Palestine—then a British mandate—in 1943. While World War II was still being waged, Begin was asked to be the commander of the Irgun *military organization, which waged a war of liberation against the British, but maintained a truce with the British during World War II. As the war in Europe was approaching its end, the* Irgun *resumed its campaign and was partly responsible for Britain's decision to leave Palestine.*

In 1948, Begin founded the right-wing opposition party Herut, *which participated in the infant state of Israel's first election. He became Israel's Prime Minister in 1977. In 1978, Prime Minister Begin and Egypt's President Anwar Sadat shared the Nobel Peace Prize for signing the Camp*

David Accords, which outlined the terms bringing peace between Egypt and Israel.

My path to Menachem Begin began in Athens. In August 1975, Arnaud de Borchgrave, then the international editor of *Newsweek* magazine, appeared at a seminar sponsored by the Young Presidents Organization. During the session, de Borchgrave and I hotly debated Middle East issues.

De Borchgrave believed Egypt's Anwar Sadat was prepared to make peace, but the Israeli leadership was blowing it. To me, it was just the other way around. Israel was ready, but Egypt was not. De Borchgrave asked me, "Have you ever been to Egypt?

"They won't let me in!" I replied emphatically. At that time, American Jews weren't allowed to enter that country.

"If I can get you into Egypt, will you come with me?"

"You bet!" I answered.

De Borchgrave lubricated the gears to open access for me, and I made a ten-day tour in July 1976. De Borchgrave himself couldn't join me on the trip because armed hostilities had broken out in Rhodesia, and he had to cover the turmoil. My purpose in going to Egypt was to assess the political support Sadat would receive if, in fact, he truly wanted to make peace with Israel. This was after the Yom Kippur War in 1973, when forward-looking Egyptians realized they would never move forward economically if some accord with Israel could not be reached.

On arrival in Cairo, Tahseen Bashir, secretary to the Egyptian cabinet, met me at the airport. He arranged contacts with the level of people I wanted to see—deputy cabinet officers, undersecretaries, colonels, assistant editors, and assistant professors. Bashir secured me a car, an English-speaking driver, and permission to travel throughout the country. He made it all possible. Every night my wife and I had dinners with English-speaking Egyptians and their guests who represented the emerging leadership of those who would be guiding Egypt over the next two decades. They told me their personal hopes and dreams, as well as what they wanted for their country. These people—the ascending elite—felt they had shed enough blood for the cause of the Palestinians and pan-Arabism. They convinced me that there were powerful political, economic, and demographic forces in Egypt that would support a peace with Israel should Sadat want to pursue it. It was evident the emerging leadership of Egypt was willing to try a different strategy. Maintaining a perpetual state of hostility with Israel was simply getting in the way of most Egyptians improving their standard of living and making a better life for their children.

On my return to the United States, I called upon UCLA Professor Steven Spiegel and an international pro-Israel think tank he had organized. I asked Steve to identify, within a month, roughly one hundred projects in such fields as medicine, agriculture, hydrofication, industry, and social welfare—projects that could be jointly done by Israel and Egypt to their mutual benefit.

When the report was ready, I flew to Israel for an urgent meeting with then-Israeli Prime Minister Yitzhak Rabin. When I told Rabin about my Egyptian trip, his aide Yehuda Avner was at the meeting. I presented the one hundred ideas as a "no-lose" deal for Israel. My argument: Here was a way to test Sadat's intentions toward peace with Israel through private, quiet diplomacy. Israel could offer to do any or all of these projects that were amenable to the Egyptians. This could become a foundation for the dialogue to begin and to make the long road to peace possible. If the Egyptians refused, Israel could then publicly offer two of these proposals a week over fifty weeks. If Egypt systematically rejected these proposals, Israel would be regarded as the peacemaker and Egypt as intransigent.

Rabin shook his head: "Crazy American! Naive American! Absolutely no chance Egypt will go for any of these ideas."

Egypt and Israel had conducted one-on-one negotiations at the famous "Kilometer 101." This was roughly sixty kilometers from Cairo, and it was the first time that Israeli military personnel sat face-to-face with their Egyptian counterparts. Rabin recounted what he proposed and the result: "Let's build a railroad that would link Egypt and Israel through the Sinai. Egypt said no. If they turned *that* down, how the hell are they going to accept any of this nonsense? Public relations: that's all this is. PR doesn't win wars. Go back to the United States, Zacks, and raise money."

What a disappointment! Still, I thought Prime Minister Rabin had a much better handle on the best interests of Israel than I did.

In November 1976, Jimmy Carter was elected U.S. president. In the spring of 1977, Rabin resigned when it was disclosed his wife had a U.S. bank account, illegal under Israeli law. Even if the matter was an oversight, Rabin took full responsibility. His resignation was a remarkable act of character. Thereafter, Menachem Begin was elected Israel's first Likud prime minister. Between 1961 and 1977, I had—through UJA—been in Israel three to four times a year, but I never met Begin because I worked with the governing Labor Party. All I knew about him was through my Labor Party contacts.

Likud was an opposition party, but it had no shadow cabinet, and it was not prepared to govern. When Begin became prime minister, the government he inherited contained some civil servants who were members of the Labor Party. Among them was Yehuda Avner. On Begin's first day in office, he asked Avner to bring in all the intelligence material on Sadat and his interest in peace with Israel. Avner retrieved the material from the archives, including the report I had given to Rabin. Begin said, "I want to meet Zacks." The next week I met him for lunch in the Olive Room of the King David Hotel in Jerusalem. After Avner introduced us, Begin and I were left to meet alone.

"Mr. Zacks, have you ever been in jail?" Begin began the conversation.

No small talk. No "How was the trip?" Just, "Mr. Zacks, have you ever been in jail?"

"Thank God, Mr. Prime Minister, I have **never** been in jail," I answered proudly.

Begin sized me up for a few seconds.

"That's a pity," the prime minister said with thoughtful confidence. "You see, I have been in jail **three times**," Begin stated with commanding pride.

I was stunned.

"The first time I was arrested," Prime Minister Begin continued, "it was during a game of chess I was playing with my wife. When they dragged me out of the house, I remember screaming to my wife that I conceded the game. The Soviets locked me up in one of their prisons. After I was there for a period of six weeks, I dreamt of being free."

A Soviet prison. With all I had read about the terrors of such places, this was a chilling thought.

"The second time I was in a labor camp in Siberia," the prime minister went on. "After I was there for six weeks, I dreamt of being in a Soviet prison. The third time I was put in solitary confinement by the Soviets and I dreamt of being back in the Siberian labor camp. Mr. Zacks, my job as the prime minister of Israel is to make sure that Jewish children dream the dreams of free people and never dream of being in Siberia."

With that, Prime Minister Begin won me over!

Hour upon hour, I answered his probing questions about my trip to Egypt. Begin had a grand vision of making peace with Egypt. To bring it about, he knew he had to engineer a visit by Sadat to Jerusalem. Through back channels, he encouraged Sadat to initiate a challenge. Sadat was to declare his readiness to come to Jerusalem to search for peace.

Menachem Begin could get away with territorial concessions that Labor could not. It was just assumed that Likud would be more hawkish than Labor. It was like Nixon going to China and getting away with opening that diplomatic door. Neither of his predecessors, Kennedy nor Johnson, could have done that. They would have been labeled Communists! Both Nixon and Begin had impeccable ideological credentials that enabled them to make bold moves.

Begin was as wise as he was well informed. "Peace through strength" was his guiding principle, as it had been during the Eisenhower administration in the United States of the 1950s. Perceived weakness leads to war, Begin believed. He was a formidable warrior, but war was not his passion in life. His passion was the safeguarding and nurturing of the state of Israel. Israel's people had to be willing to die in order for the country to live. Begin knew that young Israelis could not be asked—decade after decade—to sacrifice their lives, if the Israeli government did not make an earnest effort at the right moment to seize the opportunity for peace. Otherwise there would always be doubt if the next war was necessary. That doubt could erode the unity of Israel. Menachem Begin was astute enough to see that Sadat had made a fundamental change in course. Begin had the immense self-confidence to redefine his strategy and his lifetime posture. He was now convinced that Sadat was willing to completely alter Egypt's policy toward Israel.

While Prime Minister Begin saw that Sadat could be the man to pull off peace with Israel, Begin was also wise and knew that Sadat had to be made the hero. U.S. President Jimmy Carter believed a comprehensive settlement of the Middle East conflict, not a bilateral agreement between Israel and Egypt, would be the most effective solution. Egypt had just thrown Soviet advisors out of Egypt. He proposed a Mideast peace conference—termed a "revived Geneva Conference"—to be co-chaired by the Soviets and the United States. The last thing Sadat wanted was to reinvolve the Soviets in a strategic role in the Middle East. The idea of direct negotiation with Israel took on greater appeal for Sadat as an alternative to the American peace plan. Begin and Sadat both recognized that any other approach would grant the Soviet Union and the most intransigent Arab states effective veto power over the peace process going forward. Despite the Carter Administration's best efforts to block a bilateral settlement, the way was paved for Begin to arrange Sadat's visit to the Knesset. Back-channel communication to Sadat suggested that he publicly offer to meet with Begin any place in the search for peace, even in Jerusalem. Sadat did this, and Begin seized the moment and invited Sadat to Jerusalem for that historical visit in November 1977. I was just about to visit my daughter Cathy, who was then a student at the University of Michigan in Ann Arbor, for the Ohio State/Michigan football game—the equivalent of the college gridiron's World War III. I got a call from Yechiel Kadishai, the head of the prime minister's office, inviting me to be Prime Minister Begin's guest that weekend for President Sadat's visit. I headed to Jerusalem instead of Ann Arbor.

Arriving on Saturday, I was able to watch from the gallery as history was being made when Sadat addressed the Knesset the next day. At three in the morning on the second day after Sadat's arrival, Begin and Sadat struck the deal that would be formalized a year later at Camp David. On the evening of Sadat's departure, I was invited with three others to have tea at the prime minister's residence. At 9 P.M., Begin returned from taking Sadat to the airport. Fatigued from being up all night but still ecstatic, Prime Minister Begin declared, "Friends, there will be no more war! President Sadat and I have come to an understanding, and there will be peace." He then explained that Egypt would regain sovereignty over the Sinai in exchange for a full peace treaty and normal relations between Egypt and Israel.

Prime Minister Begin turned to his aide Yehuda Avner and said, "Let's call President Carter." Avner didn't have his black book, and he didn't remember Carter's private number. So, he called the White House switchboard number, the only number he could remember. He was finally put through to a secretary in the Oval Office and told her that the Prime Minister of Israel wanted to speak with President Carter. She dismissed it as one of the hundred crank calls they get each day. Still, she was polite and said the president would call back if the prime minister's secretary would just leave a number. He looked down at the telephone and there *was* no telephone number visible! This was the prime minister's residence and they didn't want anyone who was a stranger or a guest to learn the number. Avner asked, "Prime minister, what's the phone number of this place?" Begin had no idea, since he never called himself. He got up and walked to the stairwell and called upstairs to his wife, "Aliza, what's the telephone number of this place?" She called down the number and he gave it to Avner who relayed it to the secretary in Washington. In an instant, Carter called back.

When Menachem Begin got on the phone with Jimmy Carter, he said, "Mr. President, peace-loving people the world over—and the Jewish people for generations to come—will be forever in your debt for the role you played in bringing about this historic occasion. There will be no more war between Israel and Egypt. President Sadat and I have come to an understanding. On behalf of Israel, I want to express our deepest gratitude and our eternal love for the indispensable role you played in bringing this about. Thank you very much!" Carter acknowledged the thanks.

"God bless you, Mr. President," Begin said, concluding the call, and then he hung up.

I looked at Begin, dumbfounded.

"Why, Mr. Prime Minister? *Why?* Why did you give Carter so much credit?"

"What did it cost?" Begin answered immediately as he looked at me. "And, Gordon, think about it. Am I going to need him again?" Once more, Begin was in command of the moment putting the long-term needs of Israel above his own personal satisfaction. Now that's **wisdom!** Begin conceptualized Sadat's visit to Jerusalem. He hammered out the bilateral agreement. But, Begin was prepared to give all the credit to Carter and Sadat.

Begin's lifelong passion was to achieve and secure an independent Jewish state of Israel. His vision and his wisdom were driven by this passion for a viable Jewish state. He gave his whole life to that. Begin was a protégé of Vladimir Jabotinsky, who was the founder both of *Betar* and of the Jewish Legion after World War I, and who believed that the Jews would never get their own state through diplomacy. They would have to fight for their independence, just as America did from England. According to Harry Hurwitz, head of the Menachem Begin Heritage Center and a Begin expert, Begin's views on the proper territorial boundaries for the Jewish state were complex, and they evolved over time: "He started political life believing that the Jewish state should be on both sides of the River Jordan. He never really abandoned that belief, but pragmatically worked to have a territory from the Jordan to the Mediterranean."

As part of his later pragmatic stance, Begin believed there was already a Palestinian state (Jordan) on the other side of the Jordan River. All the Palestinians on the East Bank should become Jordanian citizens, he thought. West of the Jordan River, the entire span should be Jewish. That would give Israel the Biblical land that God promised. This would satisfy the religious Jews. It would also give

Israel the necessary strategic protection in the event of another attack. And, it would provide Israel the needed water and minerals to be economically viable. Begin was a hawk in his soul. But, at critical moments, he could correct course and make peace with the best. As Ezer Weizman once wrote, "a hawk swoops down, seizes the initiative, and takes advantage of changing situations to suit his cause."

In 1967, Yitzhak Rabin was chief of staff of the Israel Defense Forces. Levi Eshkol had succeeded David Ben-Gurion as both prime minister and minister of defense. As I said in the chapter on Moshe Dayan, Rabin became incapacitated. Begin was a member of the "wall-to-wall" coalition government of national unity, belonging to the Gahal faction. In *A History of Israel,* Howard Sachar writes: "On May 29 . . . the leader of the Gachal faction, Menachem Begin, called on Eshkol to turn over the premiership and ministry of defense to Ben-Gurion. It was an unprecedented gesture, coming from a fire-eater like Begin, a man who for years had been Ben-Gurion's sworn political enemy . . . [T]he Gachal leader was acknowledging the unifying strength of his old foe . . . The following day . . . one speaker after another implored Eshkol at least to give up the defense post—if not to Ben-Gurion, then to Dayan." On June 1, Eshkol, who was not well versed in military matters, resolved the defense leadership question caused by Rabin's temporary incapacity. He resigned the defense ministry to Moshe Dayan. But, the important element here as regards Begin is that he lobbied to have his long-time adversary Ben-Gurion assume the position of prime minister because Begin felt it would be in the best interest of Israel in a time of crisis.

On June 5, 1967, the Six-Day War began. Strategically and tactically, the war was a brilliant success. In twenty-four hours, Israel had destroyed the Egyptian Air Force, and there were stunning victories on all fronts. Toward the end of the third day, the war was literally won before Jerusalem was united. The UN and U.S. President Johnson applied intense pressure on Israel to stop the war and declare a ceasefire. Begin feared that the war would be halted before Israel reunited Jerusalem. He was also concerned Eshkol wouldn't have the strength of character to resist the outside pressure.

Begin went to see Eshkol again and explained why Israel could not stop before Jerusalem was united. You'll never have another chance, he maintained. Eshkol agreed and stood firm. This proved to be a defining moment for Prime Minister Eshkol and Israel. Begin's selfless efforts at diplomacy in serving Israel's national interest were remarkable.

Again and again, Begin showed strength of character. In fact, Begin's behavior defines the very meaning of character! Menachem Begin had a deep personal conviction in an Israel of Biblical proportions. However, when he saw the opportunity for peace with Egypt, Begin reciprocated Sadat's good faith. In 1979, Begin ordered the dynamiting of Israeli settlements in the Sinai. And, it was Ariel Sharon who was charged with blowing up the largest of them at Yamit.

Menachem Begin was a man of honor. He honored his word, and when he was prime minister, he honored the office he occupied. Begin dressed in the formal European style. Israel is a very casual country. Most of the nation's men walk around without a tie. Begin always wore a suit and a tie, no matter how blistering the heat was. For Begin, it was a matter of respect for the office he held.

Begin's sense of decency and honor was also shaped by his appreciation for the European parliamentary system. When you are accountable for a serious failing, you resign. It's generally maintained that Begin resigned as prime minister because of the death of his beloved wife Aliza several months earlier. That is in part doubtlessly true. But, even more of a factor was the issue of Lebanon. Israel had told the Americans in 1982 it would wage an offensive reaching twenty-two kilometers into Lebanon. That would be all that was needed to disable the Katyusha rockets that were plaguing northern Israel and to create a zone that would put Israel beyond their range. Soviet Katyusha rockets are fired in a battery off the backs of trucks, making their launching highly portable. They have been around since World War II, when they were known as "Stalin's pipe organs."

Israel's defense minister, Ariel Sharon, penetrated all the way to

Beirut. He sustained the invasion and created the quagmire of Lebanon that enmeshed Israel for eighteen years. (Meanwhile, Israel had Arafat in their grasp, and they still let him flee to Tunisia.) It would have been beneath Begin to say that Sharon betrayed his trust. Begin couldn't accept the formulation that Sharon was the accountable party. If Begin didn't know what Sharon was up to, Begin believed he *should* have known. Begin saw this episode as *his* breach of trust to the Americans. And, he could never forgive himself for the hundreds of Israeli soldiers killed and wounded as a consequence of this misadventure. He announced his resignation on August 28, 1983.

Whenever I visited Israel afterward, I always telephoned Begin, but I could never see him. Until his death in 1992, he lived in virtual seclusion. Begin had little money, and he lived very modestly. Sometimes, for people of great passion, there are momentous watersheds—defining moments when your own personal sense of integrity demands that you step aside and shed the mantle of power. Such a defining moment can be a sad, even tragic, consequence of being everything you can be.

I only know this: the bottom line of what Menachem Begin achieved for Israel and for the world by pursuing his passion was an immeasurable contribution from the Holocaust to the rebirth of the Jewish state of Israel.

Unjustly imprisoned political dissidents can become remarkable moral authorities. Begin, Dayan, Rabin, Shamir, Sharansky—some of the greatest men I ever knew were unjustly imprisoned in their lifetimes. So were Thoreau and Mandela. Prison can stir powerful reflections on the value of freedom and nourish a passion for it. I found Begin to be one of the real giants that I've had the privilege to know. I have met a lot of people with influence and power, but not many will be remembered a hundred years from now. Who remembers the leading toga manufacturer of ancient Rome? Who remembers the king of England of a thousand years ago? Begin is one man who I believe *will* be remembered a **thousand** years from now.

SOME KEY THINGS I LEARNED FROM MENACHEM BEGIN ARE:

Leadership requires vision, wisdom and steadfast commitment to its goals.

Prime Minister Begin wanted to be remembered for his leadership in having averted a civil war in Israel over the *Altalena* incident. The restraint Begin imposed on the Irgun demonstrated incredible character, wisdom and courage. It was a defining moment for the young state of Israel.

Be steadfast with your goals.

Be flexible with your strategies and have the courage to change them when appropriate. Menachem Begin consistently served the overarching needs of his cause. His purpose was to re-establish an independent, militarily secure, economically viable, democratic Jewish State of Israel. Menachem Begin earned respect and admiration as a warrior. He leveraged that respect and trust as he took a huge risk and led Israelis on the path to peace with Egypt. Begin had been a man of action—a fighter and a revolutionary. When he became prime minister, he transformed himself because he knew that the destiny of the nation demanded peace. To realize his passionate love of Israel, Menachem Begin focused on the relationship with Anwar Sadat and the possibility for peace.

It's amazing what can be done if you don't worry about who gets the credit.

Begin's phone call to Carter is worthy of reflection. Did it matter to Begin that he get the credit for peace or did it matter far more that Begin might need to call on Carter again as an ally in serving the interests of Israel? Begin was remarkably selfless and projected the importance of the nation first and foremost in everything he did.

This is evidenced by his readiness to make Sadat the hero and give him the credit for the trip to Jerusalem.

The leader is accountable.

Begin believed that victors write history. When they do, reality is filtered through their own paradigms and prejudices. But, Begin also believed that the integrity and the values of a nation were priceless and fundamental. These values had to be respected and upheld at all costs. When he resigned, Begin taught an unforgettable lesson, that the most dedicated leader must accept responsibility for his decisions. If your constituents have endowed you with complete trust, and those subordinates you have empowered violate the people's trust, then a leader of character will step aside and make way for a successor.

RESCUE

To save one life is as if you have saved the world.
—The Talmud

The most beautiful thing in the history of our nation is its tolerance, its hospitality, and forbearance of all who lived among us.
—Metropolitan Stefan of Sophia

The Danish Fishermen

On October 1, 1943, SS Chief Werner Best, the head of the Nazi occupation in Denmark, activated his plan to "deport" the entire Jewish community of Denmark. Of course, "deport" actually meant "transport" the Danish Jews to the death factories in the East. According to **The Copenhagen Post,** *"Best's plans had been leaked to high-ranking Danish politicians, who in turn informed key figures within the Jewish community. Most [Jews] went into hiding... Many Danes felt the German action against the Jews was beyond decency." On October 2, Sweden—neutral in World War II—offered asylum to Danish Jews, and that created a defining moment of opportunity.*

The Nazis were never welcome guests in Denmark, and King Christian X had been forced into "castle-arrest" for his outspoken anti-Nazi sentiments. When the Nazis announced their plan to deport all Jews to the East, the Danish resistance movement went into action instantly. Jews were hidden throughout Denmark and then systematically smuggled to the Danish coast. Denmark had a population of about 8,000 Jews. Of them, 7,500 were successfully evacuated to Sweden in small fishing boats over a period of three weeks.

Of course there was the occasional case in which a boat owner exacted a ransom for transportation beyond the three-mile limit. But, far and away, this was a humanitarian mission performed by normal

55

people faced with a totally abnormal moral challenge under great danger to the fishermen and their families and at no benefit. Under the cover that they were night fishing, the Christian fishermen hid the Jews beneath tarpaulins as their boats passed under the beams of spotlights mounted on Nazi patrol ships.

In 1986, a friend of mine, John Loeb, then-U.S. Ambassador to Denmark, concluded that recognition for the heroism and courage of the Danish fishermen was long overdue. He organized a dinner in New York to which I was invited to honor what these wonderful, "normal," and yet far beyond the normal, people did in a crisis. Several of these lifesaving fishermen attended and represented this courageous group.

I asked one fisherman, "Why? Why did you do what you did?"

He just looked at me. He scratched his head, stroked his long, silver moustache, and frowned in the most wonderful, uncomprehending way.

"I don't understand," he said, "why you think it is so unusual. We only did what *anyone* would do." If only that were true! Indifference to Evil is evil. These were the heroes in humanity's moment of crisis. These righteous Gentiles helped redeem mankind at its darkest time.

Ninety-five percent of Denmark's Jewish population survived the Holocaust. In Sweden, many Danish Jews were able to continue work in their professions. When the war was over, most Danish Jews returned to Denmark to a warm welcome from their fellow Danes, resuming their careers and ownership of their property. Along with Bulgaria, Denmark's treatment of its Jews during the Holocaust was a landmark stand for human decency.

One key thing I learned from the Danish Fishermen is:

Resistance to Evil is good.

One by one, these Danish fishermen seized the moment to make the world a better place. It's not enough to know what's right; you must have the courage to do it. During the Holocaust, Europe was frozen in a stupor of moral indifference with the exception of two little countries—Denmark and Bulgaria. It is outrage about Evil and the courage to confront it that caused figures like the German businessman Schindler, the Swedish architect and merchant Wallenberg, and the Danish fishermen to do what they did. Very few of us will be remembered in a thousand years. What *will* be remembered is great Evil and great Good. The Danish Resistance and the fishermen rescued 7,500 lives. They didn't just preach or express outrage. They organized themselves to act decisively and courageously. In a thousand years, the names of the rescuers may all be forgotten. The act itself, this remarkable defining moment? It can never be erased.

The Bulgarian Defiance

Before World War II, there were about ten million Jews in Europe. After the war, only four million survived. Six million were slaughtered in the Holocaust. There were 48,000 Jews in Bulgaria before the war, and there were almost 50,000 after the war. Bulgaria was the only nation in Europe during World War II to experience an *increase* in the size of the Jewish community during the slaughter of the Holocaust. Denmark and Bulgaria were the only countries to save nearly their entire Jewish populations. Not a single Jew was deported from Bulgaria proper to the deathcamps.

How did this happen? Why did this happen? What can the rest of the world learn from this experience? To try and get some answers to these questions, my wife, Carol Sue, and I went to Bulgaria recently to meet with some Jewish survivors and some of the non-Jews who saved them.

Why did this happen in Bulgaria? How? There is no single or easy answer. There are many factors that came together in time and place to create the conditions that saved Bulgarian Jewry. Among them:

> A 500-year tradition of tolerance for minorities in Bulgaria.

> Moral courage and leadership for doing the right thing, as exemplified by the heads of the Bulgarian Orthodox Church.

The courageous leadership of public figures such as the deputy chairman of the Bulgarian Parliament to confront Evil.

The shift in the fortunes of the war against Hitler in 1943.

The unprecedented acts of moral courage by citizens of Bulgaria who, at risk to their own and their families' safety, defied the Germans and the pro-Nazi Bulgarians. This particular point was the defining difference in my opinion: proof positive that resistance to Evil is good and that one person can make a difference and make the world a better place.

Bulgaria lacked the dazzling intellectual and cultural refinement of Germany. Yet, compared with Germany, Bulgaria proved to be a glistening moral star. Bulgaria's performance is vivid proof that cultural polish and education are not related to strength of conscience and depth of courage.

INSTITUTIONAL LEADERS

The Orthodox Christian Churches of Eastern Europe do not have a single religious leader as does the Roman Catholic Church in Rome. While they hold many practices and beliefs in common, the Orthodox Churches in such countries as Greece, Russia, and Bulgaria are all organized and led at a national level, and their top authorities are national figures.

Metropolitan (Archbishop) Stefan of Sofia was born in 1878 in the tiny Bulgarian village of Shiroka Luka in the Rhodope Mountains. Tall and handsome, he spent four years studying for the priesthood in Kiev, and then entered a military academy. He became an officer before his religious ordination in his early thirties. An activist who was at odds with the Bulgarian monarch King Ferdinand, he went to Switzerland and earned a PhD. On Ferdinand's abdication, he returned to Bulgaria. His rise within the church was meteoric and he became Metropolitan of Sofia, the most powerful figure in the Bulgarian Orthodox Church, the faith of 85% of all Bulgarians, in 1934.

Metropolitan Kyril of Plovdiv was also a spirited activist. He studied theology in Belgrade and became Metropolitan of Plovdiv in 1938. After the Second World War, he became the first Patriarch of all Bulgaria since the eighteenth century, which he remained until his death in 1971.

Another figure who played a crucial leadership role in the Bulgarian story was Dimitar Peshev. Born in Kyustendil in 1894, Peshev had been a lawyer and a judge before becoming deputy speaker of the Bulgarian parliament and minister of justice in 1938.

Bulgaria is a mountainous country with a sizable coast on the Black Sea. Until August 2005, its prime minister was its former King Simeon II—the only ex-monarch to return to political power in all of Eastern Europe. But, the Bulgarian royal house is not an old one. Bulgaria first existed as a country in 1878, and had been carved out of the Ottoman Empire. From the time of its independence, Bulgaria had been very much within the German sphere of influence. Principally for this reason, Bulgaria's King Boris III saw an alliance with Germany as inevitable as World War II approached.

In 1935, the Nazi regime in Germany enacted the infamous Nuremberg Laws, which eliminated rights of citizenship for all Jews in Germany and forbade Jewish intermarriage with Aryans. Partly as an effort to avoid being overrun by the Germans, Bulgaria formally joined the Axis powers and became a German ally. While an ally, Bulgaria technically remained neutral during the war and sent no troops into combat. German troops *were* allowed access to Bulgaria, which they used as a staging area for the Nazi assaults into Greece and Yugoslavia. As a reward for this support, Bulgaria received the provinces of Thrace and Macedonia in 1941, with their additional 11,384 Jews. These acts of expediency had internal consequences for Bulgaria and its King Boris III.

Bulgaria had a 500-year tradition of tolerance for its Armenian, Gypsy, Turkish, and Jewish minorities. When 200,000 Jews were expelled from Spain during the Inquisition on July 30, 1492, some fled eastward and ended up in what is today Bulgaria. After a million Armenians were slaughtered in Turkey in 1915, many of the survivors fled to Bulgaria. The Nazis demanded that Bulgaria implement a racist national policy comparable to the Nuremberg Laws. Almost all of the 48,000 Jews in Bulgaria proper lived in cities and roughly half of them made their home in Sofia. The Bulgarian Jews were historically not ghettoized and, despite maintaining their own customs and spearheading the most active Zionist movement in all of Europe, Bulgarian Jews were fully assimilated. Indeed, they were patriotic Bulgarians, with a number of valiant Bulgarian Jewish military heroes in the country's short history.

The looming tie with Nazi Germany had been evident in 1939, when 4,000 foreign national Jews were expelled from Bulgaria. Nearly all of them fled the country by ship and entered Palestine as "illegal immigrants." The 1940 Bulgarian version of the Nuremberg Laws—known in Bulgaria as the Law for the Protection of the Nation—struck a raw nerve within Bulgarian society. The law created a Commissariat for Jewish affairs headed by a German-trained, anti-Semitic attorney named Alexander Belev. Generals wrote telegrams stressing the valor of Jewish soldiers in the Balkan hostilities of 1912–13 and the First World War. Newspapers clamored against the law's injustices. According to Yad Vashem, Israel's Holocaust memorial, museum, and archive outside Jerusalem, Dimo Kazasov issued an open letter. In it, Kazasov, a non-Jewish parliamentarian and the publisher of Bulgaria's most widely circulated newspaper, declared to the king and the parliament:

> You have fallen low! In the past you fought at international conferences for the rights of Bulgarian minorities to live in peace

in their countries of residence. And now you attack the Jewish minority in your own country. In so doing, you dishonor the entire Bulgarian people. "The law for the protection of the nation" is a disgrace. You are attacking a minority which lives among us and which has sacrificed itself for this country. How dare you place them outside of the law?

For his candor, Kazasov was imprisoned by the political police.

The Orthodox Church rebuked the government for its cowardliness. Nonetheless, the Law for the Protection of the Nation took effect in January 1941. Among the consequences: Jews could only shop at designated stores; Jews and Gypsies could not cross major streets; intermarriage was banned; Jews were banished from university study, public office, and union membership; Jewish doctors and pharmacists were not allowed to practice; All Jews were required to wear the yellow Star of David, a painful and degrading statement of separation. According to Howard Sachar in *Farewell España,*

> ...all Jewish males of military age [were dispatched] to road-building camps, with the physically unfit obliged to pay a crippling indemnity tax. By June 1942...nearly six thousand Jewish men and boys were living in penal compounds. Working fifteen hours a day, they suffered freezing weather, malnutrition, illness, [and] periodic beatings.

Their meager diet consisted of a breakfast of tea and bread, bread and beans for lunch, and bread and jam for dinner. Each worker was required to break a meter-long stretch of rock each day. Many, if not most of these conscripted laborers, contracted malaria. But thousands of non-Jewish Bulgarians risked their lives to bring these Jews food, clothing, and medicine, which helped them survive.

These punitive actions satisfied neither Berlin nor the small but powerful band of Bulgarian anti-Semites with increasing power in Sofia. The Nazis turned up the heat. In August 1942, the first plans were laid for the mass deportation of all Bulgarian Jews to the death camps in Poland, and various efforts were made to round up Jews. At that time, 20,000 was set as an initial Jewish deportation target for Bulgaria. In February and March 1943, the first phase of the plan was implemented. While the Bulgarian leadership opposed the deportation, the least painful decision—they felt—was to acquiesce to the transportation of the 11,384 Jews from Macedonia and Thrace in February. Tragically, all but twelve of these Jews were murdered in Treblinka, Poland. While many Bulgarian leaders reviled the decision to allow the deportation of these Jews, the national political and church leaders were not prepared to draw a line in the sand over this point. After all, they reasoned, these territories were not an historical part of Bulgaria to begin with.

What about the other 8,616 Jews needed to fill the Nazi quota that would have to be drawn from Bulgaria proper? The collection of Bulgarian Jews began in the same month. On March 9–10, King Boris enacted a law ordering the deportation of native Bulgarian Jews. To create the pool from which these Jews would be drawn, Jews were herded into ghettos within such urban areas as Sofia and Plovdiv. The 25,000 Jews in Sofia were ordered to leave their homes and to surrender their property. That's when the Holy Synod, the top ecclesiastic body of the Bulgarian Church, went into action, spurred largely by Metropolitan Stefan and Metropolitan Kyril and confronted the King and the government. Is it enough that the Bulgarians Defiance rescued Jews based on the fact that these were *their* Jews? Courageous people throughout Bulgaria and Denmark took a stand at these defining moments and saved their Jews. It worked. If the other peoples of Europe had demonstrated the same character and courage, how many more Jews could have been saved?

Dr. Pavel Gerdjikov is perhaps the most astonishing of the lesser known figures, and I had the privilege of meeting with his wife and daughter. Today Gerdjikov, then a medical doctor in the Bulgarian army, is known as the *Bulgarian Schindler*. He observed a trainload of deportees coming from Thrace and Macedonia in early 1943. The train had stopped in Sofia, and Dr. Gerdjikov heard cries from the Jews for help. They needed water, food, and even air! Using only his credentials and the power of his personality, he bullied his way to the commander of the train and gained custody of five Jewish children, saving their lives. He claimed he had orders to provide them with medical care. In fact, he courageously pulled the wool over the eyes of the train commanders... and got away with it! After a brief stay in a hospital, two of the children were placed with a Jewish family and three were given refuge in an Orthodox monastery. This was just one of Gerdjikov's humanitarian acts. He also hid a Jewish family of ten in his home in a concealed room for two years at the risk of his and his family's lives.

Fifteen hundred Jews were arrested in Metropolitan Kyril's city of Plovdiv—the city with the second largest Jewish population. The Jews were rounded up and herded onto the grounds of the Jewish school. Kyril confronted the Bulgarian guards in the schoolyard. He told them if they tried to take the Jews to the trains, he would personally lay his body across the railroad tracks in front of the locomotive and that he would bring others who would do the same. Kyril sent an urgent message to King Boris III to demand that the Jews be released. According to Martin Gilbert in his book *The Righteous*, an outraged Kyril told the Holy Synod: "When someone comes to your house and tells you to pack up things in two hours and be ready to leave for some place unknown—this is unheard of and unseen in our country."

In Sofia, word had also reached Metropolitan Stefan. His reaction: "If our Church doesn't intervene to defend these wretched people, we should expect even worse outrages and acts of cruelty, for which one day our good-hearted people will feel shame," according to Michael Bar-Zohar in *Beyond Hitler's Grasp*. He demanded an immediate audience with the king, bringing Jewish community leaders as part of his delegation. The king feigned illness, but Stefan refused to leave until they met. According to Simantov Madjar, the current president of the Plovdiv Jewish community, Metropolitan Stefan said to Boris: "I put the crown on your father's head. [When he died,] I took it off. I also put the crown on your head and if you let the Bulgarian Jews be killed, I will take it off of your head too." When the king's response was evasive, Stefan remained steadfast. He left to return to his office, which was nearby. When he arrived, Stefan's secretary said the king's office is on the phone. Stefan said, "Hang up. I do not speak with cowards."

Deputy Speaker Dimitar Peshev, who had *not* opposed the Law for the Protection of the Nation, finally found his conscience had reached its breaking point. Bringing down Prime Minister Filov's wrath (and that of the king as well), Peshev and more than forty members of parliament signed a letter that petitioned for the immediate release of Jews and an end to their persecution. Twenty of the parliamentarians, including Peshev, were threatened with the death penalty. Peshev was dismissed from the post of minister of justice. Peshev also lost his post in parliament.

On March 28, 1943, King Boris met with Hitler in Berchtesgaden. At that meeting, the Germans made clear that it was no longer a matter of the previously agreed to 20,000 Jews. They wanted all of the Bulgarian Jews deported to the death camps. Boris agreed. Following the meeting with Hitler, Boris communicated his decision to Prime Minster Filov. When that became known, the Bulgarian Church Synod vowed to excommunicate the king if he implemented the deportation. Stefan by fiat "converted" all the Jews in Bulgaria to Christians to elude the order, but the government refused to recognize the conversion.

According to Yad Vashem documents, Metropolitan Stefan wrote the king: "Do not persecute so that you yourself will not be persecuted. Your measures shall be returned to you. I know, Boris, that from heaven God will keep watch over your actions." Finally, the king relented. The deportation order was postponed time after time. The Bulgarian Jews were dispersed into the countryside, making their assembly for deportation a logistic nightmare. And then, the Soviet "liberation" of Bulgaria occurred in 1944 and 50,000 Jews were saved.

The consequences for the Bulgarian principals:

King Boris III—whom some see as an out-and-out collaborator with Hitler—still yielded to popular will and the threats of the Church. He died mysteriously in August 1943, after his last meeting with the Führer, and it has been widely speculated that Boris was poisoned by the SS.

Metropolitan Stefan? The Communist regime sent him into exile as an incorrigible democratic troublemaker in 1948. He died in seclusion in an isolated monastery in 1957.

Metropolitan Kyril went on to run the Bulgarian Orthodox Church, but was never really trusted by either the Bulgarians or the ruling Communists because of the compromises he was seen as having made with the Communists to allow the Church to continue to exist in the country.

Dimitar Peshev? The Communists charged him with collaborating with the German Nazis. Despite Jewish community pleas to the contrary, Peshev was sentenced to fifteen years in prison after the war ended. Although he served only one of these, the rest of Peshev's life, which ended in 1973, was spent in poverty and isolation.

Fittingly, Stefan, Kyril, Dimo Kazasov, Dr. Pavel Gerdjikov, and Dimitar Peshev are all enshrined in the Righteous Among the Nations at Yad Vashem.

The Unorthodox Many

What these forceful leaders really did was fulfill a mandate delivered by Mr. and Mrs. Bulgaria. An illustrative and moving story about the courage of the Bulgarians was told to me by a woman named Beba, who was a young mother of two in 1943. Her family lived in her grandmother's home on the first floor of a two-story house in Plovdiv. A Christian family lived on the second floor. When the deportation order was issued in Plovdiv, the Christian neighbor asked Beba if she could take both of the Jewish children to live with them. Beba didn't want to break apart the family, but the offer indicated the extent of support in the non-Jewish community. This was one of thousands of acts of decency, humanity, and courage that helped save the entire Jewish population of Bulgaria.

Beba's grandfather had a good friend who was a prosperous tobacco merchant. He came to the grandfather and suggested that he put all his valuables in the tobacco merchant's care for safekeeping until after the war, when he would then return them. Beba's grandfather did so. At risk to his own family, the merchant protected all the assets and returned them intact at the end of the war.

Beba was touched personally by the events of 1943 in Plovdiv. She had two uncles who lived with the family, and one worked illegally for the Communist Party in the Resistance. In the Bulgarian central police headquarters, he learned there were plans for the 7,800 Jews of Plovdiv, already photographed and fingerprinted, to be rounded up immediately. Transportation to Poland was to happen the next day. The uncle called all of his extended family to the kitchen table. He said that they would be brought to the Jewish school. He suggested each of the family members pack separate luggage for themselves. He suspected the deportation would separate men, women, and children.

At 3 A.M., the police entered the grandmother's house with guns and demanded they immediately pack for a trip. The grandmother was not very well educated but she was very smart. She talked to the family in the Ladino[1] language and told them to move ahead with their packing very sluggishly, so that it wouldn't be finished until daybreak. Her

---

1 Ladino is a mixture of medieval Spanish and Hebrew. It is used primarily by the Sephardic Jews of Eastern Europe.

reasoning: Non-Jewish Bulgarians would then see the deportation as they started to head for work. She hoped this would cause a reaction of conscience. And, it did! Word spread quickly around town that the deportation of the Jews was beginning. Metropolitan Kyril was outraged, and made a personal pledge to the Jews of Plovdiv: "Wherever you go, I'll go!"

Simantov Madjar of Plovdiv was an eight-year-old boy in 1943. While walking home from school, he saw a German military motorcyclist run into a Jew who was wearing the required yellow Star of David, and break the Jew's leg. The German looked down at the man writhing in pain and said, "It doesn't matter. He's only a Jew." The young boy started to cry. He was deeply hurt by what he just witnessed—not just the accident, but the sense of hopeless degradation as well. A non-Jewish woman who saw this event asked the young boy to come with her to her home for milk and cookies. She sat the boy down, stared him in the eye, and said to him, "You should be very proud to be a Jew. Look what the Jews have done to make the world a better place. Moses was a Jew, and the Jews gave the world the Ten Commandments. Jesus was a Jew. So was Einstein. Walk with your head high young man!" That woman's husband was the secretary to Metropolitan Kyril.

The acts of the Bulgarian Many are—despite several recent books—little known. But, their good deeds happened day after day during the years of the occupation throughout the country. In 1942, during a round-up, one non-Jewish baker hid six Jews in his unheated oven to protect them from the police. When the Jews were dispersed to the rural areas, everyday Bulgarians—sometimes even Bulgarian police officers—made sure that they had food supply channels open from Jews in nearby villages or shared with them their own scarce food supplies. When the law forbade Jews from being taken into Bulgarian homes, some Bulgarians vacated their homes and moved in with other non-Jews. The empty houses were then occupied by Jews.

On my visit, survivors recounted harrowing encounters of how they narrowly avoided being transported to the death camps by train or ships. In one such incident, a survivor among the conscripted laborers named Natan described how the workers started to sing and dance. They were dirty and had lice in their hair, but the non-Jewish Bulgarians from the village—including the police—came to embrace and congratulate them, joined them in singing the Bulgarian national anthem. In September 1944, the Soviets "liberated" Bulgaria. Nazi influence was broken and the old Bulgarian government collapsed. The Soviet occupation continued until 1989.

Historians have also pointed out that some Bulgarians were looking over their shoulders at the changing tide of history. By March 1943, the Germans had experienced devastating defeats on the Russian front. Stalingrad was lost in February 1943, and the siege of Leningrad ended in September 1944. The North African campaign was in full swing, and the Allies were beginning their European penetration in the Mediterranean. "How will the West treat us after the war if we do *not* act to safeguard the Jews?" That's a question some Bulgarians—especially senior officials—surely asked. But, the overwhelming evidence is that the Bulgarian Defiance was waged broadly throughout the population with considerable courage and at great risk. And tragedy often compounded itself after the first threat ended, the voices of resistance against the Nazis were often punished by the successor tyranny of Communism.

About thirty kilometers outside of Plovdiv, stands the imposing Bachkovo Monastery where Metropolitans Stefan and Kyril are buried. I decided to go and say a prayer of remembrance and gratitude in this very tranquil mountain setting. It was said on behalf of decent people everywhere. The Bulgarian woman who took us to the monastery had recently accompanied a group of Israelis to the same site. She recounted the stories of Stefan, Kyril, and Gerdjikov.

Then a cynical Israeli asked her, "How do you know all of these claims about Bulgarian heroism to be true?" "Because I was one of forty Jewish children hidden in this monastery," she answered.

*   *   *

Following the creation of the state of Israel in 1948 by the United Nations (an act which the Soviets supported), the USSR permitted some 45,000 Jews to emigrate from Bulgaria to Israel. Today there are somewhere between 7,000–10,000 Jews living in Bulgaria. Some have intermarried. There is an organized and active Jewish community with synagogues, day schools, youth groups, summer camps, community centers, and homes for the aged. Much of this is made possible through the dedicated leadership and funding of the American Jewish Joint Distribution Committee (JDC), as well as the funding of the Conference on Jewish Material Claims for Holocaust Survivors and private donations from the Ronald Lauder Foundation and from the Jewish community of Bulgaria.

TWO KEY THINGS I LEARNED FROM THE BULGARIAN DEFIANCE ARE:

Acts of courage are not always pure nor simple.

If there hadn't been a Holocaust, what happened to the Jews in Bulgaria should have awakened outrage in the international Jewish community. The forced-work camps endured by the men, the loss of personal property to the state, the disruption of families, and the indignities of the Law for the Protection of the Nation were all diabolical and viciously anti-Semitic.

King Boris III remains a checkered figure for many, and yet he may have had a calculating method to what he did. When Boris was asked to explain his policy toward the Jews not long before his death in 1943 he is alleged to have said:

> It has been a difficult situation. We tried to convince the Germans that we need to keep the Jews to use their labor to build and repair the infrastructure. Our real motive was to keep the

Jews in Bulgaria and to prevent them from being deported to the death camps. Sometimes you have to choose between a big evil and a smaller evil. I have chosen the smaller evil.

For a society to make a difference, you need *both* the pillars of leadership and the foundation of leadership moments.

The daring acts of Stefan, Kyril, and Peshev are the dazzling visible tip of the iceberg of the Bulgarian Resistance, but what of the bulwark beneath it? Acts by tens of thousands of Bulgarians were done at personal and family peril. And, the impact of the two types of leadership cannot be separated. The visible leaders could not have acted effectively had the people not given a mandate to defy the Nazi-linked government. The courageous acts of the many were inspired by the courageous acts of the institutional leaders and vice versa.

When conscience is forged to courage, there is no better anvil than a tradition of honor and tolerance. With decency and dignity, the Bulgarian Defiance helped to redeem mankind in its darkest hours. This was a defining moment both for Bulgarian honor and for Bulgarian Jewry.

Remembering Wallenberg

The Wallenberg family's influence in Sweden goes back a long way.

By the nineteenth century, the Wallenbergs were formidable figures in Swedish banking, mining, and publishing. Their reach also extended into diplomatic circles. When the Nazis took over in Germany, Sweden remained a neutral nation, but Germany's power in central Europe could hardly be disregarded. During the war, the Wallenberg family juggled its relationships with both the Axis and Allied powers. Some historians contend that the Wallenberg business interests were always center stage and that some senior Wallenbergs were more accommodating than they needed to be to the Nazis and to wartime German business interests.

In 1912 Raoul Wallenberg was born. After graduating with a bachelor's degree from the University of Michigan in 1935, Wallenberg started apprenticing the multifaceted business world commanded by his family, first in South Africa, and then in Haifa in Palestine. It's important to note that Wallenberg was not Jewish—neither paternally nor maternally, nor through adoption by his stepfather Fredrik von Dardel. (Raoul's birth father died of cancer just months before Raoul's birth.) Nonetheless, in 1936 after his favorable experience in Haifa, Raoul formed his own business partnership with a Hungarian Jew named Koloman Lauer.

The two operated a Swedish-based trading company specialized in food products.

Raoul Wallenberg was an adroit linguist with a flair for diplomacy. He learned the workings of the Nazi bureaucracy, as others in his family did, because Germany was an integral trading partner for any country in central Europe. Raoul had a clear humanitarian sympathy for the Jews according to biographer Jan Larsson. He appreciated what they were going through—the degradation of the Nuremberg Laws enacted in 1935, the pandering to Nazi Germany at the Munich Conference that took place in 1938, and the infamous Kristallnacht of the same year. Hungary was an ally of Germany until 1944, and German fascist thinking was being promulgated in Hungary by a counterpart pro-Nazi Hungarian political party known as the Arrow Cross. Wallenberg was also able to visit Lauer's family in Budapest during the war when it became impossible for Lauer himself to do so. Raoul understood what was happening to Jews in Europe on the ground as it unfolded.

Until 1944, Hungary maintained relative autonomy because the Hungarians were German allies in fighting the Soviets on the Eastern front. The 700,000 Jews then in Hungary seemed safe from the Nazi killing machine, although young Jewish men were enslaved in forced labor camps. After the decisive German defeats at Stalingrad and later in Leningrad, the Hungarians could read the handwriting on the wall and wanted to end their tie with the Nazis and seek a separate peace with the Allies. Outraged at this show of independence, Germany invaded Hungary on March 19, 1944. Jews were herded into the ghettos, and the mass transport of Hungarian Jews to the death camps in southern Poland got rapidly underway.

Appalled by this turn of events, Per Anger, who had joined the Swedish legation in Budapest as second secretary two

*years earlier, came up with the novel idea of providing pro-
tective Swedish passports to Hungarian Jews. In short order, Anger issued some seven hundred such passports. At
roughly the same time, consciousness of the Holocaust had
risen dramatically within the American Jewish community.
Treasury Secretary Henry Morgenthau—the only Jew in the
Cabinet—approached President Roosevelt and convinced
him of America's urgent need to act. The War Refugees Board
was organized in January 1944 as a response, and foreign
committees became links to it. One of these was in Sweden, and Koloman Lauer was appointed a member.*

*It was obvious that the efforts to save Hungarian Jews
had to be beefed up and fast! The War Refugees Board
needed a point man in Budapest to expand the rescue effort and to maximize the impact of the foreign funding
that was now available. Despite concern that Wallenberg
was too young and inexperienced, Lauer was able to get
his business partner appointed as secretary to the Swedish
legation in Budapest. Between May 1944, and Wallenberg's
arrival in July, about 550,000 Jews were transported to the
death camps and murdered there.*

*Wallenberg's ingenious first action was to build on Per
Anger's concept of a protective passport. The documents
Wallenberg had created were multicolored and embossed
with the Swedish triple-crown national emblem. They maintained that their holders were being officially repatriated
as Swedish citizens. Jews filled the Swedish embassy to the
rafters. Wallenberg also rented safehouses in Budapest,
which were often identified as Swedish "cultural" institutions, but were actually refuges for Jews. Raoul Wallenberg
suavely cut deals with Nazi henchmen like Adolph Eich-
mann to avert or delay the transportation of Jews. Raoul
literally shoved his passports into the hands of Jews who
were crammed into the cattle cars en route to their annihi-*

lation, and he demanded the documents be recognized and these doomed people be released immediately.

Wallenberg's chauffeured car would race up to the loading platforms of Budapest's central train station. He would jump out in his trenchcoat and yell with total command, "Stop, stop! There's been a grave error!" Waving his ingeniously forged passports in the air, he would shout out the names of those marked for the death camps. "Stern, Meyer, Goldschmied—get into these trucks!" Then they would be hustled into the waiting vehicles and whisked off to the rented safehouses throughout Budapest. When those houses were filled to the brim, Wallenberg rented more safehouses to quarter ever more refugees. He never let overwhelming odds daunt either his conviction or his imagination. Wallenberg lied, cheated, threatened, and bribed. When needed, he ruptured all the niceties and norms of traditional diplomatic protocol in his defiant display of character and courage.

The Arrow Cross seized control of the Hungarian government in October 1944. Under its regime, an additional 80,000 Hungarian Jews were either murdered in Hungary or exterminated in Poland. By the time of the Soviet liberation of Hungary in January 1945, several authorities estimated that Wallenberg's unprecedented rescue efforts had saved the lives of some 100,000 Jews in Budapest. His direct efforts rescued 20,000 Jews in the city and may have saved many, many more. Indirectly he helped saved perhaps another 80,000 Jews by delaying their transport to the death camps; so that they were alive when the Soviets liberated Hungary. Unfortunately, Wallenberg's remarkable leadership had no impact outside of Budapest. Only 20,000 Jews survived the Holocaust in all of Hungary outside of Budapest. Wallenberg's heroic effort—directly and indirectly—saved more Jews in Europe than any other single initiative.

When the Soviets entered Budapest in 1945, Wallenberg was anxious that the sanctity of the safehouses be maintained. He and his driver sped to Soviet headquarters to brief the new authorities on the existence of the safehouses. The two were arrested on the spot. Why would this scion of a wealthy Swedish family, the Soviets wondered, put himself at risk to do what he did for Jews? He must have been a madman or an utterly unmanageable rebel in the least; a certain threat to a proletarian totalitarian regime, which was also fundamentally anti-Semitic in its mindset. And, what's more, because of his involvement with the War Refugees Board, probably an American spy to boot. Then for decades, the thread of Raoul Wallenberg's life and the memory of his momentous accomplishments vanished. There is one exception to this neglect, and that occurred within Israel itself. In 1966, Raoul Wallenberg received the Righteous Among the Nations honor, but this was scant recognition for his enormous achievements.

Annette Tilleman was twelve-years-old when the Nazis occupied Hungary. Her father was a prominent figure in the Jewish community of Budapest. The Arrow Cross had already imprisoned him in a forced-labor camp. When the Nazis rolled into Budapest in 1944, one of the first SS targets was the home of the Tilleman family. They were on the Nazi liquidation A-list.

Intuitively, Annette saw the inevitable. She told her mother that she wouldn't stay a minute longer in their apartment. "Where can we go?" her mother asked. "Let's try to hide with the grandparents before the SS get us. They've already blocked all the streets!" Annette answered. Shortly afterward, she and her mother arrived on the doorstep of Annette's maternal grandmother. The next morning, the grandmother called a cousin, an assistant to the Portuguese ambassador to Hungary, and asked for sanctuary for Annette and her mother in the Portuguese embassy. Portugal, like Sweden, was also a neutral nation during World War II. The embassy was able to offer them refuge, and they were sequestered there for nine months. Then they received protective passports through the Portuguese government. When the Portuguese ambassador was recalled to Lisbon, he took six Jews with him including Annette and her mother on these passports. (The concept of protective passports innovated by the Swedes was replicated by other neutral nations with diplomatic legations in Budapest.) En route to Portugal, Annette and her mother were able to stop in Switzerland, which is where they remained from December 1944 through November 1945.

After the war ended, Annette and her mother returned to Budapest to discover the fates of their loved ones. Annette's grandmother was killed by the Nazis or the Arrow Cross as was everyone else in her family, except for one uncle who had gained refuge in Budapest's Vatican embassy. In addition to family members, Annette was desperately trying to learn the whereabouts of a boy named Tom Lantos— the love of her life. Born in 1928, Tom was only sixteen and Annette was a mere thirteen and a half, but both knew that their relationship was very deep. Annette discovered Tom had been given refuge at one of the Wallenberg safehouses. Annette and Tom remained in Budapest for about a year. Tom recalls today: "There was this Swede in a trenchcoat. If you could get to him, you had a chance of surviving." Wallenberg, in fact, used Tom, with his blond hair and Aryan features, as a courier when he needed deliveries made in the city. Today Tom believes he owes his very life to Wallenberg.

Tom was able to win a scholarship at the University of Washington. Among the 3,000 applicants for these grants worldwide, only fifty won grants, but not all of these ultimately got to attend the university. The University was now overrun with U.S. war veterans returning to college on the G.I. Bill and filling the dormitories. Of the fifty scholarship winners abroad, only ten were able to attend, with their fate decided by raffle. Tom was one of the lucky ten. In 1950, Annette and Tom married after he had become a faculty member at San Francisco State University. In America, Tom and Annette revived a relationship begun long ago in Budapest. The couple shared a common debt to Wallenberg. How to repay it was the challenge.

By the late 1970s, the general presumption was that Wallenberg had died in a Soviet prison. As Annette was getting ready to attend a wedding reception in 1977, she heard that Simon Wiesenthal had given a news conference in Rome, and said that Wallenberg was probably alive in a Soviet "mental hospital" in Siberia. She was shocked. This was a defining moment in her life. "Wedding receptions can come and go," she said to herself, "but, if Wallenberg was still alive, I had to become involved in trying to save his life and free him." This was her opportunity to make a difference, and that is what she intended to do.

It didn't happen over night. Annette was a housewife with neither wealth nor connections. In 1980, after thirty years as an economics professor, Tom was elected to the U.S. House of Representatives. Tom and Annette finally had a platform from which they could mobilize support for finding Raoul Wallenberg. No, it didn't happen overnight. But, there is one great thing about networks: They percolate!

Jack Anderson wrote one of his syndicated columns about Wallenberg. That column appeared in the *Columbus Dispatch,* and it mentioned Annette Lantos's campaign to find out what had actually happened to Raoul Wallenberg. I was stunned and appalled by what I read. I had been involved with Jewish causes since I was fifteen, and I never knew of this Swedish hero. In all those years of Jewish life, I had never even *heard* of Raoul Wallenberg. Why didn't I know about this remarkable hero? I called Elie Wiesel to verify if the Wallenberg story was true. Elie wasn't sure if the number of Jews saved totaled 20,000 or 100,000, but true it was and "what," Elie said, "did the number matter?"

After sending Annette Lantos a modest check to support her efforts, I called her to find out what I could do further. I helped Annette raise money to aid her development of an organization to free Raoul Wallenberg, and aided Tom Lantos in getting a bill through Congress on May 19, 1981 to make Wallenberg only the second honorary citizen of the United States. The first was Winston Churchill.

The whereabouts of Wallenberg was a topic raised from time to time during East-West talks in the 1980s. Chapters of books—indeed *entire* books—were written about Wallenberg. Television documentaries were produced and aired. People were sought who might have any information about him.

A few members of the Wallenberg family, I have been told, disowned Raoul. If he had been alive, they didn't seem anxious to have had him released. They saw him as an embarrassment and discouraged the Swedish government from finding him. In Stockholm, Annette Lantos, working with Wallenberg's half-sister, Nina Lagergren, and Per Anger organized a full-scale inquiry on Wallenberg's fate to provide a central clearinghouse for all the information and possible whereabouts. I went to Stockholm to attend the inquiry and met with Nina Lagergren and with Per Anger, who had since served as Swedish ambassador to Australia and Canada.

Wallenberg may have been anti-Nazi and pro-Jewish, but those weren't decisive factors for the Soviets. In all likelihood, the Soviets considered him an American spy because of his link to the War Refugees Board. When the KGB files ultimately were opened, not a single piece of paper was found. The KGB, it is contended, tracked down and killed people who had evidence about Wallenberg. They deliberately purged all the records from their files. After exhaustive research, it was ultimately concluded that Wallenberg died as a victim of the Soviet prison system, probably as early as 1947. It wasn't until 1989, that the then-teetering Soviet government finally returned Wallenberg's personal effects to his family.

He was recognized by the Knesset on what would have been his seventy-fifth birthday on August 4, 1987. The Holocaust Memorial Museum in Washington is situated on Raoul Wallenberg Place. There are Wallenberg statues in Hungary and Israel and a tree in his memory on the Avenue of the Righteous in Yad Vashem. These are tributes, no doubt, but it is shameful that this is all that has been done. Do students in the free world today know about Wallenberg's defining moment? Is he used as an example of heroic leadership, character, and courage in courses about ethics and values? I constantly hear the refrain that there are so few heroes. Raoul Wallenberg was one of the great heroes of modern times, but his name is scarcely known. Why aren't we holding Raoul Wallenberg up as an heroic example of how to make the world a better place?

TWO KEY THINGS I LEARNED FROM WALLENBERG AND HIS COMMEMORATION ARE:

One person can make a difference.

Raoul Wallenberg was a handsome, wealthy, non-Jewish young man in his thirties, and the citizen of a neutral nation. Why did he put his promising young life on the line to save thousands—perhaps a hundred thousand—Jews in Hungary? Here is one of the great heroes who understood that resistance to Evil is good. For those of true conscience, it is not only doing good, doing otherwise is unthinkable. In certain respects, we know little about Wallenberg the person and *very* little about his motivations. I would maintain that Wallenberg was undeniably a leader of enormous character. When the moment arose to make a difference, it was this foundation of character that defined the moral compass on which he could act with great courage.

Congressman Tom Lantos uttered some poignant words when he memorialized Wallenberg in Stockholm in 1989:

> Raoul taught us two things. Raoul taught us that a single individual committed to an idea can achieve miracles, and Raoul taught us that human rights are indivisible; it is not enough just to be concerned with our own human rights.... Raoul Wallenberg not only fought evil, but he also fought indifference, and indifference is the twin of evil. Those who kill are murderers but those who stand by and do nothing in the face of murder share a complicity in crime.... Raoul's message was clear and loud. We had to fight evil, but just as hard we have to fight indifference.

Commemorating courage is crucial.

Annette Lantos embraced a personal mission to memorialize the person who saved Tom's life and the lives of a hundred thousand other Jews. When it became clear that he was probably dead, she and her husband Tom embarked on a program to memorialize Wallenberg's great and courageous acts. This led to his posthumously awarded honorary U.S. citizenship and his remembrance as the street address of the Holocaust Memorial Museum in Washington, D.C. The obligation to commemorate Wallenberg was every bit as great as it was to rescue him. How could we neglect the character, courage, and leadership of Raoul Wallenberg—one person who acted to redeem mankind at its darkest hour?

There is no deadline for setting the record straight. Wallenberg's legacy contains a shameful lesson. How could the Jewish people, the Swedish people, the American government, and those devoted to democracy worldwide ignore the contribution of this courageous leader for decades? Annette Lantos was a catalyst and I was caught up in the intensity of her cause. The bigger challenge is that the cause of character and courage always needs heroes. And, it's our moral responsibility to ensure that they are recognized and celebrated.

Postscript

When the Hungarian Revolt broke out in October 1956, many Hungarian Jewish parents feared a second campaign against the Jews as one result of the Soviet crackdown against this democratic uprising, some Jewish Hungarian parents made the courageous decision to send their children to the West. The Hebrew Immigrant Aid Society scrambled to find homes for these youngsters. My parents, who had raised two sons, said they would be willing to take a third. Well, life doesn't always turn out as expected, and they were offered a sixteen-year-old girl instead, by the name of Erica Schick, who was welcomed into a loving home in Columbus, Ohio. We later discovered that Wallenberg had been responsible for saving Erica and her mother, Piri, through the Wallenberg system of protective passports and safehouses.

They remembered vividly how Wallenberg's masterful strategy slowed deportations and saved lives. And, Erica's family experienced all of the other degradations of this unforgettable persecution. They suffered life and death in the forced-labor camps and factories. (Her father died in one.) They had to live by their wits—bartering a wedding ring for safe passage from forced labor and her grandfather's World War I medals for military heroism as a bribe to the Arrow Cross to block deportation.

Learning of my foster sister's own Wallenberg experience has one overarching significance for me. Those selfless people who make the world a better place weave their impact over time. So, it is with Raoul Wallenberg. They glisten as beacons of moral decency and their beam glows time and again from places we might never thought of searching for it.

George Bush and the
Ethiopian Jews

*The Jews of Ethiopia are the black Jews of Africa. They
trace their ancestry back to Menelik I, who was the son
of King Solomon and the Queen of Sheba. The Jews in Ethiopia, which numbered 30,000 in 1983, were life-loving
people abandoned to the backwaters of history. By the late
1970s, the political conditions in this country had seriously
eroded. The Jews in Ethiopia began to flee the country to
neighboring Sudan. By 1979, Israel started covert operations
to bring Ethiopian Jews to the Jewish homeland. A new
surge of Ethiopian refugees entered Sudanese camps in 1984.
It was increasingly apparent Israel would need U.S. governmental and private help to complete the rescue of the
Ethiopian Jews. However, Israel was technically at war with
Sudan at the time. And, the U.S. was doing its best to maintain good relationships with Sudan because its coastline was
a strategic access route to Middle East oil. That was the
backdrop against which Operation Moses was organized.*

Operation Moses was a secret undertaking that rescued around 8,000
Ethiopian Jews between November 18, 1984 and January 5, 1985,
but the mission was not completely achieved. Richard Krieger in the
U.S. State Department did an admirable job of organizing Operation
Moses. He obtained the necessary permissions from the U.S. Govern-
ment, Israel, and Sudan to participate in Operation Moses. However,

83

when the Ethiopian Jewish rescue initiative was announced at a meeting of the Knesset and a subsequent press conference took place, the word got out, and Operation Moses was halted by Sudan. Within days, the exit doors were shut by the Sudanese. The Jews who were stranded either returned to their villages in Ethiopia or remained in Sudan, where they thought they had better prospects of safety. Unfortunately a number died while waiting in the refugee camps of Sudan.

The Ethiopian Jews who were stranded in Sudan were mostly women and children. After the cover for Operation Moses was blown, it was believed that about 2,000 Jews in total were affected. The leadership of the Republican Jewish Coalition was asked to come to New York in January 1985 to meet with Meir Rosenne, who was then Israel's ambassador to the United States. The meeting took place in a law office and I was an attendee.

A stranger identified only by his first name, David, was introduced to us. He later proved to be David Halevi, who went on to head the Mossad—Israel's equivalent to the CIA. At the time he was the third-ranking official in the Mossad, and his mission was to try and rescue as many of the Ethiopian Jews who were stranded in Sudan as he could. He described the conditions in Sudan and said that the Jews who were trapped there were in great peril of starving to death. These Ethiopian Jews were also plagued with disease. Sudan was politically unstable, and there was a very serious risk that the government could fall. In the aftermath of a civil war, anti-Semitic violence could be waged against the remnant of this Jewish community stranded in Sudan.

Separately, it was known that Vice President Bush had a trip planned to Sudan in thirty to forty days to meet with the Sudanese President Gaafar el-Numeiry. Phil Blazer, who is the publisher of the newspaper *Jewish Life* on the West Coast and host of his own TV show, had been to see Dick Krieger about doing something to save the Jews in Sudan. Blazer had learned of Bush's trip. Phil wanted to charter a commercial plane and man it with a group of mercenaries. Their mission: Fly the Jews out of Sudan. The idea seemed so off-the-wall that Dick told Blazer he would never be allowed to fly out of this country to Sudan and desperately tried to talk Blazer out of this scheme. A mercenary action staged out of the States would have been a terrible embarrassment to the U.S. Blazer was adamant that he would carry out his plan with or without government support.

Phil Blazer knew Jerry Weintraub. Jerry is a very powerful movie executive. He produced *Starlight Express, Oceans 11* and *12*, and *The Karate Kid* series. But more importantly, he was, and is, a close friend of George H. W. Bush. Jerry had been involved with Bush since 1966, when Bush ran for Congress and won. Jerry's wife Jane Morgan, an internationally acclaimed singer, and Barbara Bush are also good friends. The couples regularly vacationed together at Kennebunkport, Maine. So the Weintraubs and the Bushes went back a long way.

Blazer called Jerry to explain what was going on with the Ethiopian Jews. Blazer asked Weintraub to intervene and to get him an appointment with Vice President Bush. This was the first time Weintraub used his relationship with Bush to advance a Jewish agenda issue. "You've got to see Phil Blazer," Weintraub told the vice president, "and you need to be attentive to what he says." Blazer asked Dick Krieger to set up a meeting with Vice President Bush. Krieger called Don Gregg, Bush's National Security Advisor, who agreed to see him. Vice President Bush walked in and remained for the rest of the meeting.

Independently Blazer and I met with Secretary of State George Shultz, who wasn't enthusiastic about the idea of Bush meeting with Blazer or helping the Ethiopian Jews. Neither was Jim Baker, who was Reagan's Chief of Staff at the time. Nor was Bush's Chief of Staff, Craig Fuller. Fuller's position was understandable: Craig was smart enough to grasp what the risk was, and risk avoidance was his business as chief of staff. The upside seemed minimal, and the downside considerable. When he raised the matter with me, I said, "Craig, there are certain issues where you have to do what's right. You can't let concerns about political risk guide your behavior. How many chances do you get to save the surviving remnant of persecution that goes back thousands of years?"

Vice President Bush and I met privately, and I urged him to help rescue the Ethiopian Jews, that it was the right thing to do. Then

Ambassador Meier Rosenne met one-on-one with the vice president, pleading with him to accept responsibility for leading the rescue effort. The vice president realized he had a chance to do something to save Jews who were imperiled. He was in a unique position and determined to make use of it. With considerable courage, George Bush took command of this defining moment.

Bush then met with Reagan and told the president: "I'm going to Sudan to meet with Numeiry and his second in command, Omar Tayeb. Here's an important point on my agenda. I think it's the right thing to do. I'd like your blessing to be able to (a) negotiate an agreement to let these people go, (b) and, if successful, to organize and mobilize an airlift that would bring these people out in a timely way." To his credit, the president let Vice President Bush negotiate a deal with Numeiry and approved the use of American military planes to effect a rescue if this negotiation were successful.

What happened afterward is unprecedented in the history of the United States. Vice President Bush and the Sudanese struck the deal. Omar Tayeb engineered the logistics of the interface with the Americans in arranging for this exodus. The mission was dubbed "Operation Sheba." To the best of my knowledge there's never been an instance, prior to this one, where an airlift occurred using the planes of the United States military to rescue non-American citizens and take them to a country other than the United States. Bush bought into this because of his moral compass. The world had been absent while Jews perished in the Holocaust. Vice President Bush wasn't going to sit idle while there was a chance to do something to save these Jews from imminent death.

George Bush wouldn't have been aware of the situation if there weren't people around him to sensitize him to the fact that this crisis existed. In the normal scope of his briefings, before going to Sudan, he wouldn't even have known there was a Jew over there. However, when he did know, he acted. One particular person who played a central role in Operation Sheba was Don Gregg. Many were convinced that Gregg was an Arabist. They were dead wrong. Don was totally dedicated to organizing the operation with the CIA, the Mossad, and the U.S. military. He was with the program from the start and could have stopped it, had he chosen to do so. The conditions under which this emigration was allowed to take place were stringent because the mission was being conducted from a chiefly Islamic Arab nation. The U.S. was told the refugees couldn't leave Sudan in Israeli planes and they couldn't go directly to Israel. In total, 494 Ethiopian Jews were rescued in this exodus on U.S. planes.

Two weeks after Operation Sheba was completed, Numeiry's government fell and a Communist, pro-Soviet regime took over in Sudan. The new government used Numeiry's and Tayeb's involvement in Operation Sheba as a basis for imprisoning Tayeb to two consecutive life sentences. Behind the scenes, Vice President Bush was trying to find a way to get Tayeb released from prison. Tayeb had been tried as a traitor, and the vice president didn't want to implicate Tayeb further for fear that he would be killed while in prison. Bush insisted on a total blackout of U.S. involvement and of his personal role, because of the threat to Tayeb's life, if the real connection between Bush and him were known. He would talk about it in a private group, but he would never discuss it or permit any of his staff to reveal it to the press.

In 1986, I persuaded the vice president that it was the right time for him to go to Israel again. One part of the visit included encounters between George and Barbara Bush and Ethiopian children rescued through Operation Sheba. In one little Israeli village, there were 400 Ethiopian children either orphaned or with parents still stranded in Ethiopia. Through a visit there, I wanted the Bushes to have a sense of the incompleteness of what had been done. They also went to an absorption center, where they saw whole families who were being integrated into Israeli life. These kids pleaded with the vice president of the United States not to forget their parents. That whole experience had a very profound and positive effect on George Bush, the man. Since 1986, an additional 15,000 Jews have been brought out of Ethiopia, and that exodus continues to this day.

Rescue should always be a human imperative. *You* **should** *just do something!* But, 6,000,000 Jews died because nobody *did* anything. And, today there is wide-scale suffering in Sudan and elsewhere because **no one has done anything!**

ONE KEY THING I LEARNED FROM GEORGE BUSH'S LEADERSHIP IN RESCUING ETHIOPIAN JEWS IS:

Have the courage to do the right thing, because it's the right thing to do.

George Bush has an unerring moral compass. He never asked what the political fallout of this initiative would be. If everything went right, it wouldn't have amounted to a mini-blip on the political radar screen. Had it failed, it could have destroyed Bush's career. It might have cost him the presidency in 1988. What mattered to George Bush was that the right thing be done. Save one life and it is as if you save the whole world. He had no interest in being recognized for his contribution. In fact, he actively suppressed knowledge of it. And, to make the mission of rescue complete, Israeli society took up the challenge of assimilation after the Ethiopian Jews arrived. The challenge of rescuing and reassimilating the Ethiopian Jews continues to this day.

MORAL RESOLVE

In any moment of decision, the best thing you can do is the right thing, the next best thing is the wrong thing, and the worst thing you can do is nothing.
—Teddy Roosevelt

The minute you start talking about what you're going to do if you lose, you have lost.
—George Shultz

You are not required to complete the task, but you are called upon to begin it.
—The Ethics of the Fathers

Sazo Idemitsu

In 1968, on his eightieth birthday, there was a surprise party for a Japanese industrialist and 250,000 people showed up! In late 1971, when I read an article about this gigantic happening, I was overwhelmed. What would cause 250,000 people to appear at a private surprise party? The guest of honor was Sazo Idemitsu. As I read through the article, I learned that his company, Idemitsu Kosan, was one of Japan's largest oil companies. It was the leading firm in sales and profit per employee in Japan. Anybody who could achieve those results while creating an atmosphere that would prompt a quarter-million people to show up for his birthday was special. I decided I wanted to meet him on my forthcoming trip to Japan.

I wrote to him. Idemitsu agreed to meet, provided I sent him questions in advance. It took me an entire weekend to figure out exactly what I wanted to ask him. When he got the questions, he liked them. Idemitsu identified a time and place that meshed with an upcoming business trip I had in Kyoto. I visited him on May 19, 1972.

Idemitsu started out selling industrial oil to factories and supplying kerosene to fishing boats. He founded his own company in 1911. Idemitsu was a member of the Japanese Diet (parliament) and had a thriving oil business prior to World War II. He opposed the attack on Pearl Harbor and the war with the United States, but the warlords prevailed. After the end of hostilities, the postwar administration headed by American General Douglas MacArthur classified him as a defense industry supplier during the war. As such, he was placed on the blacklist and denied the opportunity to operate an oil business, since oil was a strategic industry.

Idemitsu's company was privately held. He also had a personal collection of Impressionist paintings. They were worth a fortune. His board of directors advised him to sell the business and his art collection. They told him to invest the proceeds in U.S. government securities and to clip coupons for the rest of his life.

At the end of the war, the Idemitsu Company employed about 1,000 people. Most of them had served in the army, and many were in prisoner-of-war camps, but they were starting to return home. Idemitsu's two passions in life were his employees and his paintings. In this defining moment, he chose the greater passion—service and dedication to his people. Idemitsu told the board he would not sell the company, but he *would* sell the paintings. His reasoning: "The people of Idemitsu came to us when we needed them. Idemitsu will not abandon his people when they need *him*." He asked the board to figure out what business he could enter with the proceeds from selling the paintings that would offer employment to the people of Idemitsu.

After reviewing the marketplace, his directors counseled him to go into the bicycle repair business. Bikes will be big, they contended. Idemitsu resolved to totally redefine himself. He could have ignored this rather mundane suggestion, no matter how pragmatic it was. Instead, he met the test of the moment. He took all of his highly trained oil refinery workers and educated them in bicycle repair. Then Idemitsu bought a bicycle manufacturer and put them to work building bikes. Bicycle-making gave the people work. It also held them together as a team. Meanwhile, he kept doggedly pursuing MacArthur, contending that the firm really belonged on the "white list." Idemitsu was not a defense supplier by choice and had opposed the war. In three years, he was given the green light.

He sold the bicycle repair and manufacturing businesses, but kept his people. He was able to immediately and fearlessly redeploy them into the work they knew best. Overnight he was back refining crude oil. The business prospered. In 1954, Idemitsu flew to Iran, and made a deal with the shah to become the exclusive importer of Iranian oil in Japan. A driven and tireless leader, he introduced larger and larger super tankers and extended his sources of supply to include the Soviet Union and Kuwait. When I visited with him in 1972, Idemitsu Kosan employed 50,000 people. Later, his son, Akira, ran the business, which extended into such areas as petrochemicals, power supply, and real estate. Today, the annual sales of Idemitsu Kosan are roughly $20 billion!

Sazo Idemitsu was a memorable presence, wielding a big horn hearing aid when I visited with him. We met in a vast conference room at his Tokyo corporate headquarters, and he entered the meeting with an entourage of five people. On my visit, I learned that Idemitsu managed the company in accordance with the Japanese Way. The essence of the Japanese Way is to answer trust with trust: Assume that people want to do the job right. It is your responsibility as a leader to train them so that they know what *right* is. Even if people stole or lied, they weren't fired. He considered *their* flaws to be the *leader's* fault.

Idemitsu's passion was to make the Japanese Way live for people—a living, breathing example for the rest of Japanese industry to emulate. While he considered his firm's most important resource to be its people, Idemitsu believed businesses should develop people, not use them. He felt Japanese industry had lost its way and was emulating the West. He was disturbed that it had resorted to using American management practices. He chose to fight back and operate in the classic Japanese way. For example, there was no mandatory retirement age in his company. He was confident that people knew when it was time to cut back and to take a different job in the company or to retire.

I asked Idemitsu how he motivated people to create these spectacular results. First, he believed that people should enjoy their work. "Enjoying work," he said, "is not working at the direction of someone higher up." The leader's challenge, however, goes far beyond making the workplace enjoyable and challenging. "The leader's job is to know the needs and wants of his people, especially to understand that people have different wants at different stages of their career," he said. He believed you can have people of various ages in similar jobs with markedly different needs. You had to fit fulfilling their needs in the context of advancing the enterprise. This was undoubtedly the richest and most important lesson I learned from him.

Idemitsu's philosophy of fulfilling needs deserves exploration. At different times, people need money or power or recognition. When they start out, they need money to provide for their families. You find ways to reward them with money so they can afford to buy homes and take care of their children's education. Later, they want to exercise power, to demonstrate they can manage and control outcomes. As they get older, they want to be recognized and appreciated, and you have to provide a platform that permits this. Money, power, recognition. At any one time, all three needs are active in any one person, but the mix is different.

Listening to Idemitsu brought my thinking to a whole new plane. Assume that the needs and wants of people change over a lifetime. Then the effective leader will recognize this. He or she will both fuel and fulfill those personal aspirations. In so doing, the leader will harness the energy necessary to move the organization forward.

Idemitsu's philosophy had a great similarity to the organizational development theories of the productivity-improvement researcher Rensis Likert, which I had put to work in my own business. Idemitsu also believed deeply in empowerment and teamwork. I learned from him that the "servant leader" must have a selfless commitment to meeting the employer's obligations—again, through a thorough and tireless identification and fulfillment of the employees' needs as they serve the needs of the enterprise. To quote Idemitsu: "A servant leader can't be self-willed."

Idemitsu could have lost everything, but got it all back because he was able to keep the motivation and loyalty of his people. By doing right by his people, they did right by him. And those 250,000 people at the surprise birthday party? Were they all from the ranks of Idemitsu? Indeed not! Thousands of them came from firms that did business with Idemitsu Kosan, and thousands more from firms that had been caught up with the authenticity of his approach to the Japanese Way. Everyone praises the importance of people, but few actually practice what they preach. Talk about the leadership and how one person channeled his passion in a purposeful way to reverberate in the lives of thousands! Here was a leader who had the character and the courage to do the right thing because it was the right thing to do, and his people rewarded him with the loyalty and dedication that built Japan's most successful oil company.

Idemitsu was a true servant leader, and he had the opportunity to practice his beliefs for years more, until his death at the age of 93 in 1981. Our conversation became part of a book that was published in Japanese and twenty-six other languages. He asked if he could publish our conversation in English. I agreed only if I could edit my section. That translation, titled *The Eternal Japan,* appeared in 1975. I talked with him about productivity improvements in our own firm's factories. For example, in 1969, we had 350 people producing 16,000 pairs of shoes a day. In 1971, those same 350 completed 24,000 pairs. Idemitsu said that I must have changed my trust level toward people and "given them their head." They cooperated better and enjoyed their work more. He said that this was "way off the American beat" and contended I was "a rebel in the ranks of American business." He asserted I was thinking Japanese in the way the workforce was being managed. He was exactly right!

When I gave him permission to publish our interview chapter in English, Idemitsu surprised me with an antique Imari cloisonné plate in a hand-crafted box. Totally unexpected, an associate of Idemitsu arrived in my office one day to deliver it. He flew from Tokyo to Columbus with this box on his lap. The aide brought it in, bowed, and presented it to me. He simply said, "Gift from Idemitsu."

"May I buy you lunch?

"No, must go back Japan. Sayonara," he said, bowing his way out the door.

That bowl and a picture of Sazo Idemitsu remain important remembrances for me today.

Needless to say, Idemitsu built another art collection even grander than the first. In fact, there are several. The first includes great paintings by Georges Rouault and the Californian Sam Francis. Experts deem another of his collections, of Japanese and Chinese ceramics, to be one of the finest in the world. Since 1966, the various collections have been housed in the Idemitsu Museum on the ninth floor of Tokyo's Imperial Theater. (If you would like to see a sampling of the collections, go to the Idemitsu website at www.idemitsu.co.jp/e.) While imposing in themselves, these exhibits don't include the vast collection of Middle Eastern art that he also established back in 1979 in Tokyo's Middle Eastern Culture Center.

If you have a chance to visit the Idemitsu Museum in person—it's very close to the Imperial Palace—you should take time to look at something else. The docents. They are Idemitsu retirees. Remember those employees who knew it was time to cut back and take on a different role in the company? When I visited the museum in the 1970s, the docents I saw were the veterans of the bicycle factory. They were exhibiting this glorious art collection to the public. Their lifetime careers had been made possible through Idemitsu's sale of his first art collection. It seems fitting that those careers be completed in overseeing the second collection, such a vibrant symbol of Idemitsu's rebirth.

TWO KEY THINGS I LEARNED FROM SAZO IDEMITSU ARE:

Reward loyalty with loyalty.

Servant leadership means doing the right thing for your people—no matter what. The needs of people must be served with respect, dignity, and intelligence. Idemitsu was a great servant leader. In a defining moment when the chips were down, Idemitsu fulfilled his obligations to his people and sold his passionately loved art collection. Character matters. It is the readiness to do the right thing even when it hurts. Destiny brings many ups and downs in life. Idemitsu was able to go from oil entrepreneur to bicycle maker and back to oil entrepreneur on a far more dramatic scale because he kept his skilled and loyal people.

Leaders must respond sensitively to the changing needs and wants of their people.

Better than any leader I have ever met, Idemitsu grasped how people need money, power, and recognition at different points of their lives in different proportions. Be sensitive to where people stand in the pursuit of well-being for themselves and for their families. And, be aware of where you yourself stand in this life's journey. When you sensitively align meeting people's needs with a clear vision for the organization, you unleash the latent potential and imagination of people to make the organization all it can become.

Elie Wiesel

Elie was born in 1928 in the little Romanian village of Sighet. It is located in Transylvania, a region that has been tossed back and forth between Hungary and Romania over the centuries. He spent much of his young life in Budapest, until he was transported to the death camps at the age of sixteen.

It was Elie Wiesel who first publicized the plight of Soviet Jewry. His 1966 book The Jews of Silence *documented his journey through the Soviet Union to meet some of what were then three million Jews. When the Six-Day War happened in the next year, thousands of Jews tried to move to Israel. The repression began almost immediately. Jews around the world feared that the Soviet Union, with its totalitarian regime and history of pogroms and ethnic exterminations, could be the site of a second Holocaust.*

It seems I have known him forever, but I can't actually remember when I met him. Elie Wiesel is a man shrouded in sadness and pain. Elie was an Eastern European Jew, and deported to Auschwitz. He lived through the Holocaust, but the brutal memories plague him all the time. In his family, only Elie and two of his sisters survived. Elie believes with a passion that the lesson of the Holocaust is: **Indifference to Evil is evil.** That it is his responsibility to the memory of the six million who were slaughtered in the Holocaust to make sure that the world remembers them, so he tells their stories.

Elie's entire village was deported to Auschwitz in 1944. In his book *Night,* he wrote:

> Never shall I forget that night, the first night in camp, which has turned my life into one long night, seven times cursed and seven times sealed. Never shall I forget that smoke. Never shall I forget the little faces of the children, whose bodies I saw turned into wreaths of smoke beneath a silent blue sky. . . . Never shall I forget those moments which murdered my God and my soul and turned my dreams to dust.

Elie survived not only Auschwitz, but Buna, Buchenwald, and Gleiwitz as well. In April 1945, the camps were liberated. He was sent to an orphanage in Paris. Then he studied at the Sorbonne and became a journalist. He won the Nobel Peace Prize in 1986 and has been chairman of the President's Commission on the Holocaust.

For decades a New Yorker, Elie was criticized by the Israelis for not moving to Israel. I'm sure that he feels his purposes can be better served from New York. He married a wonderful woman, Marion, in 1969. Their son, born in 1972, remains the apple of his father's eye. They are great comforts for a man who lives every day with the pain of the world.

Elie believes in God, but he can't and won't explain the Holocaust in terms of God. He blames man, not God for the Holocaust. Elie is convinced that even a writer or a thinker must act in order to change the world. When nearly the entire journalistic and literary community locked arms to oppose the American invasion of Iraq in 2003, Elie's profound sense of integrity made him take a stand. He saw this as a defining moment and went to see National Security Adviser Condoleezza Rice. Within seconds of entering her office, President Bush came in and remained during Elie's entire presentation. With all his commitment to peace, Elie urged President Bush to invade Iraq. Elie's reasoning: If Saddam doesn't possess weapons of mass destruction, he aspires to and he will. If he doesn't collaborate with terrorist organizations today, he will in the future. In Elie's view, this moment was comparable to when Hitler could have been stopped if the Free World had acted and not caved in at Munich in 1938. The terrible costs of World War II might have been avoided. If everyone in Germany had stood up for what was right in their little piece of the world, Elie has argued, then Hitler and the Holocaust could have been stopped. Hence Elie's famous words: "To remain silent and indifferent is the greatest sin of all."

When Elie survived the Holocaust, he felt a moral obligation to tell the story of the Holocaust. He felt obliged to be the advocate of those survivors in speaking to the world's humanity. He wanted restitution to be made to ease the remaining years of the survivors' lives. It became, and is, the passion to which he has dedicated his own life. Elie came to embrace suffering throughout the world, beyond the sufferings of the Jews. The plights of people in Cambodia, Uganda, and Darfur in Sudan have caused the same pain for him. Wherever there is human suffering because of intolerance and Evil, his position is: You have the moral responsibility to demonstrate against it and I—Elie—have the responsibility to lead by example. The cases I can point to in which Elie has stood up for principle are legion. One was particularly memorable. It was an instance where Elie, who is someone I deeply admire and value as a friend, and I had to take a stand against a position held by a man who remains a beloved president for me: Ronald Reagan.

During a visit to the United States, German Chancellor Helmut Kohl had extended an invitation to President Reagan to come to Germany. The fortieth anniversary, in 1985, of the end of World War II was an occasion Kohl was eager to mark. So, presidential aide Michael Deaver went to Germany to find some symbolic site to memorialize a final reconciliation of this conflict. It would be a place where Reagan and Kohl could demonstrate that a new relationship had begun. At the same time, it would show mutual respect for soldiers who died in the war.

In the background, there was also an IOU outstanding. Kohl had supported Reagan on retaining Pershing missiles in Europe. Reagan knew he was obliged to repay the favor. There was nothing inherently wrong with the idea of going to Germany, but Deaver didn't do his homework. He proposed a cemetery in the town of Bitburg where nearly 2,000 German war dead were buried. That too would have been understandable, but more than forty of those graves contained the remains of the reviled SS. Inadvertently paying tribute to the ground where the SS were buried was a totally different symbol than that which was intended for the trip in the first place.

President Reagan's chief of staff, Don Regan, arranged a meeting on April 16, 1985, with some leaders of the American Jewish community. They included: Dick Fox, Morris Abrams, George Klein, Max Fisher, Elie Wiesel, and myself. Joining Don Regan in the meeting were Ed Rollins, the political director; Marshall Breger from the Office of Public Liaison; and Pat Buchanan, the communications director. Within the administration, the only staff member really sympathetic to our viewpoint—Elie recalls—was Ed Rollins. Ostensibly, the Jewish leaders were invited to the White House to talk about the Bitburg issue. We were really brought there with the administration hopeful of cutting a deal. In other words, somebody had advised President Reagan to add a stop at Bergen-Belsen on this trip and it would atone for the visit to Bitburg.

Don Regan, I believe, had this scenario in mind: The Jewish leadership would bless the deal. Then we would see the president. We would all kiss and make up. We would appear before the press and say the problem was solved with video rolling and camera shutters clicking. Don Regan kicked the meeting off, and I'm sure apologized for the Bitburg decision but said that nothing could really be done about it. Of course, we were horrified that the White House would even conceive that this would be an acceptable alternative to us or to the broader Jewish community. We said this was no longer a political issue—it was a moral issue! You can't honor the SS and the victims of the SS at the same time! You can honor one *or* the other. You can't honor both. From our point of view, Bergen-Belsen was irrelevant.

The issue was Bitburg, where 47 SS troops were buried. If Reagan did or didn't want to visit the death camp, that was his choice. The issue was he shouldn't visit Bitburg at all! While I immediately voiced objections, it was really Elie Wiesel who eloquently articulated the overwhelming sentiment of the Jewish community.

We offered alternatives that would symbolize this reconciliation. Why not visit the birthplace of Konrad Adenauer, Germany's first postwar chancellor? Or, the tomb of the German Unknown Soldier? We even said go to Bitburg, but don't go to the cemetery. Go to the chapel at Bitburg and say the appropriate things about soldiers who die in battle.

From the White House side, the issue became the president not backing down in the face of political pressure. This would be interpreted as a sign of weakness. The president gave his word to Kohl, and the White House—indeed—had picked the site. Kohl was the only one who could release the president from his word, and Kohl would have to initiate this. The president wouldn't request it. We told Regan that we thought he was doing a terrible disservice to the president. We pointed out that the president's ability to govern was as much reliant on projecting a moral force as demonstrating sheer resolve. Why not just admit the error? That was the last meeting I ever had with Don Regan.

I left the meeting and I went to see former National Security Adviser Dick Allen because he was very close to Chancellor Kohl. (Allen studied in Germany and speaks German fluently. He had introduced Ronald Reagan to Helmut Kohl two years before Reagan was elected.) I asked Allen to call Kohl to suggest to the chancellor that he make the generous gesture, recommending the president visit someplace else. In return, the chancellor would earn the enormous long-term gratitude of President Reagan for taking him off the hook, and worldwide public admiration for his statesmanship. Allen called Kohl. The chancellor was engaged in a bitter internal fight for his political life, and he rejected the proposition. Bitburg for him, within Germany, had become the symbol of true reconciliation. Backing down would have been terribly costly to him politically.

We failed in convincing the White House staff, but Elie Wiesel would not accept no. Elie would not let the challenge of this moment pass. On April 19, he was invited to the White House and President Reagan conferred him a Congressional medal. In his remarks, Elie used the occasion to address the president with the words: "That place [Bitburg] is not your place. Your place is with the victims of the SS." Elie failed, but he tried, even to the point of frontally raising the issue with the administration while the president was honoring him at an official ceremony.

One thinks about people like Elie Wiesel—so few of them exist— as otherworldly and beyond being mortal. The truth is Elie is very human in the best sense of the word. That's why he understands human nature so well. He is a very caring and compassionate person.

One day, before a trip to Washington in 1981, I stopped in New York to have lunch with Elie to seek his counsel. Having forgotten my watch, I asked him what time it was, he took off his watch and gave it to me. Two weeks later, I had occasion to be with him again. I wanted to return the watch. He refused to take it and said it was his gift to me. I have that watch framed and hanging in my office. Whenever I look at it, I remember what he said as he presented it to me: "Gordon, you can't go to Washington and not know what time of day it is. You'll be just like the rest of those politicians."

Two key things I learned from Elie Wiesel are:

Indifference to Evil is evil.

Confronting Evil requires courage. It also demands conscience. Often Evil is not as clear or as overwhelming as it was or should have been in the Holocaust. How do you recognize Evil? What face does it wear? To be driven to seize the moment and act, you must have the sensitivity to spot Evil in its subtle, early stages. The character to know has to precede the courage to *act*. Neither is courage always clear cut. Often, courage is not the black-and-white of battlefield courage. Courage can often require tenacity, an unwavering dedication to principle, and a willingness to search for the Evil that the world would rather ignore.

Look for the inspiration to fight the pain of darkness.

Elie Wiesel has—every day of his life—accepted the responsibility of fighting man's inhumanity to man in all corners of the world. He has done it at great personal cost. His commitment shows moral leadership at its pinnacle. He knows that he will never drive Evil out of the world. He will never win that war, but he must still be an active participant in the struggle against Evil. I maintain that detailed questions about the death camps such as these can never be forgotten:

> Who cut the hair off the corpses?
> Who dug their fingers into the anuses and uteruses of the dead in the search for jewels and gold?
> Who threw an infant—still alive from the gassing—into the crematory ovens, knowing if they did not, they would be thrown there themselves?
> How many were forced to burn the remains of their mother or their brother in this assembly of horror?

These were inmates, too, and this is what has driven Elie and people like him to take that stand day after day. They cannot afford to grow tired and say it is someone else's task—as long as they are living—as long as they are breathing—and, neither can we! Only a select few have Elie Wiesel's boundless strength. If there is a drawback to his enormous sensitivity, it is this: Most human beings would find living in such a profound state of sadness to be a paralyzing condition. I know Elie would say: Never let the gravity or tragedy of a situation prevent you from acting at all. Be open to the world, but above all, when the sinister signs of Evil appear, act and act decisively! The Talmud doesn't require that we complete the task, but it does require that we begin it.

Natan Sharansky

Natan Sharansky was born in Ukraine in 1948. His father was a journalist. He was five when the Soviet dictator Josef Stalin died. On the day of his death, Sharansky's father told him that Stalin was a fiend, and he also advised his son to carefully keep that opinion to himself. Sharansky grew up in the total repression of the Soviet Union at the height of the Cold War. As a student at the Moscow Institute of Physics, he came to know the great scientist and human-rights activist Andrei Sakharov, for whom he was to become a translator and communications advisor. In 1973, Sharansky applied for an exit visa from the Soviet Union. Natan married Avital—whom we met toward the beginning of this book—in 1974. In 1977, Sharansky's outspoken views on human rights led to a nine-year nightmare of brutal imprisonment and coercion by the Soviets.

Since his release in 1986, Sharansky has written two internationally acclaimed books. He became an important political leader—especially for Israel's burgeoning community of Eastern European Jews. An Israeli cabinet minister, he resigned his ministerial post in May 2005, when the Sharon government decided to cede Gaza to Palestinian rule. True to his lifelong standard, Sharansky was driven by a matter of principle. He rejected personal power and perquisites because he felt the Palestinian leadership needed to do much more on human rights before their control of Gaza was

justified. Sharansky remains a member of the Knesset and
is a distinguished fellow at the Shalem Center in Jerusalem,
which publishes the journal Azure.

My first trip to the Soviet Union happened in the summer of 1974. There were approximately three million Jews in the Soviet Union at the time. The Soviet Union refused permission to most of the Jews who wanted to leave the country. The international Jewish community kept their cause alive. My "cover" for learning about the condition of the Jews in the Soviet Union was a business trip organized by the Young Presidents Organization—a professional association of business presidents under the age of fifty. YPO had a trip planned to Moscow, Leningrad, Tbilisi, and Vilnius in Lithuania. The membership of the organization was curious about what the Soviet Union was really like, and the Soviets were anxious to have us visit, because the U.S. had enacted a trade bill called Jackson-Vanik—named after the bill's sponsors, Senator Henry Jackson from Washington state and Congressman Charles Vanik from Ohio. That bill effectively restricted trade with the Soviet Union until the latter cleaned up its human rights practices, and the Soviets wanted it repealed. They thought that influencing the Young Presidents Organization would serve that objective. So they were very responsive to the YPO visit.

My overriding goal in visiting the Soviet Union was to study the conditions of Jews there. I wanted to meet with Jews who had applied for permission to leave and were denied. The refuseniks. They were not only denied permission to leave, they were also forced out of their jobs and humiliated by the KGB—the target of reprisals and KGB surveillance. They were a symbol of resistance to the Soviet system. The refuseniks fervently wanted the Jackson-Vanik Amendment to stand. They saw it as their hope for a better life.

In advance of the trip, I was carefully briefed by the U.S. State Department, the National Conference on Soviet Jewry, and the Israeli government. They told me what the rules were. I wanted to be sure what the Soviet law permitted me to do and not do, what I could and couldn't bring in. I also called my senator, John Glenn of Ohio, and said, "John, I'm about to go into the Soviet Union. I'm coming out through Berlin on July 25, 1974. If I don't call you on that day by 5 P.M. your time, please raise hell 'cause I'm in a jam."

"Gordy, don't get in too much trouble cause I don't have too much influence there," John answered.

When my wife, Carol Sue, and I arrived in Moscow, I asked her to check in with our Young Presidents Organization group at the Europa Hotel on Gorky Street. It was about 7 P.M. I went on to meet an engineer by the name of Vladimir Slepak, who was to be my lead contact in the Jewish refusenik movement. Slepak was the fountainhead of the resistance, the leader of leaders. His apartment was also on Gorky. It was about a mile and a half away, so I decided to walk. Later, when I did need a taxi, I learned how to hail a cab in Soviet Moscow and, it wasn't with brandishing worthless rubles: Wave a pack of American cigarettes!

What a first impression on the street. I smiled at people and said hello along the way. No one smiled back or said anything. They immediately stared down at the pavement. When I reached the address, I climbed the stairs to Slepak's sixth-floor apartment, knocked, gave the password, and was admitted. By coincidence, a meeting of the leadership of the Moscow-based refusenik community—including Natan Sharansky—was going on when I arrived. I asked them to tell me their stories.

Vladimir Slepak told his story first. Slepak was born into a family of academics—many of them mathematicians. His father had left tsarist Russia, gone to the United States, and returned to Russia to help "make the Revolution" with the Bolsheviks in 1917. Slepak's mother was Jewish. Slepak's father grew up with no connection to anything Jewish other than having "Jew" stamped on his passport, Slepak himself had no relationship to or connection with anything Jewish. And, Slepak had an amiable, functioning relationship with non-Jewish people.

In 1956, Slepak was a student at the University of Moscow during the Suez War. The Soviets published erroneous information about what was happening in the war, saying that Jerusalem was being bombed and that the country was about to fall. The false news reports unleashed a furor of latent anti-Semitism among Slepak's non-Jewish "friends." They basically said, "You Jews are getting what you deserve!" For the first time, Slepak felt very uncomfortable being Jewish. He decided that things weren't right. So he went to see his father and asked how such bias could survive in this "worker's paradise." His father told him he had to be patient. "You don't change human nature overnight," his father said. "The system takes time to cleanse and to purge all the bad things that happened before and it's going to take another two generations, but it's going to happen." That persuaded Vladimir to stay in the fold. There were more incidents of anti-Semitism. In 1969, after the Six-Day War is when Slepak finally decided it was time to get out.

At the time, Slepak was working in a research institute involved in the development of Soviet color television. In order to get a visa for his family and him to leave the USSR, he needed his boss to sign an affidavit that Slepak had no access to state secrets. The boss said he couldn't sign it.

"What do you mean you can't sign it?" Slepak asked dumbfounded,

"Everybody knows that we are at least fifteen years behind the West in developing color television!"

"Comrade Slepak, *that's* the secret!" was the answer. We all laughed.

"But, every school child knows that is the case!"

"But, Comrade Slepak," his boss concluded, "*you* know it better."

"How can you still have a sense of humor with all the restrictions you face in your daily life?" I asked Slepak with some amazement.

"Without humor you couldn't survive," he explained. "My kids were thrown out of college. One of them drives a cab. They're bright kids, but they can't go to school. My wife is a talented academic. I don't remember how long she's been out of work. The entire country lives in a huge cage, except for us. We fly above the cage because of you Americans and other foreigners. You're here and you care. We know they know you are here. Because of that, they won't kill us. As long as you Americans come and visit me, I know *they* know what's going on in here. As long as they know you're here, there isn't anything else they can do to me. They can't kill me, because then the world will know. It's a paradox. We can test the limits of what the authorities and the KGB can and will do to break our spirit. That's why we can and must laugh to make it from day to day."

After Slepak had told his story, it was Natan Sharansky's turn. Natan said that when he grew up, the word "Jew" was synonymous with the phrase "fifth line" on nationality forms—the entry space for national origin. For Jews in the Soviet Union, it was also synonymous with why Jews didn't usually have entry to the best schools or land the best jobs. When Natan applied for an exit visa in 1973, he was working as a computer specialist. At a group meeting organized by a KGB front, the group was asked, "Does anyone have a question for Sharansky, who has betrayed us all?"

Natan still had his computer job during my visit. He explained that he and Avital had been married just months ago, in July 1974. Then he recounted the hair-raising story about Avital being given a visa to Israel on the day they were married, with the condition that she leave in twenty-four hours. At this defining moment, they both decided Avital should seize the window of opportunity. He asked me to look her up on my next visit to Jerusalem, to say that he was well and to communicate his love. He had promised to see her in Jerusalem in six months. Well, he was working on it, though he might be a little late. Natan had chutzpah galore and humor to boot!

One after another, the stories of frustrated and sometimes shattered lives were told. None stuck with me as poignantly as that of Natan Sharansky. His entire aura communicated such resolve and defiance. I was certain of two things: First, matters were sure to get worse for Natan before they got better. Second, if anyone had the prospect of leaping over the Iron Curtain to his beloved in Israel, this little fireball of a man was the one to do it.

*   *   *

When I came back from Slepak's at 1:30 or 2:00 in the morning, my wife was panicked. This was before the age of cellphones and she hadn't heard from me. She's thought I'd been captured by the KGB. After she was reassured I was okay, she said: "I've been here for the better part of six hours and I can't get any towels to take a shower." We had been in transit for nearly an entire day. I told her I would get her towels immediately.

"OK, big shot. Get me towels," she said skeptically.

I knew the rooms were bugged. I called the American embassy in Moscow at 2 A.M. and a Marine answered the phone. I launched in with, "What kind of propaganda have you been spreading in the United States?! You told us the Soviet Union was a modern, urbane, sophisticated society. This is a primitive, backward place. We can't give even get towels to take a shower!" While I was still on the phone, there was a sudden, loud, knock at the door. Was it the KGB in trenchcoats, who were onto my visit with the refuseniks and ready to hustle us off to Ljubyanka Prison? No, it was the maid. Finally, thanks to the walls with ears, the towels were being delivered! The refuseniks' insight was validated. You could use the intrusive surveillance of the KGB and turn it on itself to your own ends, once they *knew* the outside world was listening.

Natan Sharansky lost his job as a computer specialist in 1975, and went to work as an interpreter for Andrei Sakharov. By this point, Natan was used to being called *Zhid* (the derogatory Slavic term for Jew) by state loyalists. He was hounded and tailed ceaselessly by the KGB. The political situation grew intolerable for Natan. During this time, he was frequently picked up and interrogated for periods of ten to fifteen days. After a while, he became such a major tenant of the punishment cell, they nearly named it after him. In 1977, the Communist Party newspaper *Izvetsia* reported that he had been indicted as a

CIA spy. He was convicted of treason in 1978. Natan was sentenced to thirteen years in prison to be served in the Gulag.

What was prison life like for Natan?

> In the punishment cell, he lived off bread and water. And, he only got that twice a day. On "full" days, there was sour cabbage boiled in water with little bony fish or thin gruel.
>
> He was interrogated more than a hundred times.
>
> The towels he was given were always too short to serve as a noose, should he harbor thoughts of suicide.
>
> The cell toilet—and there were often six prisoners to a cell— was a crude hole in the cement floor, Natan and the other prisoners would drain the water out with rags and shove their faces into it in order to communicate with inmates in neighboring cells.
>
> When he was arrested in 1976, Natan weighed about 150 pounds. After his 1983 strike, he was a mere shadow of himself and had lost more than half his body weight! When this hunger strike ended—they forced nutrients into him through his rectum—he went on to stage other strikes as he felt the situation warranted it.
>
> His heart suffered terribly through the entire ordeal, and he received no medical care. In Avital's earlier account, she describes the angina he felt as being so bad that he wore a hole in his shirt from massaging his heart.
>
> He retained his sanity by playing chess games in his head, reading a book of psalms in Hebrew given to him by Avital, and reflecting on two refined photos that he had of her. Near the end of his imprisonment, he engaged in readings of the Bible with a fellow prisoner.

Throughout his imprisonment, Natan lived with the conviction that the Soviets could not humiliate him. Only he could humiliate himself.

Then, through Avital's pressure, through Reagan's pressure, through the pressure of the most determined voices in the free world, the day finally came in February 1986. Natan was released—nine years after his imprisonment, eight years into his official sentence, but five before his scheduled release. Actually, he was expelled from the Soviet Union.

But, then he refused to go until the KGB gave him back his Hebrew psalm book. They had tried to confiscate it as a last gasp of control. When they finally returned it to him, he was flown to Berlin. After the plane landed, he was brought to the checkpoint to be transferred to the West. The KGB told him to march directly toward a parked car. Natan said he was not about to cut a deal with the KGB about what he would and would not do, expecially not now.

And in a wildly and wonderfully crooked way, he zig-zagged to the waiting automobile.

What did he say when he reached his darling Avital? *"Sorry I'm a little late."*

Israeli Prime Minister Shimon Peres and a host of Israelis greeted him at the airport in Israel. Ronald Reagan made a call to him when Natan arrived in Jerusalem. Natan telephoned Sakharov's home to give this giant further determination in his campaign for human rights. In April 1986, Sharanksy made his first trip to the United States, with only two months to orient himself to the real world. He had been in the clutches of the Soviet penal system for nine years, many of them in solitary confinement. Nine years out of communication with the outside world.

When he arrived in New York, I had the privilege to escort him to a huge rally organized in his honor by organizations that had played such a key role in focusing attention upon the plight of Natan Sharansky in particular and Soviet Jewry in general. Sharansky came on stage without notes. He looked out at 150,000 cheering people gathered on the Plaza in front of the United Nations. After five minutes of uncontrollable screaming jubilation, Natan quieted the crowd and said:

> In the deepest, darkest moments of my solitary confinement,
> your love was an echo that warmed my soul and inspired me

to resist and maintain hope. I could feel your love and your support 12,000 miles away and it nourished me and it gave me strength and it brought me freedom and may God bless you. I thank you from the bottom of my heart and I urge you to continue to do what you've been doing until every Jew who wants to leave the Soviet Union is free to do so and has left.

The crowd went crazy.

We then proceeded to Washington, D.C., for Natan to personally thank the Reagan administration for its support in gaining his release. I accompanied him on his visit to Vice President Bush when Natan thanked the vice president for his help. George Bush wanted to know: If any Jew who wanted to leave the Soviet Union *could* leave, how many Jews would go?

Natan began his answer by telling a story in which President Gorbachev is having a conversation with his Foreign Minister Edvard Shevardnadze:

> "Comrade Shevardnadze, how many people do you think would really leave the Soviet Union if they had the permission to do so?" Gorbachev asks.
>
> "Well," Shevardnadze says scratching his head, "I don't know about you Comrade Gorbachev, but I think *we'd* all be gone."

Sharansky said he felt that two million Jews would go. Then Bush started to describe what was happening politically inside of the Soviet Union. "What will be the likely outcome of glasnost and perestroika?" he asked.

"Don't be seduced by Gorbachev," Sharansky answered. He said it would a very dangerous time for the Reagan-Bush team to tie themselves too closely to Gorbachev. He could tumble at any time. It was not the case of changing one man, Sharansky contended. It was a matter of changing the system. Prophetic words given the coup that was later to befall Gorbachev and the eventual dissolution of the Soviet Union.

Vice President Bush was impressed with Sharansky. I think anybody who ever really spends any time with Sharansky has to be. He has the irrepressible spirit of a man who can not be broken. He retains great optimism and great faith in mankind. He maintains a positive belief that the world could be better. He is able to hang on to this wonderful sense of humor, in spite of all of his persecution and hardship. George Bush developed a warm relationship with Natan Sharansky, which remains close to this day.

After our meeting with the vice president, I took Sharansky to a meeting hosted by the Washington press corps honoring Natan. His message was memorable. To my best recollection, he said:

> You have been on the front line of man's struggle to be free. There could have been no movement of resistance inside the Soviet Union, there could have been no refuseniks: if there hadn't been honest, free information and this information was the key to nourishing the resistance. The honest flow of free information is the enemy of totalitarianism and you in the press have been in the front lines, battling for man's right to be free. The job is not done. Keep doing what you have been doing till freedom rings throughout the world.

The "cynics" of the press corps gave Natan a standing ovation. Then came the first question, "Mr. Sharansky, you are clearly recognized as one of the foremost international figures in the human rights movement. How do you feel about the manner in which the Israelis are oppressing the Palestinian people?"

"That's a very serious question," Sharansky answered, "and I was deeply troubled by it—so concerned, in fact, that I decided that I would do a study before coming here, to try and get an understanding of what the real situation is. There are very few subjects on which

I am truly an expert. However, one of them is prisons. I am a very, very qualified authority on prisons. I've spent nine years of my life in the Soviet prison system. I decided I wanted to see firsthand how the Israelis were treating Palestinians that were interned in Israeli prisons.

> I called the head of the Israeli prison system and said I would like to have the names of the prisons in which you are interring Palestinians who have been arrested for terrorist activities against Israel, as well as the names of Israeli prisons where you are housing Israelis. He gave me the names of four, and I made this request: I want to be able to go to any one of these four unannounced and without an escort. I'll bring my own Arabic interpreter. I walked through the prisons and talked to Palestinian and Israeli prisoners both. I asked to see the punishment cell and was shown it. Having been a guest of the Soviet prison system and having now visited the Israeli prison system, I was proud as a Jew and as an Israeli at the level of humanity and the decency with which the Israelis were treating the Palestinian prisoners. The average Palestinian prisoner eats healthier meals and sleeps in more living space than the average citizen of Moscow. I am here to tell you that the Israelis are doing a much better job than I had been led to believe from the reports I have read in your press.

What an incredible and effective response to a very hostile question. He succeeded in using his authority of competence to defeat the unfounded and scurrilous attacks against Israel and its handling of the Palestinians in a very convincing way. But what foresight and what preparation for someone out of touch with the outside world for nine years and free only three months.

Natan wanted to focus attention upon the 2.6 million Jews who were locked behind the Iron Curtain in the Soviet Union and whom we could not fail to rescue. His vision was to organize a rally of

400,000 people on the Mall in Washington, in conjunction with President Gorbachev's summit meeting with President Reagan. Most of the leadership of the organized Jewish community cautioned him that he would never get more than 15,000 people to rally in the middle of winter, and further, there were not 400,000 Jews who wanted to leave the Soviet Union in the first place. And, the Jewish community didn't want to jeopardize the steady trickle of emigration to Israel that was already taking place. They said he would be foolish to even try. The Washington Jewish Federation said it would be impossible to attract more than 15,000. It's too cold! Natan traveled throughout the U.S. speaking to Jewish communities urging their attendance at the rally—telling them it was a moral imperative that they do so. He reminded them of the consequences of the failure to organize such a protest in the 1930s against the rising tide of Nazi sentiment that emerged even in the United States.

It was December 6, 1987, the day before the forty-sixth anniversary of the attack on Pearl Harbor. It was cold, but 250,000 people showed up!!! They came from all over the U.S.A.—mostly, but not all Jews—young and old, men and women, half the members of the U.S. Congress, and the national media. Soviet Premier Mikhail Gorbachev was in town to sign the treaty regulating intermediary nuclear weapons with President Reagan. Vice President Bush was the keynote speaker at the rally. I introduced him. The vice president's central message was a demand that Gorbachev and the Soviets permit the Jews to leave the Soviet Union. With Gorbachev staying down the street at Blair House, this was an enormous political gamble for the vice president. He didn't have to stick his neck out. The Reagan/ Bush administration was to meet with Gorbachev the very next day, and Bush was staging a provocative confrontation.

The night before the speech, I met with Natan. He asked me if there was anything in Vice President Bush's speech about the Jackson-Vanik Amendment? I said no. Natan emphasized it was very important that Jackson-Vanik be reaffirmed before the summit. After seeing Natan, I met with George Bush and pointed out the omission. "Mr.

Vice President," I said, "we made a mistake in the speech. There's no reference to Jackson-Vanik. It clearly should be included."

Vice President Bush agreed with me. Now, you don't just add a line to a speech from the vice president of the United States with policy ramifications the night before a talk. There's a whole procedure of clearances you have to go through in order to make a change. George Bush asked me to get it done and told me that I had his backing. I contacted Don Gregg, the vice president's advisor on national security affairs. He dug in and got the clearances. The next day Jackson-Vanik was reaffirmed in Bush's reworked speech—a commitment that remained throughout the Bush presidency. His speech set a policy tone toward the Soviets when there was a temptation to abandon it. In a world of glasnost and perestroika, wasn't a trade reciprocity measure like Jackson-Vanik simply a dinosaur? Not at all. Sharansky saw the peril in the omission. Bush saw Sharansky's wisdom.

When the vice president reached the dramatic zenith of his talk I remembered Avital's relentless demand: **"I . . . want . . . my . . . husband . . . back."** Over the Mall, George Bush rang out the words: **"Mr. Gorbachev, let . . . these . . . people . . . go!"** Four words. Same cadence. Same pounding at the gate. Could Gorbachev hear it just down the street at Blair House? You bet he could and he did! From 1989 until Gorbachev was ousted in 1991, 1.5 million Jews were permitted to leave the former Soviet Union, of whom a million emigrated to Israel. Today, less than a million remain in the former Soviet Union.

In December 1989, Andrei Sakharov died in Moscow. For Natan, the greatest hero of the twentieth century was, and is, Andrei Sakharov. He saw in Sakharov a man of enormous character, moral force, and invincible courage. If you ask Natan who is responsible for the collapse of the Soviet Union and brought its people democracy, he would say that they were: Sakharov, the dissidents within the Soviet Union, Senator Henry Jackson, and Ronald Reagan. These were the prime movers behind that achievement. The guiding light of the dissidents in the Soviet Union was Sakharov, and Sakharov was *not* Jewish. Sakharov was the symbol of human rights, freedom, democracy, and decency for all people, regardless of race, creed, or color. That's what he was about and he inspired people like Natan and others who struggled for the same values. Then, Natan would say Ronald Reagan contributed significantly to the pressures that brought about the collapse of a system that inevitably had to collapse because of its own inefficiency and corruption. In his mind, the pace of that self-destruction was accelerated by the courage of Sakharov, the dissidents, Jackson through the Jackson-Vanik legislation, and President Reagan.

Natan called me shortly after Sakharov's death. He wanted to meet with President George Bush. Natan wanted to personally convey Sakharov's last message to the West. For that purpose, I took him to see the president in the Oval Office in February 1990. A second agenda item was to be the growing number of Jews who were trapped in the Soviet Union because of a breakdown in implementation of an agreement on direct flights between Moscow and Tel Aviv.

I remember the last-minute preparations before we set out for the White House. Sharansky asked me if he should wear a tie: "Would the president be offended if I did not?"

"No," I replied, "but he would be very pleased that you should show such respect for his office if you did."

Sharansky agreed but he said I'd have to tie it for him. I tied his tie. He was turning red. "Gordy," he gasped, "you've got to loosen it. I don't think the president would appreciate it—after I spent all those years in the Gulag—if I died of suffocation in the Oval Office!" Although he compromised in wearing a tie, Sharansky insisted on wearing his military cap. Orthodox Jewish men must keep their heads covered all the time, although he didn't want to wear a yarmulke. Natan's negotiations about ties are something of a legend. (In 1998, Bibi Netanyahu—then Prime Minister of Israel—took a delegation to the Wye Plantation in Virginia for a Mideast summit with Yasser Arafat under the auspices of President Clinton. Near the end of the meeting and anticipating the signing of an accord, a protocol chief told all the members of the Israeli delegation that they had to wear ties. Natan asked if Arafat would be wearing a tie. The U.S. staffer didn't think so. In *The Case for Democracy,* Natan reports his answer: "So, we'll offset each other.... Here at least we will have real reciprocity.")

Sharansky's visit with President Bush was a press event. So Press Secretary Marlin Fitzwater was there, as was Deputy National Security Director Bob Gates and Middle East expert Richard Haas, both from National Security Advisor Brent Scowcroft's staff. After photos and the exchange of pleasantries, Sharansky outlined his agenda. He said he was compelled to communicate Sakharov's message face-to-face with the president. But, Sharansky said he also needed to update the president on the evolving situation for Jews in the Soviet Union.

"Mr. President, events are running away from us and I must use the limited time we have together to speak to you about Soviet Jewry. So while I initially came here to deliver a message that Sakharov had for you, the urgency that I feel about the conditions that are unfolding for Soviet Jewry cause me to first want to talk to you about their plight and to make a request of you about their situation.

"Because of you and President Reagan, the doors have opened and Jews are able to get visas. Thousands are leaving, yet hundreds of thousands of Soviet Jews want to leave, but can't. All flights out of the Soviet Union connecting to Israel are booked through March 1991. Anti-Semitism is on the rise. It's pervasive. Leaflets are being published, and Jewish academics in the institutions of learning are being threatened. There's a tremendous disillusionment with the failure of the Soviet system among the people. The people need a scapegoat, and they're blaming the Jews for Bolshevism and Marxism and for the failure of the economy."

Natan explained that there was a long history of anti-Semitism dating back to the bloody pogroms in tsarist Russia. There was also a lack of confidence that perestroika and glasnost would succeed. Jews in the Soviet Union feared the return of a vicious, violent outbreak of anti-Semitism. When that happens, Natan argued, the Jews know the doors will close. If they fail to get out now, they may never be able to get out.

Two big issues loomed behind the problem. One was the matter of direct flights from the Soviet Union to Israel. This measure had been negotiated, agreed upon, and then collapsed in implementation. Direct flights would have made it possible for many more Soviet Jews to get out much faster. Otherwise there was a limitation on the number of air seats that were available to take people out of the Soviet Union to Eastern Europe, as a transit point to Israel. Under the El Al umbrella, the Israelis were prepared to charter and operate direct flights to move tens of thousands of people out in a compressed period of time. Natan pinpointed the problem as a shortage of planes. He said that the December 6, 1989, agreement between Israel and the Soviets to permit unlimited flights had not been honored.

President Bush turned to Gates and asked what the U.S. knew about this and why the Soviets weren't living up to that agreement. Haas explained that Natan was correct. There *was* an agreement, but the Israelis violated the agreement by publicly announcing the fact that such an understanding in fact existed. This embarrassed the Soviets, and they reneged on the commitment. The president told Natan that he would try to move the matter along, but that the U.S. feared Gorbachev was very vulnerable, and the U.S. had to proceed carefully.

Natan had managed to put the Soviet Jewry agenda item— technically the second of the two issues—skillfully to the fore. But, President Bush wanted to know about Natan's conversation with Sakharov before he died. Sakharov's message, as relayed by Natan, was both profound and prophetic. Natan said that Sakharov believed Gorbachev had to decide between economic growth and empire. The U.S. should downplay the emphasis on supporting Gorbachev the man. "Don't foster hope in Gorbachev that he can have both. He cannot," Natan quoted Sakharov, "and, there's no such thing as a little bit of freedom. You're either slaves or you're free. If you want economic growth, people must have free markets and free choice. As soon as you provide people with the conditions under which they can freely express themselves politically and economically, the Soviet empire has to fall apart. Commonwealth is possible, but not empire. The West must send clear, unambiguous signals that it will support commonwealth and free markets. For the people in the Soviet Union to embrace the West, the West must back political and economic freedom and human rights in that country."

Essentially, what Natan told President Bush were some of the seminal ideas that underpinned Natan's own book *The Case for Democracy*, which was to appear some fifteen years later. What the U.S. needed to do, as Natan recounted Sakharov's position, was to align America's policy in support of political and economic freedom and human rights advances. If Gorbachev and the Soviet leadership supported policies that nurture and encourage that condition, America should support them as well. However, if the Soviet leadership moved in a different direction, then the U.S. shouldn't back Gorbachev. Gorbachev should be replaced. If the Soviets reverted to repression to hold the empire together, the Americans should withdraw their support of Gorbachev altogether. Only democracies can make peace. Furthermore, the Baltic Republics must be free to chart their own course. This will be the first step in the disintegration of the empire. The U.S. had given Gorbachev a big boost by supporting his use of troops to quell the uprising in Azerbaijan, which had happened shortly before this White House meeting.

"Mr. President," Natan summed up Sakharov's message, "you have to use the moral force of your office to compel Gorbachev to make a choice."

"I'm afraid Gorbachev is experiencing great pressure from both the left and from the right," President Bush acknowledged, "I *did* decide to escalate our support for perestroika, to support Gorbachev's use of troops in order to give him some encouragement." In other words, the President thought Gorbachev was very vulnerable. While he appreciated what Sakharov was saying through Sharansky, George Bush felt that the U.S. was really better off with Gorbachev than with any of the other apparent options. In the end, the Soviet system collapsed under its own weight, as Natan had predicted, and Gorbachev was not a long-term factor in the situation.

Natan Sharansky is an inspiration to all. He suffered nine years of harsh imprisonment. When he was released, he left prison with his faculties intact, with his energy unabated, with his humor bubbling, and with a full sense of responsibility for the two and a half million Jews he left behind. What proof that one person can make a difference!

Natan and Avital Sharansky are two of the most extraordinary people I have ever met. They have touched the future with their children, born and raised in Israel. Through the impact of their character, courage and leadership, millions of Jews from the former Soviet Union are also now free to live their lives and raise their children in freedom.

SEVERAL KEY THINGS I LEARNED FROM NATAN SHARANSKY ARE:

Integrity matters.

Character is doing the right thing, especially when it hurts. Natan aligned himself with Sakharov because Sakharov's stance on human rights was the right position—even though it exposed him to huge political pressure and ultimately imprisonment. Natan refused to sign the letter that would have gained him a release from prison because it implied he was guilty. He knew he was an innocent victim of Soviet repression, not a criminal. Later he resigned as a cabinet minister from the Israeli government to voice his disagreement with the Israeli pullout from Gaza. He believed that the Palestinian Authority had made no significant movement toward democracy and human rights.

Don't debate abstractions.

Reduce issues to human terms. Talk about realities in the concrete. Don't let the ground rules of the debate shift to empty rhetoric. Emphasize your direct experience in areas where you have a clear authority of competence, as Natan did in confronting the press on the treatment of Palestinians in Israeli prisons.

It is very difficult to maintain moral authority and engage in politics.

Politics requires too many compromises and has too many gray areas.

Natan decided that he had a moral imperative to enter politics. As always, he is out to make a difference, not to make a living. But, now he is irreversibly linked to the political arena. He cannot return to the revered and irreproachable role of prophet. Yet, he retains a remarkable ability to register an authoritative voice on issues of the moment. Advocating vigorous dialogue among Jews inside of Israel after the Gaza withdrawal, Natan wrote in the *Jerusalem Post,* "We must continue knocking on each other's doors. Breaking down the walls of ignorance and indifference is critical not just to our strength against external enemies, but our ability to address the many societal challenges facing us in the days ahead."

What makes Natan such a special leader is his remarkable blend of so many positive attributes:

> His character and integrity,
>
> His moral and physical courage,
>
> His constant and invincible sense of humor,
>
> Staying true to his roots,
>
> The power of his and Avital's love to sustain each other and to overcome hardship,
>
> His relentless optimism,
>
> The focus of his passion,
>
> His incredible energy.

No one person captures the essence of character, moral courage, and leadership better than Natan Sharansky.

In the Oval Office on May 28, 1981. Avital Sharansky's single-mindedness and tenacity brought Natan Sharansky's unlawful imprisonment to President Reagan's attention. At this dramatic meeting, described in the Avital Sharansky chapter, the President made Natan's release a top U.S. policy priority.

Natan Sharansky urgently requested the meeting pictured here to relay the human rights activist Andrei Sakharov's last warnings to the West before his death. Sakharov's words were prophetic, but the most amazing milestone of this Oval Office session may have been Natan's agreeing to wear a tie!

With Egyptian President Hosni Mubarak. My contacts with Egypt have spanned thirty years, starting with my carefully arranged first trip to Egypt, which took place in 1976, during Anwar Sadat's rule. At that time, it was illegal for American Jews to enter Egypt.

Israeli Prime Minister Yitzhak Rabin's boundless courage in pursuit of peace between Israel and the Palestinians led to his assassination by a right-wing Jewish extremist.

You can barely see President George Bush beside me in this receiving line with Russian President Boris Yeltsin. When President Bush commented to Yeltsin that I had helped Soviet Jews to emigrate to Israel, he quipped, "Can you get him to send them back? We need them to jump-start our economy!"

At a 1986 reception hosted for Vice President Bush by Israeli Prime Minister Shimon Peres. Peres has served Israel for some sixty years as head of every top cabinet ministry at one time or another. His strategic and diplomatic skills secured critical French armaments and nuclear technology in the early years of the Israeli state.

If I met Ronald Reagan once, I met him twenty times. On the twentieth visit, he still didn't remember who I was, and this was long before the ravages of Alzheimer's. His mind was programmed in a different way — totally focused on his vision to secure the future of an America he loved deeply.

In the Oval Office with President Reagan and Vice President Bush.
Max Fisher is to my left on one of our frequent White House visits.
The Reagan administration was always open to discussing
American-Israeli issues; and during that time period,
there were many.

In the Oval Office with President George Bush. His building of the
Coalition for the 1981 Gulf War was a masterpiece in diplomacy.
Being able to persuade Yitzhak Shamir and Israel to not respond to
the Iraqi missile attack was evidence of his ability to inspire trust,
even among skeptics.

With Israeli Prime Minister Yitzhak Shamir in his Jerusalem office.
Shamir displayed uncompromising integrity and great wisdom in
not foreclosing the options of a future Israeli prime minister in
trading land for peace. That discussion keynoted one of the most
remarkable meetings I ever had with an Israeli PM.

My meeting with Sazo Idemitsu in Japan in 1972 taught me much
about a wise leader's recognition of how people's motivations
change during their lives. His leadership principles were so
widely respected that 250,000 people attended his
surprise 80th birthday party in 1968.

Vice President George Bush and his wife Barbara at an absorption center in Israel in 1986. They were visiting some of the children he helped rescue in the 1985 Operation Sheba airlift from Sudan.

In President Bush's office at Kennebunkport with the president and National Security Advisor Brent Scowcroft. The topic was loan guarantees for Israel in the wake of the 1991 Gulf War.

Introducing Democratic Congressman Tom Lantos before a meeting
of U.S. House members. Tom and his wife, Annette, led a campaign
to make Raoul Wallenberg the second honorary citizen of the
United States after Winston Churchill. As Tom said,
"Raoul taught us that a single individual committed
to an idea can achieve miracles."

My wife Carol Sue and I on the vice president's boat in
Kennebunkport with the Bushes. On the porch of his summer home
there, George Bush once said to me, "In the last analysis, Gordy, the
three things that really matter in life are faith, family, and friends."

HEALING

If you drain the Pacific Ocean, you should not be surprised to find that islands are all connected.
—Dr. Judah Folkman on the holistic nature of the human body

Discovery is to see what everyone has seen and to think what nobody has thought.
—Dr. Albert Szent-Gyorgi

Dr. Judah Folkman

Judah Folkman was born in Cleveland in 1933. He grew up in Columbus, Ohio, and I had the great good fortune to grow up with him. Judah attended Ohio State University and went on to the Harvard Medical School. It was there— as a student—that he helped develop the first pacemaker. During service in the Navy, he invented an implantation for the time-release of drugs—an invention he later donated to the World Population Council. It was in the Navy that Judah made a dramatic observation. He had been monitoring some isolated human organs with tumors that were being kept in glass containers. The tumors stopped growing when they reached a certain size. Why? Because their blood supply had reached its capacity. This flash of insight was to lead to the theory of angiogenesis—that tumors require a blood supply to grow. What, Judah reflected, would happen if tumors were deprived of the blood that enables them to overwhelm the body's natural processes and structure? He then set about to develop a variety of angiogenesis inhibitors to do exactly that. This was a defining moment for Judah and for the entire field of cancer research. What hope this has unlocked for far more targeted cancer treatment, in a medical world dominated by often drastic surgery or the ravages of chemo- and radiation-therapies that subject the entire body to enormous physical punishment!

Judah's research since has been centered on ever more sophisticated techniques for withdrawing the blood supply from malignancies without damaging the surrounding organs or healthy tissue. Judah's cancer concepts, first published in The New England Journal of Medicine *in 1971, form probably the most revolutionary and promising thinking done on this dreaded disease. Seizing this defining moment and walking out on that limb in 1971 took courage, but he knew the risk of holding back. It would have retarded progress toward a cancer cure in a massive way. Indeed, it would have harmed the world by slowing down the most promising avenue of cancer research ever pursued.*

Judah's teaching and research work have been breathtaking. From 1967 to 1977, he served as a full professor of surgery at the Harvard Medical School. Today he is Professor of Cell Biology on the Harvard Faculty. As a lecturer, his capacity to hold audiences, technical and lay, is dramatic to witness. He was the pioneer in using Interferon in cancer treatment and has developed increasingly potent cancer compounds. The drug Endostatin, which he developed, may well have benefits in preventing stroke and heart disease as well as combating cancer. His research work has been coupled with a brilliant career as a surgeon. He was named chief of surgery at Children's Hospital in Boston when he was just thirty-four. His involvement with complex infant cases is legendary. Today Judah serves as the director of the Vascular Biology Program at Children's Hospital. Over his career, he has won the Soma Weiss Award, the Boylston Medical Prize, and the Borden Prize. It's safe speculation in my view that when a cure for cancer is found, Judah Folkman will have been in the forefront of that victory. Not to be overlooked are the collateral treatments Judah's concepts and investigations in angiogenesis inhibitors have spawned. They are already at work combating arthritis and actually reversing the blindness caused by macular degeneration.

Judah Folkman's father Jerome was a rabbi, and Jerome hoped his young son would be a rabbi as well. There had been rabbis in the Folkman family since—well, forever. On Sunday, his father would take Judah with him on his rounds to comfort the sick who were hospitalized. When he was seven, Jerome took Judah on a visit to a woman named Miriam with an incurable and particularly painful disease. She was deeply depressed. Judah, who was wise well beyond his years, saw the woman lying there in agony and asked himself, "How do you handle this? What do you say to somebody suffering in this way?"

Rabbi Folkman took Miriam's hand and said, "God must love you a great deal."

"What?!" she asked with astonishment. "How can you possibly say that, Rabbi Folkman?"

"Because, Miriam, He has *chosen* you to deal with this condition," he answered firmly. "He must have great confidence in your ability to work through this or, he would never have put you in this situation. Don't let him down."

Miriam never recovered physically, but her attitude and endurance changed seismically in the coming months. Watching Miriam rally, Judah understood his passion and purpose in life. It was *not* to be a rabbi. It was to be a doctor. Judah felt that his father had given him a precious gift in that visit with Miriam. The gift was the secret of healing itself—hope.

In later years, Judah Folkman, the physician, told the *Boston Globe:* "If patients have been given no hope, I try to provide some . . . . You constantly have to skate between no hope—the worst thing a physician can do; patients are terrified of being abandoned—and false hope."

How does a person like Judah Folkman come to be? Much of the answer stems from how **he was** raised. When I was a teenager, I got to know the family well. My parents were not devout Jews, nor was I, but I actually changed my temple affiliation to belong to Rabbi

Folkman's congregation. There was something magical about the Folkman family. Judah's mother, Bessie, was plagued by a painful curvature of the spine that made many of her days agonizing. Never did I see her any way except meticulously but modestly groomed with a serene smile on her face. Bessie had the simplest and perhaps the best definition of happiness I have ever heard. It is three-pronged: "Someone to love. Something to do. Something to look forward to."

The Folkman family had a remarkable custom. During their family vacation, Judah and his younger siblings, Joy and David, would sit in a circle around their parents Jerome and Bessie. Each of the children would then make a brief presentation: What had they accomplished in the last year? What were their goals for the coming year? What would be the chief obstacles they would need to surmount? How would they tackle them? How would they measure their success? This tradition continued with the grandchildren until Rabbi Folkman's death.

Wow! Can you imagine the sense of accountability for living life responsibly that such expectations would engender? Is it any surprise that Joy went on to become an outstanding medical doctor in her own right? Is it any surprise that David developed into a merchandising wizard in the retailing industry, running premier department store chains like Gump's, the Emporium, and Magnin's on the West Coast? Is it any surprise that Judah became Judah?

Judah Folkman has never been content to be a practitioner or a researcher. You can sense he feels an obligation to be an inspiring and provocative communicator. He is capable of taking the most complex medical ideas and rendering them in images and metaphors that register with the lay mind. Once, the Reuters news service asked him to explain the connection between leukemia and angiogenesis. His response: "'The leukemia cells are like grapes growing on a bush and the branches are the blood vessels...thinner than a hair...the leukemic cells stimulate new blood vessels in the bone marrow cavity and then grow on them." In his communication, there is only one thing that surpasses the boldness of Judah's imagery, and that is his personal modesty. It's in his character, and it is also part and parcel of his pragmatism. "Scientists are excited about someone else's discovery," he once told the *Jerusalem Report,* "but not if it makes them a celebrity."

The Public Broadcasting TV series *Nova* once interviewed Judah and asked him if it was easier to be a practicing physician or a researcher. "Clinical medicine has tremendous feedback," he responded. "Research is just the opposite. It's just years of frustration.... You've got critics all over, and scientists are sometimes mean to each other; they criticize the ideas in the name of scientific skepticism ... it's easier to be a physician than to be a researcher. I've been both and physician is easier." What makes Judah both a better physician and a better researcher is his deftness in crossing between these two different worlds. When the human body is at stake, for example, there is a peril for researchers to live in a world of pure science. "...Many of them," Judah says, "had never seen cancer except in a dish."

Over the years, I have had the chance to drop in on Judah in his offices. My estimate is that he receives and *answers* between fifty to one hundred phone calls and e-mails a week from people seeking his help. He is never too busy to answer a call from an anxious parent whose child is facing a life-threatening cancer crisis. The source of Judah's empathy is not casual. Laura, Judah and his wife Paula's first child, was born with cystic fibrosis. They later lost an infant son to the same dreaded illness. He tasted anguish firsthand and has never forgotten. The sense of command Judah radiates with patients and parents and his inexhaustible persistence have earned him the sobriquet "the Lance Armstrong of oncology." He handles every challenge tossed his way with poise and a positive spirit.

Judah has had his setbacks. Skepticism toward angiogenesis inhibitors in the traditional scientific community has been an obstacle since the early 1970s. Bold ideas are not readily accepted in this often petty world. Giordano Bruno was burned at the stake for forwarding the theories of Copernicus. Galileo was ultimately banished to house arrest when he challenged the presumption of an earth-centered universe. Darwin's notions were savagely attacked, and still are.

In response to Judah Folkman's angiogenesis theories, colleagues have undermined funding for grants. Scientific journals have challenged the premises he and his team have used and declined to publish the findings. Scientists have been warned off taking posts in his departments. Judah never lost courage or retreated to more comfortable positions. He even went on to support new applications for the controversial drug thalidomide—the source of tragic birth defects in the 1960s—and showed how it could, nonetheless, play a powerful, positive role in cancer therapy. Over time, many leading voices in the scientific community, such as Nobel Prize–winner and DNA co-discoverer James Watson, were won over to many or all of Judah's positions.

In addition, Judah's formal work was disrupted a few years ago by a patent dispute, and Judah was named a party to the litigation. The suit was ultimately dismissed. Tests and procedures might have been postponed, but his mind didn't miss a beat in its conquest of cancer or in its care for his patients. If there were long faces in the labs during those trying days, colleagues are quick to say that one individual's courage, confidence, and positive attitude remained invincible—Judah himself.

As a practicing physician, Judah's bedside manner rivals his father's in ease, sincerity, and optimism. Hope is Judah's métier, his invincible mainstay. I have seen him say to a patient: "If you can just hang around, the answer seems right around the corner. Don't throw in the towel." Judah knows exactly how to inspire hope.

Judah has been a masterful mentor. He is ever willing to credit young colleagues like Dr. Michael O'Reilly, whom Judah acknowledges as the discoverer of Angiostatin—a critical compound in the angiogenesis equation. Judah has groomed countless leading surgeons like Dr. Marshall Schwartz and Dr. Steven Fishman. The researchers who have grown under Judah's guidance are legion and include MIT Professor Robert Langer, the author of hundreds of articles and the source of countless patents. Many of Judah's protégés are in charge of their own laboratories today and create a powerful network that can only advance the conquest of cancer.

With all of the activity in this bustling life, Judah and Paula, a gifted musician, have done a remarkable job of raising their two lovely daughters, Laura and Marjorie. The family tradition has come full circle. The Folkmans are for Carol Sue and me ever identified with family because it was Rabbi Folkman who married us more than fifty years ago. When the rabbi retired from the pulpit, he became a faculty member at Ohio State University, teaching a course in family life. I remember asking him once what was the most accurate predictor if a person would remain committed to Judaism in later life. He said that there was one factor that mattered more than anything else—if the mother lit the Shabbat candles for the family dinner each week. Tradition matters. Symbols matter.

Two key things I learned from Dr. Judah Folkman are:

The power of tenacity.

It's nearly thirty-five years since Judah Folkman first proclaimed his theory of angiogenesis—the work of one courageous scientist. Despite the rejection of many of his colleagues, he has persevered in his beliefs. Early on, Dr. John Ender, who discovered the polio virus, said to Judah that his theory would take about "10 years before anybody is going to believe this." Judah had the character and the courage to seize the moment and take on the scientific establishment. And, the world is a better place because of his leadership.

A towering giant of hope can also be a paragon of humility.

While wearing the hat of the dauntless researcher, Judah has never abandoned his mission of serving humanity as a skilled practicing physician. Helping one person at a time and energizing people with hope, Judah is a master of healing and a great embodiment of what it means to be truly Jewish. Vision, tenacity, and love. Judah Folkman has lit countless candles of hope in others and made the world a better place in so many ways . . . and has done so person by person, one individual after another.

DIVINE POWER

You want to change the world? Start by changing yourself.

—The Rebbe

The Rebbe

Menachem Mendel Schneerson was born in the Ukrainian town of Nikolaev in 1902. The son of a rabbi who was a noted Talmudic and Kabbalistic scholar, he followed in his father's footsteps and became proficient in both disciplines at an early age. In 1928, Menachem married the daughter of the sixth leader of the Lubavitcher movement, also named Schneerson, in Warsaw. Menachem Schneerson developed a strong interest in the sciences and, accompanied by his wife, moved to Western Europe. There he studied at both the University of Berlin and the Sorbonne in Paris. There, too, he spent most of his time engaged in the study of the Talmud and other Jewish scholarship. In 1941, after the Nazi control of France the preceding year, the couple were able to make their way to the United States, where his wife's father had already emigrated. That emigration, the Holocaust, and the death of his father-in-law formed a defining moment that changed one person's seeming destiny to be a world-class scientist to that of a publicly engaged leader for the Jewish people.

A rabbi, of course, is a teacher and leader of the Jewish faith. Some rabbis lead a congregation, but all rabbis are expected to be knowledgeable in Jewish law and some are scholars on particular subjects. A rebbe occupies a different role. His involvement is far broader. A rebbe is spiritual leader of a Hasidic community. The title is generally dynastic, but not always. Hasidic Judaism originated in Eastern Europe in the eighteenth century. While there are several different Hasidic groups, they share some traits in common: They are all Orthodox, all inclined toward mysticism, and all are recognizable—especially the men—by the strict dress code they adhere to. The latter includes black coats and hats, and white shirts. One of these groups is the Lubavitchers. Among reformed and conservative Jews, the words "black-hat communities" are often used to describe Hasidic Jews. In the last century, this one particular rebbe, Menachem Schneerson, had an impact surpassing all others. In a loving way, he considered the agenda of the Jewish people as his very own, reaching out to develop Jewish awareness in every area he could. Indeed, he was a daring leader on a global scale. For many, he is known simply as the Rebbe.

In 1950, Menachem Schneerson's father-in-law died. Normally a birth-son would have taken on the role of rebbe, but Menachem Schneerson's capabilities and presence were so overwhelming that he was selected as the successor to head the Lubavitcher movement—a role he reluctantly assumed in 1951. For the next forty-three years, until his death in 1994, he presided as the Rebbe of the Lubavitch group with its network of Jewish schools, programs, outreach centers, and thousands of students. The Schneersons had no children. Since his death, he has not been replaced by a new rebbe, because many of his followers were persuaded he was the Messiah and none of them have found a person of his caliber. They still aren't sure he isn't coming back! I'm not an Orthodox Jew, but I can say this with complete conviction: The Rebbe I knew was one of the most unforgettable people I ever met.

In 1969, I was the Chairman of the Young Leadership Cabinet of the national United Jewish Appeal. As such, I was invited to deliver the keynote address to the Council of Jewish Federations and Welfare Funds Annual Conference, being held that year in November in Boston. The theme was "Youth Looks at the Future of the American Jewish Community." I spent six months preparing for this talk. Usually, I speak extemporaneously with at most a one-page outline. This time—because of its importance—I elected to read the entire speech.

In it, I thanked my parents' generation for supporting the creation of the state of Israel and rescuing survivors from the Holocaust. In its aftermath, two million Jews had been delivered through their efforts from lands of oppression and resettled to lands of freedom. Nonetheless, I pointed out that we faced a disaster in the field of Jewish education. We ran the risk of losing more Jews through assimilation than we had saved through affirmation. We needed to address the failure of our Jewish educational system to inspire many young Jews to continue to be Jewish. I recommended that we create a national Jewish research and development venture capital fund to invest risk capital in innovative approaches to make Jewish education relevant to young people and to create an Institute for Jewish Life that would manage the process.

To fund this Institute, I proposed that the Jewish community endow the Institute with $100 million of State of Israel bonds for a period of ten years. The purchasers would receive a tax deduction. At the end of ten years, they would get their principal back. The Institute would get the use of the interest. Annually it would provide about $6 million in revenue. We would have ten years in which to evaluate the results. If the concept didn't produce worthwhile results, that would be the end of the Institute. Ultimately the idea was adopted in an abbreviated form with funding of $3.5 million. In this truncated version, it failed in its mission and was eventually closed. Still, it stimulated a lot of discussion about Jewish education, and placed it right behind rescue as a priority for the American Jewish community.

In December 1969, I received a call from a man named Leibel Alevsky. He was a rabbi with the Lubavitch movement in the Crown Heights section of Brooklyn. He said the Rebbe wanted to meet me. Given the tone of the phone call, I thought I was being invited for a royal audience. I immediately said yes to a date in January, but I didn't even know who the Rebbe was! My rabbi gave me some background and urged me to go ahead with the meeting. On the appointed day in January, Alevsky and I were finishing dinner in his home at 11:15 at night. We got a call that the Rebbe would see me now. I walked with Alevsky to a modest building to find 300 people—from around the world—each waiting at the Rebbe's headquarters, the *Chabad* Center, in the middle of the night for an audience with the Rebbe!

Later I learned that the Rebbe held these audiences three times each week, lasting from sundown often until the middle of the night.

I went in alone to see the Rebbe. In his office, illuminated by a single ceiling light, books were stacked from the floor to the ceiling. He was a slight man with translucent skin and absolutely clear whites of his eyes—the sclera encircling his sparkling blue irises, his beard outlining an impish grin. The Rebbe was sixty-seven at the time. He looked at me in such a penetrating way that I felt like I was being x-rayed.

"Mr. Zacks, I have read your speech," he began, "and it's clear you have taken good care of your mind. I can look at you, and it's clear you have taken good care of your body. *What* have you done to take care of your soul?"

No small talk about how I was or if I had a pleasant trip. I was stunned.

"The Jewish house is on fire," he continued. "We have an emergency, and this is not the time to experiment with new ways to put out the fire. Instead, you call the proven and tested fire department. We *are* that fire department. We—the Lubavitch—don't have drugs or intermarriage problems with our children or kids opting out of Judaism. Our tradition works, and our children are being educated. We have a worldwide outreach program that contacts and impacts non-observant Jews and saves souls. Give us the $100 million, and we will spend it to correct the problems that you are concerned about."

"Rebbe," I asked after pausing for a moment, "what if the house is on fire, but people have forgotten your telephone number?"

"God will provide," he answered me.

"There are millions of Jews whose houses are on fire," I said to him. "Most of them are Jews who will not call you, either because they have lost your number or they won't accept the lifestyle compromises you expect. They're still worthy of saving in their own way, and they are entitled to a quality Jewish education that makes Judaism relevant to their lives. That's why we need this Institute."

"Do you believe in revelation, Mr. Zacks?" he asked me next.

"I believe in God and I believe he inspires . . . but I don't believe he writes," I answered.

"You mean, Mr. Zacks, that there is this vast structure God has created of plants, animals, food chains, stars, and planets. And, that the only creature in all of creation that doesn't understand how to fit in and live their life purposefully is the human?"

I told him *yes*.

"What about the complexity of the human body? What about the jewel of the human cell? How does the body ingest food and renew itself with absolute consistency?"

I had no answer.

"Why, Mr. Zacks, is the nose always where the nose belongs? Why are the eyes always on the face for generation after generation?"

I could only shrug my shoulders, but my respect for him deepened by the moment.

"And, how can you account for the brain and the mind? How do they steer this remarkable system in a purposeful and precise way? And, what about how we fit into the earth's ecosystem, where we inhale the oxygen that plants so wonderfully manufacture for us? Could this all be accidental?"

How could I answer him?

"And, beyond what happens on earth. What about all the heavenly bodies in the sky that seem to follow such a perfect order and don't collide with each other? Is man the only creature on the planet earth without guidelines for living its life? Should man ignore the Torah given to us by God as a roadmap to guide us? This is the missing link which connects us to the complexity of Nature!"

So it went. Comment after comment. More times than not, I could not begin to answer his points.

He quoted Kazantzakis' book *Zorba the Greek* to me during our conversation. "Do you remember the young man talking with Zorba on the beach, when Zorba asks what the purpose of life is? The young fellow admits he doesn't know. And Zorba comments, 'Well, all those damned books you read—what good are they? Why do you read them?' Zorba's friend says he doesn't know. Zorba can see his friend doesn't have an answer to the most fundamental question. That's the trouble with you. 'A man's head is like a grocer,' Zorba says, 'it keeps accounts.... The head's a careful little shopkeeper; it never risks all it has, always keeps something in reserve. It never breaks the string.' Wise men and grocers *weigh* everything. They can never cut the cord and be free. Your problem, Mr. Zacks, is that you are trying to find God's map through your head. You are unlikely to find it that way. You have to *experience* before you can truly feel and then be free to learn. Let me send a teacher to live with you for a year and teach you how to *be* Jewish. You will unleash a whole new dimension to your life. If you really want to change the world, change yourself! It's like dropping a stone into a pool of water and watching the concentric circles radiate to the shore. You will influence all the people around you, and they will influence others in turn. That's how you bring about improvement in the world."

"Rebbe, I'm not ready to do that," I told him. I remained firm despite the incredibly woven tapestry of the universe he presented to me.

"What do you have to lose?" he asked, "One year of your life? What if I'm right? It could gain you an eternity if I'm right, but only cost you one year if I'm wrong."

"I'll think about it," I said as we wrapped up our hour-and-a-half conversation. The normal audience with the Rebbe was thirty seconds to a minute. Three hundred people were still waiting to come in at one in the morning.

The Rebbe took people the way they were. His ultimate goal was to bring you to the ways of Jewish life, but his means were not confrontational and demanding. You could literally feel his warmth and love in addition to the power of his vast intellect. Once he established the *Chabad* Center at 770 Eastern Parkway in Crown Heights, I don't think he ever left it. Yet he was totally wired into the events of the world. I sensed this in my first meeting with the Rebbe. He radiated compassion, love, and respect for others—a servant leader totally committed to serving God through helping others.

The Rebbe wrote me letters encouraging me to devote myself to Jewish education. Over a series of years, I received five letters from him saying that he wanted to send his representative to me to spend a year teaching me how to be Jewish. I responded to each of them and declined.

Beginning in 1986, the Rebbe had a receiving line on Sunday in which he passed out a dollar bill to be given by the recipient as *tzedakah* to charity. His reasoning: "When two people meet, something good should result for a third." People waited in line for as long as four hours to be greeted by him and receive his blessing and the dollar bill. The Rebbe was eighty-four when he started doing this. An older woman in the line asked him how he could manage to perform this demanding task. "Every soul is a diamond," he answered. "Can one grow tired of counting diamonds?"

In 1987, my youngest daughter, Kim, had just returned from Israel and she wanted to participate in the custom of Sunday Dollars. I said fine I would take her. I neither called nor told anyone who I was when we arrived. I stood in line with her. It had been seventeen years since I had seen the Rebbe and ten years since he wrote me his last letter. When it was our turn to speak with the Rebbe, he looked at me and asked "What are you doing for Jewish education?" His eyes had the same penetrating look that had scanned me seventeen years earlier and asked, "*What* are you doing to take care of your soul, Mr. Zacks?" It was as though I had just walked back into his office. In truth, hundreds of thousands of people had filed past him over those years.

"You are amazing!" I exclaimed to him.

"What has that to do with saving Jewish lives? What are you **doing** for Jewish education?" he retorted. He may not have gotten exactly what he wanted from me, but the Rebbe surely taught me the power of changing yourself to influence others. He wanted to enlist me as *his* fundraiser for Jewish education. While I certainly considered his invitation, I declined it. Still he may have been the most charismatic man I ever met. He had an incredible aura to him, partly because he was such a combination of charisma *and* pragmatism. This man came out of the scientific community to return to the religious life. Every Israeli prime minister and Israeli chief of staff found his way to the Rebbe's doorstep when they came to the United States. The most amazing thing? The Rebbe didn't believe in the state of Israel! For him, no Israel could exist if it wasn't ushered in by the coming of the Messiah. The Rebbe saw himself as perfecting God's will. He had no power in the sense that a police commissioner, a general, or a tax collector does. He had no one enforcing his decisions. What he *did* have was the authority of his holiness, which caused others to connect to him. It wasn't his title that gave the Rebbe authority. It was his presence and his profound grasp of bringing the principles of the Torah to life in himself and in others. The Rebbe didn't declare himself a leader. His overpowering presence inspired those around him to declare him their leader and to revere him. Through earning respect and trust, people endowed him with leadership.

About ten years after I first met the Rebbe, I attended a dinner in Cleveland at the home of Leibel Alevsky. At the table with us was the man the Rebbe sent to the Soviet Union to save Jews. When the Rebbe sent him on this mission, he didn't give him a plan or give him money! This was during the Stalin era. The anti-Jewish, anti-Zionist mentality of the Soviets may have been at its very worst. The Rebbe's designate went to the Soviet Union, lived and worked by his wits, and figured out how he could smuggle Jews out to Poland by train. He succeeded. At the same time, he was smuggling *in* prayer books, religious articles, and calendars for those still in the Soviet Union. And, he set up secret schools to teach Hebrew. The Lubavitchers are incredibly resourceful people, whose outreach is one-on-one.

The Lubavitchers are the essence of true believers. As I traveled abroad, I first noted their presence in Morocco. They ran schools for kids in the ghetto. That may sound noble, but not earth-shattering until you understand the kind of "social security system" that pre-vailed in Morocco at the time. Children *were* the system. At birth, many infants—Arabs and Jews both—were maimed and deformed by their parents so the kids could beg more effectively! The Luba-vitchers *bought* the children from their parents for one more *dirham* than the market value of the child begging on the street for a year, and then they gave the children an education.

You could see the evidence of the Rebbe's positive work all over the world in places like the Soviet Union, Morocco, and Iran. How did these devout Lubavitchers get there? The Rebbe would simply say, "Go to Morocco and save souls." They didn't get a dime or an ounce of organizational help. They saved thousands and thousands of Jews physically, and they spiritually changed many more. The conviction they are doing God's work carries them forward. Their passion brings them to college campuses all over the United States. They will send out a representative wearing *payos* and a black frock coat and open up a *Chabad* house on campuses like University of California at Berkeley. They get kids off narcotics and give them a spiritual jolt instead of a buzz on drugs. "Get high on God!" they preach. Their individual mis-sions are great illustrations of the power of one. The Rebbe's passion for saving Jewish souls lives through them.

Unlike every other Jewish figure in this book, the Rebbe was not a Zionist. Though very supportive of the state of Israel and its defense forces, he felt that redemption would only be ushered in by the Mes-siah. He also drove home the point that a commitment to the state of Israel does not exempt us from fulfilling age-old Judaic command-ments. In fact, it should actually elicit more loyalty to the Torah. The Rebbe was completely devoted to fulfilling God's will.

The essence of the Rebbe's teaching is celebration of God. The *Chabad* radiate a wonderful joy of life that is a reverberation of the Rebbe's spirit. I wish I could believe the way they do, with their absolute confidence in their answer. Their sheer love in celebrating the Jewish traditions with singing and dancing is unmatched. Noth-ing equals the celebration of a Shabbat with a *Chabad*-nik. The food is homemade, delicious—though not necessarily healthy for your arteries—but it's only the beginning of the positive energy that flows in each Shabbat from celebrating the birthday of the world!

TWO KEY THINGS I LEARNED FROM THE REBBE ARE:

Want to change the world? Start by changing yourself!

Although I did not agree with his overriding viewpoint, the Rebbe motivated me to set standards for myself that I would never have dreamed of earlier. The Rebbe caused me to champion the goal of assuring that all Jewish kids have a chance to receive a quality Jewish education, regardless of their parents' ability to pay. He helped me to become a strong supporter of Jewish day schools. And, he inspired me to become a lifelong Jewish learner.

Being a leader isn't always a role one seeks or even desires.

In Jewish history Moses is the greatest of all leaders. The Torah ends with the words "In front of the eyes of all Israel." According to Rabbi Areyah Kaltmann, The Rebbe told the following story—a story that had the power to bring tears to the Rebbe's own eyes. When Moses shattered the Ten Commandments, he made a statement about saving the people of Israel. As much as Moses loved the Torah—and he cherished it above all else in life—he did so to save the people of Israel, who had become lustful, idol-worshipers. He shattered the Torah because he knew that the Torah was not an end in itself. It had to be a living mission to perfect the world and make it a better place. Moses' job as a leader was to help bring the spirit of the Torah alive in the Jews. To do so, Moses acted out of moral courage and exercised the power of one in an epic way. No doubt Moses would have preferred to study the Torah just as the Rebbe might rather have studied sciences at the Sorbonne. Instead, they each submitted to a greater need to serve the Jewish people. They both reluctantly served God in continuous leadership roles to make the world a better place.

TEACHING

I touch the future, I teach.

—Christa McAuliffe

The Learning Team

Perhaps the most important learning in my college education was how to choose the best teachers in the school. Any school. Take as many courses from them as you can. Develop personal contact with them. The subjects they teach are secondary. Greater mentors and teachers share methods: how to think, how to learn, how to defend your positions, and how to embrace change in a world which redefines itself with lightning speed. Their challenges make you grow. In addition to learning how to think and articulate your views, they can teach you the values that will enable you to have courage when you face the defining moments of your life.

Two of the most memorable professors I had at Dartmouth were in astronomy and religion. Professor George Dimitrov was an Eastern European refugee and taught astronomy. His English was fractured, yet he would fill lecture halls with five hundred people. The class would then break up into small groups of twenty to visit the observatory. From Dimitrov, I learned that the most important thing in life is enthusiasm. He was a great astronomer, but an even better expert in the passion for living. Every day—he preached—do what you love and love what you do. "If I can't make this class interesting enough for you to come, don't show up," he said. (True to his word, he refused to take attendance.) "But, if you come, I expect you to be prepared and if you aren't, I will *throw* you out of class!" he said. We became great friends.

Professor Dimitrov served on the National Science Foundation that made grants for basic scientific research. "Professor, how do you decide who gets money?" I asked him. And he replied, "I have one criterion: Enthusiasm! Who has enthusiasm for what they want to do? No one is smart enough to anticipate the outcomes of raw basic research. So, I bet on the person, never knowing about the outcome. Nor am I smart enough to figure out the application of a new discovery. Give me a person who is totally committed to what they want to do and the likelihood of finding successful end results is far greater than if you bet on the idea and the man or the woman hasn't got the commitment to really make it happen. Invest in the person, and you may not win all the time, but your batting average will be better than if you bet on the idea."

In my second year at Dartmouth, I was a typical sophomore, rebelling against my parents and whatever authority was in my life. People would ask me what religion I believed in, and I would shoot back, "Zacksology!" Not Jewish, not Christian, but very conscious of moral principles. Our home was a Jewish home, but not a religious home. Saturday we went to the movies. Sure, we celebrated Jewish holidays, and my mother found a way to make them relevant. My parents demanded I go to Hebrew School—time which I resented spending—and make my bar mitzvah. But, I dropped out afterward.

I was outraged about the Holocaust and the indifference of the world to the slaughter of six million Jews. It was ironic that I was passionate about saving the Jews, but I was indifferent to Judaism as a religion. That year, I took a course in comparative religion from a Protestant minister by the name of Fred Berthold. He helped me to discover that the very essence of Zacksology was all about being Jewish. It was almost as if by osmosis these very fundamental values of Judaism had crept into my being and were influencing my thinking. This shocked me because my Jewish background was so shallow and my Jewish education so poor that I could not understand how these ideas could have influenced me without my being aware of it.

As a result of this realization, I made a critical life decision. You can't be successful doing anything in life if you don't know yourself. If I was so much influenced by Jewish thought and Jewish values, my first responsibility was to understanding *who* I was as a Jew. That began my lifelong study of Judaism, Jewish history, philosophy, and religion. It helped me to grasp the centrality of Sinai—the giving of the Torah and the Ten Commandments. The Jewish people are defined by this event. I concluded I would never understand myself unless I understood Judaism. I became a lifetime learner of Judaism and remain so to this day.

Another defining moment for me happened after my second year at Dartmouth. I met the woman I was sure I would marry—and did. Carol Sue was a powerful magnet drawing me back to Columbus. We have been together for more than fifty years. When I returned to Columbus, I was anxious to become involved in the family business. What could be a better way to do that than study business in the College of Commerce at Ohio State while working in the family firm R. G. Barry? The thinking proved flawed, but the reasoning seemed compelling at the time. As soon as I arrived on the Ohio State campus, I set out to find the Buckeye equivalents of Dimitrov and Berthold. Student opinion was clear. Go study under a political science professor named David Spitz. His reputation was well earned. Before graduating, I took every course he offered.

Abraham Lincoln was the subject of my first class with Spitz. The first session was on a Monday, and he passed out Carl Sandburg's book on Abraham Lincoln. "Read this book by Wednesday," he said. "Class dismissed." So I went home and read it. It is one thick book! And, it's a condensation of the six volumes on Lincoln that Sandburg completed in 1939. Sandburg says Lincoln was the greatest human who ever walked the planet. Sandburg believed Lincoln was the new prophet: a man unselfishly dedicated to serving humanity and mankind.

In class on Wednesday, Professor Spitz began by saying, "I want to talk to you about the most malicious, the most vindictive, the most unprincipled, the most inhuman man who ever occupied the White House: Abraham Lincoln. This man was self-serving, politically ambitious, ruthless in dealing with his adversaries. Lincoln absolutely had no quarrel with the most vicious methods."

A student raised his hand and asked, "Wait a minute Dr. Spitz, what are you saying? We just read this book by Sandburg, and it said—"

"Who's Sandburg?" Spitz interrupted him, "He's just a man. When does he write? Eighty years after Lincoln died. What did Sandburg think? When was he telling the truth? When did he lie? What did he *really* know? What do you know? What do I know? Why did you come to class today? To hear me tell you what Sandburg wrote? If so, you didn't need to read the book. If you read it, you don't need to hear me repeat it. I'm not concerned with what Sandburg said. Nor should you be. I want you to be concerned with what you think and what you say. I want you to sort through the evidence and come to a conclusion. Then I want you to be prepared to defend it." That was the essence of the course. Analytical thought and debate. If you were a capitalist, Spitz was a communist. If you were a communist, vice-versa. David Spitz taught me how to think and the importance of having the courage to defend my ideas. I learned the significance of rational, analytical thought as well as deft argumentation and persuasion, and I'm indebted to him to this day.

Herb Friedman

Born in New Haven, Connecticut, in 1918 to immigrant parents, Herb Friedman was educated at Yale and Columbia, and trained for the rabbinate. Following America's entry into World War II, he enlisted as a chaplain. With a fluent command of German, Herb became a valued staff aide to General Joseph T. McNarney. Responding to the defining moment created by World War II and the Holocaust, Herb leveraged his position to help smuggle Jews—illegally— to Palestine. He commandeered trains and directed food, water, and medical supplies to help rescue camp survivors. More than once, he could have been court-martialed. Later, as a pulpit rabbi in Denver, Herb smuggled arms to the infant state of Israel through Palestine and arm-twisted the military establishment to grant illegal Palestinian visas to European Holocaust survivors. If there is ever a person who defiantly and even recklessly seized the moment with courage—time after time—it has been Herb Friedman.

Initially affiliated with the United Jewish Appeal as a volunteer, he ran the organization's national speaker's bureau while ministering to a large congregation in Milwaukee. He went on to become the UJA's chief executive for sixteen years. During his tenure the organization's annual campaign rose from $40 million to a half billion dollars.

Throughout his colorful career—from smuggler to spiritual leader—Herb has been one of the greatest modern

networkers on behalf of Jewish causes, especially rescue.
His relationships with U.S. Presidents date back to Harry
Truman and his contacts with Popes started with Pius XII.
Herb's experiences are wonderfully documented in his auto-
biography Roots of the Future.

In December 1960, Herb, then the professional head of the National United Jewish Appeal, invited a selected group of forty young Jewish men, twenty-five to forty years of age, from throughout the U.S. to an all-day conference of the UJA. I was fortunate to be among them. Each of us was active in our local Jewish communities and all had been identified by the local leadership as having potential for future national leadership.

At this conference, Herb delivered a six-hour lecture on the history of the Jewish people. The launching point for his talk was Moses receiving the Ten Commandments. Then Herb described the Assyrian conquest in 722 B.C.E. the destruction of the First Temple in Jerusalem by the Babylonians in 586 B.C.E., and the destruction of the Second Temple in 70 A.D. The central theme of his talk centered on how Judaism became a portable religion as Jews dispersed throughout the world, and why such concepts as the minyan and the Torah were essential to the Jewish Diaspora. A minyan is the quorum of ten Jewish adults who constitute the minimum needed for a Jewish service and the basic rites of the community. The portability of the Jewish faith is reflected in the Torah as the centerpiece of each Jewish synagogue, the core creed that is designed to be rolled and transported. With this emphasis on movement also came a focus on Judaism as a belief in deeds rather than a reverence for physical structures. Herb's speech then outlined the contributions that Judaism and Jews had made to improving humanity.

He demonstrated the relevance of Judaism to the present and the future of the civilized world. His concluding comments dazzled us. Because he believed that Judaism had something important to contribute to improving the world, he cared deeply about Jews who carried the values of Judaism. And because he cared about Jews, he was committed to establishing a secure homeland, a safe haven for Jews to live without fear. He pulled everything together into one integrated, systematic structure that was coherent and compelling to all of us. Herb's talk was a spellbinding defining moment for me.

From his audience, Herb selected those who would accompany him to greet Romanian refugees in Vienna in 1961, and to go on with him to Israel. My associates and I were to become the founding members of the Young Leadership Cabinet of the United Jewish Appeal. Herb summarized the Cabinet's mission eloquently:

> Raising people by strengthening their individual Jewish identities, linking their hearts and souls to the land of Israel and the worldwide people of Israel, influencing their children's attitudes in the same direction, is the central purpose of the Young Leadership Cabinet.

That 1961 trip to Vienna was another milestone event for me, which I described earlier. I learned it was not enough to be committed with your head, you had to be committed with your heart. After Europe, we traveled to Israel, where we met with Prime Minister David Ben-Gurion. The trip to Israel was another spiritual and emotional landmark; the excitement of the rebirth of the land and the rescue and the resettlement of Jewish refugees from over 100 countries speaking over 60 languages to the new state of Israel. Here we were on the same land, speaking the same language, praying to the same God, guided by the same Torah as our ancestors 3500 years ago.

Among Herb's multitude of skills is his expertise as a fund-raiser. "The power of the UJA, and its appeal to the contributors," he has written, "stemmed partly from the fact that it dealt with monumental crises and thus shaped history. Responding to historic challenge was the core of every speech, advertisement, rally, film, and conference that I had the authority to design." Through his capacity to transmit this intensity, Herb was able to raise billions of dollars for Jewish causes. In his classic *Roots of the Future,* Herb's profile of the effective fund-raiser is the best I have ever encountered:

> [T]he most significant assets in the fund-raiser's arsenal are *knowledge* of the cause he or she is representing, a *passionate belief* in that cause, and a strong *self-confidence* that produces clear articulation, an easy manner, and an ability to rebound from rejection.

Herb grasped that a fund-raiser had maximum impact when he was not positioned as the individual setting the level of the solicitation. That task was best left to the minyan.

> [I]n case the prospect should ask, during the solicitation: "What right do you have to ask me to contribute such and such an amount?" The solicitor can then honestly reply, "It is not I doing the asking. The minyan has established this rating. The whole community is doing the asking."

During trips to Israel, Herb employed tactics he innovated, such as the "back-seat-in-the-bus." He describes it this way:

> When a busload of mission members were traveling on a day's itinerary, the back bench would be held empty, and selected individuals would be invited there one at a time for a private conversation with the chairman or myself to settle that individual's contribution to the current UJA campaign.

Herb Friedman has been a lifetime teacher who brought Judaism, Jews, and Israel together for me into a cohesive experience. Herb is one of the most self-confident people I ever met. His self-confidence has at times stepped over into hubris. In Herb, I recognized a valuable lifetime lesson: People's greatest strengths, when pursued to the extreme, can often prove to be their greatest weaknesses. This was the case when Herb tried to run the UJA from Israel when he lived there. He thought he could leave the management of the annual campaign to the able UJA Executive Vice Chairman Irving Bernstein. The fact was you couldn't steer a large, complex organization like the UJA from the back-of-the-bus cruising toward Jerusalem.

In my opinion, one of Herb's greatest contributions was his role in framing the Wexner Heritage Foundation. This concept was a worthy sequel to Herb's pioneering achievements with the Young Leadership Cabinet.

Les Wexner is founder and CEO of Limited Brands. He is both one of the great retailing geniuses of our time and one of the most devoted philanthropists to Jewish and non-Jewish causes. In 1983, I called Herb and relayed an idea which Les had of recruiting and developing young Jews with exceptional leadership potential.

Les's idea was to identify, recruit, educate, and develop high-potential Jewish leaders for the future. For Les, this was the most important thing he could do to make the American Jewish community stronger. While these individuals were active at the local level, the training would be centralized. When Les asked me who would be a talented leader to spearhead this program, Herb came to mind instantly as a natural fit. Les engaged him to organize and run the program. In 1985, the Wexner Heritage Foundation emerged in its present form. For the first of these retreats, Les, Herb, and I took a group of seven young people on a whirlwind trip to meet leading Jewish authorities in Eastern Europe and France. Ever since its inception, the Wexner Heritage Foundation has been a remarkable success in instilling common leadership principles in individuals who are dispersed throughout the United States.

Several key things I learned from my Learning Team are:

It's the teacher, not the subject, that matters.

Find the best teachers! Take as many courses from them as possible. Let them share with you the excitement and the vision that causes them to be what they are. It's often contended that college is when we begin to narrow the scope of our pursuit of knowledge. I'm convinced that the opposite is true. The subject matter is far less important than the teacher. Great teachers teach you how to learn and, they teach you how to learn for the rest of your life. They teach you how to think, how to research, and how to communicate and defend your views whether orally or in writing. Great teachers exhibit passion, dedication, values, and focused thinking. They teach you how to *know* what is important. We can never forget that the foundation of genuine leadership is believing in what is right. Great teachers can help you learn the wisdom of essential, timeless values.

Bet on the player, not on the idea.

Professor Dimitrov taught me the secret of investing money for research grants: It's the person, not the idea that matters. It's been more than fifty years since I learned that great advice, and I can tell you that every time I have invested in a great idea rather than a top-notch person behind an idea, I have made a mistake—sometimes a serious one.

Raising people is more important than raising money.

Herb Friedman has been my foremost mentor in developing concepts of Jewish-leadership education. He has articulated his driving principles this way:

> [M]y fundamental beliefs have been these: the primary sacredness of Jewish survival . . . the inestimable value of Israel as a

physical and spiritual center; the responsibility of every Jew for every other and for the homeland.

Leaders are the key to sustaining Judaism and its commitment to Israel. If you raise the people who will be dedicated to the cause, then you have created the mechanism that will find the money and sustain the cause on tangible terms.

At eighty-seven, with his white hair flowing *everywhere,* Herb speaks and looks like a prophet. He retains his matchless gift as an orator. Both Judaism and Israel have been blessed with such a devoted and effective leader and a living symbol of what it means to seize the moment with courage time and again, and to do so with stalwart conviction.

Max Fisher

*Max Fisher was a unique figure in American Jewish life.
He grew up in a small, rural farm town. He played football at Ohio State on a scholarship. His sense of gratitude
to OSU ran deep and he repaid it with a $20 million gift
toward the building of the university's Fisher College of
Business. He had a keen knack for teaching others to give
back as well. Not long ago, his nephew, Steve Ross, made
a $100 million gift to the University of Michigan.*

*When Max went into the oil business in Detroit with his
father, he studied it very thoroughly—as he did everything
else in his life. He borrowed $38,000 in the form of an
installment loan for an investment in new technology from
a man named Henry Wenger. When he completed repaying
the loan (on time as always), Max owned a "cat-cracker"—
at the time, a revolutionary new oil-processing machine.
Against his father's desires, he changed the nature of their
business from retailing commercial lubricating oils to selling gasoline at cut-rate prices to general consumers—first
as a refiner and then as a retailer. Max's strategy proved
right.*

*Max's first passion in life was to make money. He
started out dirt poor and had no desire to taste that life
again. His early business career showed both the character and the courage that were later to characterize Max's
contribution as both a political leader and diplomat. As he*

*built his gas station business before World War II, Max
had a contract to buy oil at a certain price from a supplier.
The wholesale price plummeted unexpectedly. Max told
his supplier that he would pay the agreed upon amount,
which was significantly higher than the market price. In
exchange, he asked for a commitment: When oil got scarce,
Max expected to be guaranteed a supply line. It worked.
When nobody else could get it, Max had oil.*

*Eventually, with Henry Wenger as a partner, Max bought
a retail gas chain called Speedway 79. The two acquired
independent filling stations and changed the signs at the
pump. The previous owners continued to operate the stations. Max's goal was to harness entrepreneurship. It was
a form of franchising before franchising became fashion-
able. To make sure the entrepreneurial drive remained,
Max carefully studied the mindsets of independent station
owners. Why were some hesitant to sell their businesses?
Max found that they feared the perks of owning their own
business would disappear—perks like writing off lunches
and joining country clubs. When Max understood that, he
"grandfathered" the one-time owners. Whatever ownership
perks they had prior to selling would be covered by the
new owners. The condition was that these former owners
had to stay on to run the business. The enterprise Max built
was hugely successful. In 1959, it was acquired by the
Ohio Oil Company, which changed its name to Marathon
in 1962.*

*As his business success grew, so did his network of
contacts. During World War II, Detroit was the industrial
capital of the United States and the Arsenal of Democracy.
Through the 1960s, it was also the automobile capital of
the world. Max developed a strong friendship with Henry
Ford II, grandson of auto pioneer and Ford founder Henry
Ford. Max reached out and built friendships with people
who were financially successful and politically powerful.*

Leonard Garment, the Washington attorney, once said that the two most powerful engines in life are envy and boredom. Max Fisher, Garment told Peter Golden, "doesn't have a lot of envy, but he's deathly afraid of boredom." "Max was like a great underground river," said his close friend Henry Ford II, "invisible, constant, relentless in nourishing the soil and getting water to the flowers, the trees, and the grass. Presidents [of the United States] came and went, but Max remained." Steadily. Invisibly.

Max didn't grow up in an observant Jewish household. In fact, he wasn't bar mitzvahed until more than sixty years after the usual age, albeit at the Western Wall. After he had made his fortune, and while his network of contacts was blossoming, Max Fisher's passion changed. His first trip to Israel was the defining moment of his life. It happened in October 1954, and was part of the first United Jewish Appeal study mission. He was impressed by the idea of Israel and appalled by the living conditions. On that trip, he had a memorable encounter with then Finance Minister Levi Eshkol, later to become Israel's prime minister. It's cited by Max's biographer Peter Golden:

> Because you're short on money," Fisher asked, "wouldn't it make sense for Israel to shut down immigration for a while?" Eshkol's reply ... "Every Jew in Israel remembers how six million fellow Jews died under Hitler because they had no place to go," the finance minister said. "Even if you don't give us another dime, no Jew is ever going to add to that six million."

Max described that exchange as "the greatest lesson I would ever learn about Zionism." After that visit to Israel, he committed to provide leadership to the cause of Israel's security. He became chairman of the Jewish Welfare Federation of Detroit in 1957, and raised nearly $6 million—the most in the Motor City campaign's history. His success caught the attention of the gentile community, including the Ford family. It wasn't long before Max was the first Jewish chairman of Detroit's United Way campaign.

Max got involved in the National Council of Jewish Federations of Welfare Funds and the UJA In 1968, Max was one of the first Eastern European Jews to lead the UJA—an organization dominated since its inception by German-Jewish immigrants and their offspring. He became chairman and president of both. He was involved with the Anti-Defamation League and the American Jewish Committee. Max was a part of all the organizations that were supportive of Israel.

Max Fisher was my mentor in learning how the political arena is organized and works. He taught me how to play within the system to advance one's goals. He understood power and how to maximize its impact. He mastered the art of negotiation better than anyone I ever met. Max avoided confrontation and was a healer who brought people together. This did not mean he was soft. Max never underestimated an adversary. He would spend as much time understanding an opponent's objectives as his own. In a negotiation, he drilled deep to try to grasp other people's objectives and aspirations. He also learned their strengths and weaknesses. Who was supporting them, and who was not, and why? Who could act as bridges of compromise in a particular situation? He was a man of action, but a thoughtful one. He was only interested in information as it related to courses of action. Les Wexner once shared this thoughtful analysis of Max with me: "Most people are focused on the past. Some dwell on the future. Max lives in the moment."

When Max took over the leadership of an organization or a project, he was relentless in prioritizing objectives. He felt that a leader's biggest limitation was that of time. Max's magic number was three. Only have three priorities. A leader also had to have the necessary authority and to know the measures of success. Max was a model for others in the way he deferred instant gratification in favor of achieving long-term ends.

Max was no memo writer. He received (and retained) a lot of information orally. He was relentless about driving for particulars. In his later years, he worked out of his homes in Detroit and Palm Beach. The telephone was his medium, and it's hard to imagine that Max Fisher could have existed before Alexander Graham Bell had changed the way we communicated. He could lead many initiatives and projects at the same time. He knew how to pick managers, delegate assignments to them, and monitor relentlessly. If you were assigned a task, you could expect three or four phone calls a day. His follow-up was incredibly thorough and the closest to infallible of anyone I ever met. Max didn't have a Rolodex. He *was* a Rolodex. He—at one point—could literally remember a thousand numbers. Despite the avalanche of follow through, Max was warm, humorous, and soft-spoken. I never heard him tell a joke, but he was a natural kibbitzer. If there was an amiable way to weave the Ohio State football team into the conversation, he would find it. Max could charm anybody. He had a very soft and soothing phone style—a necessary counterbalance to the incessant contact he maintained with people on issues that were front burner for him.

Max Fisher was not confrontational. He supported evolutionary not revolutionary change. He managed his downside in everything he did. He was a master of power and how it works. He knew exactly how decisions were made in Washington and Jerusalem. No American Jewish leader ever understood better how to orchestrate the use of power to achieve goals and objectives. Max was a unifier, compromiser—a bring-people-together guy. In a person's great strengths, as I have said, you will often find their great weaknesses. So it was with Max. At times, he may have been too willing to compromise, as with President Reagan's decision to visit the German cemetery at Bitburg.

Max was one of the first nationally prominent Jews to align himself with the Republican Party. He provided invaluable national guidance to U.S. presidents, primarily the Republican ones, and certainly to every Israeli prime minister. Ira Milstein of the law firm Weil, Gotshal, Manges declared Max was a national treasure. Ronald Reagan said he "inherited" Max. Max Fisher became the most powerful non-elected figure in the Republican Party. He never lost sight of his local power base. Until his death, he remained Mr. Republican for

Detroit and for Michigan. He always believed that you had to build your base at the local level.

Max Fisher understood that you didn't need a title to lead. He was offered many cabinet posts and ambassadorships by President Nixon, which he declined. He understood that money and votes were the currency of political power. They created IOUs. He wanted to make them payable to the Jewish people. Instead of a post, Max wanted and needed access to the President of the United States, and the wisdom and power of that decision never paid greater dividends than during the Yom Kippur War.

While Max was close to Richard Nixon, indeed, Max was one of Nixon's lead fund-raisers, Max was totally untouched by the dark clouds of Watergate and the other blemishes of that administration. With all the scrutiny of the investigators hounding the Nixon team, they would have found a misstep had Max ever committed one, but they couldn't because he was always scrupulously honest.

Every Republican Party National Chairman would make a pilgrimage to Palm Beach each year to see Max. He was a master of political access and fund-raising to advance the Jewish agenda. He gave a quarter million dollars to the Richard Nixon re-election campaign and he gave early. He saw widespread voter mistrust of George McGovern in the 1972 presidential election, and used it to bring an unprecedented number of Jews to the Nixon camp.

While Max declined official positions in government, he maintained regular access to the president to talk about significant issues of the moment. Max did accept the non-paying chairmanship of the National Center for Voluntary Action in the first Nixon administration. That gave him a White House pass, an office with a secretary in the Executive Office Building, and a diplomatic passport. His second portal to the executive branch was influencing the choice of the contact person to the Jewish community in the Office of Public Liaison. He talked with this person several times a day. That's how he kept up with what was going on. Access was Max's long suit.

*   *   *

By spring 1973, the internal U.S. debate over how to best enable the immigration of Soviet Jews to Israel was intensifying. At the end of March, the first $31 million payment was made from the U.S. State Department to the United Israel Appeal for absorption of Soviet Jews in Israel. Max backed President Nixon in opposing the Jackson-Vanik Amendment and even met with Soviet Ambassador Dobrynin to search for new ways to increase Jewish immigration from the U.S.S.R. so that Jackson-Vanik could be avoided. By April, however, Congress was pressing for this legislation's passage.

The year 1973 was to prove pivotal in U.S.–Israeli relations, and no month was more important than October. In 1973, Golda Meir was Israel's prime minister when the Arab sneak attack occurred at 2 P.M. on Saturday, October 6. It was Yom Kippur, and I was a National Chairman of the United Jewish Appeal at the time. Israel had lost more than a hundred planes in that attack—twenty-five percent of its aircraft. Another hundred planes were badly damaged and desperately needed parts if they were to be repaired. The Israeli armed forces were running short of ammunition. The Egyptians had crossed the Suez Canal into the Sinai and stopped to hold their position. Syria had penetrated the Golan Heights and had halted, but they were terribly close to breaking through. Fortunately, the Syrian troops were Soviet trained and taught to be cautious at a moment of success. The Soviet doctrine was wait, stop, it could be a trap. If they had not followed this military policy, the Syrians could have pushed all the way down to Haifa and the Egyptians could have thrust forward all the way up the Sinai. The Israelis were reeling from the loss of planes and equipment and were in desperate need of resupply from the United States. This promised to be far different from the previous Six-Day War when Israel had the advantage of surprise and a need for far lower levels of matériel and supplies.

Israeli intelligence had failed on a nearly catastrophic scale. However, according to historian Daniel Yergin, signs that trouble was in the offing were there to read—from the sudden emptying of hospital beds in Egypt to the excavation of huge graves in Syria. On the day war broke out, Prime Minister Meir called Israel's Ambassador to the

U.S., Simcha Dinitz, to press for U.S. resupply. Dinitz approached U.S. Secretary of State Kissinger for U.S. aid on Monday, October 8. As the Soviets began a massive air- and sealift to resupply Syria and Egypt on Tuesday, October 9, Israel shifted its remaining reserves from the Sinai to the Golan. Awareness of the gravity of what was happening had just *started* to sink in at the White House.

On Tuesday afternoon, October 9, Max met with President Nixon in the Oval Office and requested resupply. This was a defining moment for Israel and the Jewish people, which Max seized. According to Peter Golden, Max pressed President Nixon with the words: "I've worked hard for you and I've never asked anything for myself. But I'm asking you now. Please send the Israelis what they need. You can't let them be destroyed." On the same day, Nixon and Kissinger met, and Nixon approved the replacement of Israeli aircraft losses. In the evening, a Jewish national leadership convocation took placed at the Shoreham Hotel in Washington.

One must remember that the White House Watergate crisis was in full swing, as was the scandal surrounding Vice President Spiro Agnew. Ten days after Nixon's second inauguration, two aides implicated in the Watergate break-in were convicted. Max had once again weighed in early with support for Nixon in a letter in April. On Wednesday, October 10, with Israel's fortunes becoming drastic, Vice President Spiro Agnew resigned. One can only imagine the high-voltage tension in the Oval Office on that day.

On Wednesday, October 10, the situation was desperate for Israel and the resupply was not underway. Late that evening, I got a phone call from Max Fisher. Max asked me if I knew Congressman Sam Devine, a local congressman from Columbus, Ohio. Indeed, Sam was my representative. I had supported him in each one of his campaigns, contributed to them and raised money for him. We had a good relationship. "Can you call him?" Max asked, "He sits on the Armed Services Committee in the House, and he's the ranking Republican. Tell him I have learned there is a problem with re-supplying Israel. President Nixon made a decision to resupply. The Pentagon is dragging its feet, deliberately holding back a rapid, immediate resupply.

The decision was made Tuesday, and this is already Wednesday night."

It was at night, but I called Sam immediately. He was outraged. He said he would call the Armed Services Committee into session that night. "I'll get in touch with the chairman and we will deal with this. When the President of the United States makes a decision, it's the responsibility of his Cabinet to carry it out. This is treason!" Sam shouted. It was approaching two days after the decision, and nothing had moved. They couldn't find this and couldn't find that—they'll handle it tomorrow. The excuses didn't stop. The Pentagon's rationale for opposing the resupply: Sending matériel to Israel would have drawn down United States' reserves and made it impossible for the Pentagon to carry out its global mission of defense for the free world. Nixon said do it anyway. Either Secretary of Defense James Schlesinger or Undersecretary of Defense William Clements, later Governor of Texas, was blocking the directive. Other sources dispute this and contend that it was Kissinger himself who was blocking the resupply.

Pressure was also mounting from Democratic Senator Henry Jackson for the White House to act. Decisive intelligence came to Jackson on Thursday, October 11, when U.S. Navy Admiral Elmo Zumwalt called the senator and told him that Israel would lose the war unless the U.S. aided it immediately. Jackson believed that Kissinger, not Schlesinger, was the roadblock to resupplying Israel. Jackson met with Nixon the same day as he received the intelligence from Zumwalt. It was really Nixon who saw the danger of not backing Israel. (It was also Jackson, according to his biographer Robert Kaufman, who interceded to get the Portuguese to allow the U.S. to use the Azores as a refueling station. All the other European nations had refused the U.S., because of fear of incurring Arab wrath.)

The administration finally saw the true magnitude of the stakes. Unless the U.S. resupplied Israel, the Middle East's balance of power would be lost. The Arabs would not only have prevailed, they would have prevailed almost solely because of the supply of Soviet arms. President Nixon issued a crystal-clear directive to begin the emergency airlift to Israel. The resupply effort had truly begun. The replacement Phantoms were stalled by heavy winds in the Azores. By Sunday, October 14, C-5A cargo jets were landing at Lod (Lydda) Airfield in Israel every half hour.

The most massive resupply effort in the history of the western world was underway—on a scale not seen since the U.S. ramping-up of Berlin during the Airlift of 1948–1949. We took everything we owned in Europe and moved it on a massive scale to Israel. The rest is history, including the arrival—in the nick of time—of the armaments that allowed Israeli forces to regroup and virtually destroy the Syrian army.

Henry Kissinger's feud with Defense Secretary James Schlesinger was an open book. The allegations that Defense was responsible for the delay are certainly plausible. That is not to say that Kissinger was a total enthusiast in the resupply campaign, especially in the early stages. After some bizarre schemes were considered, including sending aid in unmarked planes, Kissinger proposed sending three C-5A military transports. Nixon asked how many the U.S. had available. Kissinger said twenty-six. In a later interview included in Peter Golden's biography of Max, Nixon described how he responded :

> "Just send them all," I said. My point was that if you send three, then we were going to get blamed by the Arabs just as much as if we had sent twenty-six. It's important to do enough. Always do enough.

The U.S. conducted over 500 resupply flights between mid-October and mid-November. Max Fisher made literally hundreds of calls and lots of people did lots of things. My contact with Congressman Devine was just one more drop of water into the cup. We may have been doing a great job of fund-raising, but when I gave my speech at the community fund-raiser on October 11, I had a personal epiphany: **I realized you can't fly dollar bills.**

*   *   *

A peace in the Middle East was ultimately brokered, but it was achieved in the context of vast and unrelated turbulence in the White House. On October 20, while Henry Kissinger traveled to Moscow to work out a Mideast ceasefire with Soviet head of state Leonid Brezhnev, the infamous "Saturday Night Massacre" happened during which President Nixon dismissed three Justice Department officials, including Attorney General Elliot Richardson. Two days later, the UN approved the U.S.–Soviet brokered deal and urged the first direct negotiations between Israel and Egypt. In the White House, Nixon's doom was all but sealed when Leon Jaworski was named Watergate special prosecutor eight days later. Max was ecstatic about the resupply of Israel, as were we all. But, he and Nixon were less happy roughly forty days later when Jackson-Vanik passed the U.S. House. Max always did what he believed was in the best interest of Israel and the U.S. On this one, he made the wrong call, as Jackson-Vanik proved to be one of the most powerful tools ever in liberating Soviet Jews and contributed to the collapse of the former Soviet Union.

Succeeding Nixon after the Watergate scandal and his ensuing resignation, President Gerald Ford occupied the White House for two and a half years. Max and Gerald Ford had a relationship that went back a long way. Peter Golden reports Max visited Ford in the Oval Office twenty-five times. Max specialized in getting the Ford White House "the background information on what the unofficial thinking of the Israeli government was." Max's White House access was perhaps even stronger than it had been in the Nixon era. But the job of developing support for Ford was difficult.

For forty years, I had the privilege of working closely with Max Fisher. Our relationship was that of mentor and protégé. Most of the time. There were also instances when it seemed like that of rebellious son and aggrieved father. I publicly disagreed with him on a number of different issues. They were honest disagreements.

On his ninetieth birthday, the guest list for Max Fisher's party was stellar: former Presidents Ford and Bush, Kissinger, the Israeli ambassador, Michigan's governor, Detroit's mayor. They were all there. Max Fisher passed away at the age of 96 in 2005. The family was offered the opportunity of interring his remains in Israel's national cemetery on Mount Herzl. Only two other non-Israelis are buried there. One of them is Herzl himself. Instead, his wife Marjorie and the family chose the Fisher plot in Detroit. An array of family, friends, and admirers spoke their tributes. The most moving eulogy for me came from his daughter, Jane Sherman, who repeated the story of the role Max played in the 1973 resupply that saved Israel. And second from an African-American who remembered how Max Fisher dug in to help restore housing for blacks after the devastating 1967 Detroit riots. Max was a man of many dimensions. The Detroit Symphony Orchestra lost its most cherished patron upon his death. It's no surprise that Detroiters refer to their newly renovated concert hall simply as **The Max.**

SEVERAL KEY THINGS I LEARNED FROM MAX FISHER ARE:

Think about your long-term objectives.

When Max agreed to purchase oil at prices significantly higher than market, he was prescient enough to guarantee supply later when oil stocks were scarce. When Richard Nixon, who had already lost a presidential election, was struggling to build support for a comeback, Max was there in the early days. Later the relationship he built proved to be essential to Israel's survival in the 1973 war, when Max rose to his defining moment in helping to secure Israel's vital resupply.

Clarify your goals for any role that you accept before you take the job.

For countless civic leadership roles and for his initiatives on the part of Israel and the Republican Party, Max knew exactly what he wanted to achieve. He also had an idea how long realization of those goals would take, the people he would need to do the job, and what would be necessary to motivate the people he would recruit to meet the challenge. His rule of thumb: Identify and stick to the top three objectives in any role you accept. Max focused his efforts on those critical few priorities. He was a walking textbook in leadership.

Retain integrity at all costs.

Max was a man of honor. When he gave you his word, the matter was settled. His motives were always driven by his sense of what was right. Whatever he did politically, he perceived to be in the best interests of America and Israel.

Bring people together under a broad tent.

Max was a master of the art of compromise. He believed you didn't have to win every point. Wisdom resides in knowing which points are "must-win" situations for the cause you want to further.

FOLLOWING YOUR MORAL COMPASS

To be is to stand for.

—Abraham Heschel

America is never wholly herself unless she is engaged in high moral principle.

—George H. W. Bush

George H. W. Bush—
First Encounters

When President Jimmy Carter came to office, George Herbert Walker Bush was unemployed. He was a former everything. In 1976, under Gerald Ford, his last political appointment was as director of the CIA. Before that he had been special envoy to China, U.S. ambassador to the UN, Republican National Committee Chairman, and a U.S. congressman from Texas. During World War II, he was the youngest pilot in the U.S. Navy and decorated for his wartime achievements. At Yale, he had been captain of the baseball team. Most of his life, through remarkable dedication, discipline and energy he had been "captain" of nearly every team he had served on. When I first came to know George Bush, he was totally committed to become President of the United States.

In October 1978, I got a call from Gus Hoster asking me to attend a gathering to meet George Bush, who was seeking the Republican presidential nomination for 1980. Gus explained that Bob Mosbacher, who had worked in the Ford campaign in 1976, was running Bush's finance committee. Bush had few Jewish contacts with truly national reach. His staff wanted to recruit me to raise money for his campaign nationally. When I asked who would be at the meeting, I was told eleven other non-Jews would be there—all of them industrialists and bankers who were heavyweight Republicans from Ohio. I said I didn't want to go. Why? Either I would monopolize the agenda talking about the issues of concern to me, or I would spend time learning about issues that weren't critical to my support of Bush. Would I meet with Bush privately? Gus asked. Anytime and anyplace, I said, provided I have at least an hour with him.

Bush had made the decision to go after the presidency about four or five months earlier, and he had just started his run for the nomination. This was his full-time occupation. Bush called me and proposed that we meet in Columbus in March 1979. I went to his suite at the Sheraton Hotel and spent two hours with him. I really liked the man. I liked his views of the world—his sense of what the major issues were—and his grasp of the geo-strategic, political, and economic matters vital to our country. He understood that an interconnected global economy was emerging. And, that struck me as remarkable. This was 1979, and people weren't talking that way yet. I also identified strongly with his view of the strategic power struggle between the Soviets and the United States and its ramifications. Bush had a very strong conviction about the need to improve America's energy independence. He was certain that America was never going to be able to find or fulfill its role in the world if it remained a net importer of oil. He believed we had to be energy vital and energy independent.

Philosophically, I was in harmony with George Bush's moderate-conservative view of the world overall. Most of all, I was struck by the basic decency of the man and the clarity of his moral compass. He radiated true character and compassion. Here was a leader who really had a sense of responsibility toward improving the conditions of people's lives at home and around the world. Bush had only one large deficiency in my book: I judged his level of knowledge on the Middle East as a one on a scale of one to ten.

Bush had been all over the world and visited a hundred or more countries, but he hadn't really been to the Middle East, so he never had any occasion to really come to grips with that part of the world. He may have had headed the CIA, but the CIA was not a policy formulating agency. Bush believed it should be an intelligence-gathering entity and an analytical service to policy makers, though not a policy formulator itself. Bush was an envoy to China, the precursor of being an ambassador to China. However, ambassadors don't make policy, they implement policy. When he was ambassador to the United Nations, he was in a spokesperson position. He contributed to policy, but policy was made in the State Department. Also, his preoccupation was with East/West relations. He was never focused on the Middle East outside of its role in East/West relations.

At the time we met, Bush couldn't have answered any of the detailed questions he can answer today. He just wasn't aware of the fundamentals of the Arab-Israeli conflict or the Arab-Arab conflicts within the region. He didn't know the nuances and simply couldn't talk about them intelligently. Remember, he had had no need to be involved in these fine points. In any of the roles that he had played, he had no significant responsibility for policy formulation that would have caused him to have a command perspective or to contribute to the policy process.

At the end of our meeting, I said: "Mr. Ambassador, I'm very, very taken with you and very comfortable with your positions, but I must be candid, your knowledge base on the Middle East is shallow. For that reason, I would be highly uncomfortable with you as President of the United States. You could make very poor judgments that could prove to be damaging both to Israel and to the United States."

"Gordon, I think that is very fair," he said. "I've traveled everywhere in the world, but I have never really been to the Middle East. I have spent eight hours in the Middle East—all of them in Jordan. I don't feel comfortable with my knowledge of the Middle East. Can you teach me? Will you help me?" I said certainly, and he asked what we should do. Initially, I asked for one day of his time to bring in an expert who would brief him.

We scheduled a date in Houston in April. I brought in Professor Steven Spiegel, from UCLA, who is a political scientist and well versed on the geo-political and economic structure of the Middle East and the religious tensions within the region. (You'll recall I had enlisted Professor Spiegel in developing the report on Egyptian-Israeli cooperation opportunities that I had prepared for Yitzhak Rabin.) Professor

Spiegel came equipped with the necessary maps and diagrams. George Bush is very bright. He absorbs information readily. He got an exhaustive eight-hour briefing. It included all of the essential perspectives on the region: Israel and Arab neighbors, Arab/Arab, Shia/Sunni, and then East/West. It contained a strategic history of the Palestinian/Arab/Israeli conflict. George's wife, Barbara, attended as did his chief of staff. Over dinner that night, George thanked Steve and me for coming and praised how informative the briefing had been.

"Gordon," he said, "I am really grateful, and I can't tell you how beneficial and useful this has been. I would really like to have you come on board my campaign and take a major role."

"George, I'm sorry I can't do that yet. Here's why: Unless you go to Israel and stand at Qalqilyah, you'll never understand the border problem. It's the narrowest point in the pre-1967 border, and you can see Tel Aviv and Haifa from that location. Unless you go to the Golan, you'll never appreciate the security problem from the Israeli point of view, and you'll never understand and be sensitive to the things that Jews and Israelis are terribly concerned about. Have you seen the borders? Have you stood at the strategic vantage points? You've never been to Israel. Until you have had the experience, you'll never appreciate what Menachem Begin said—that the greatest general in the history of the Israeli army was 'No Choice.' The power of one and the power of unity—the compelling power of a people unified under a common vision, who believe they have no choice. How could I go out and talk to the Jewish community to raise money on your behalf, if I can't say you've been to Israel? You'll never play in this community if you haven't been there."

"Will you take me?" Bush asked.

"I'll need four days of your time."

"OK, provided I have a legitimate reason for being there, I will go. But, I'm not going to pander to the Jewish vote, just like I'm not going to go to Ireland and to Italy as a typical politician would." I agreed to his terms and got him an invitation as the former head of the CIA to attend the Jonathan Institute Seminar on International Terrorism run by future Israeli Prime Minister Bibi Netanyahu. Barbara joined him.

We went to Israel on the Fourth of July. Before he came to Israel, Bush spent five hours in Egypt.

Prior to the trip's start, I was telephoned in the U.S. by an unknown caller. He introduced himself over the phone this way: "You don't know me, but I'm the head of the 'company' in Israel. When Mr. Bush was head of your 'company' in the United States, we did many joint ventures together. I would like very much to have dinner with Mr. Bush when he is in Israel." I agreed to have him host a dinner for us on a Friday night at the restaurant Chez Simone in Jerusalem. "By the way, who is meeting the Bushes at the airport?"

"I am," I said. The mysterious caller was Nahum Admoni, the head of the Mossad.

Two days before Bush was to arrive, I checked into the Hilton Hotel in Jerusalem. On the day of his arrival, I got a call from the American ambassador to Israel to confirm my plans to pick up the Bushes at Ben-Gurion Airport. He said, "Mr. Zacks, Senator Scoop Jackson is visiting Israel. He has requested and been given a military plane by the Israeli government so he could fly to Cairo for the day. He has learned that George Bush is in Cairo and he is extending an invitation to the Bush party to join him on the trip back to Israel. I just don't know if George Bush has accepted that offer."

My assumption was simple enough: Bush would just cancel his commercial flight from Cairo to Israel via Athens. I found out where Jackson's helicopter was to land and arranged to meet it at the heliport. As a contingency, I sent my car and driver to Ben-Gurion Airport, which is twelve miles from Tel Aviv, to meet the Bush party in the unlikely event he had flown in commercially. The two separate arrivals were just five minutes apart. Senator Jackson got off the helicopter and, to my astonishment, Bush was not with him. Scoop explained that he extended the invitation to Bush, but Bush wasn't comfortable taking a gratis trip underwritten by the Israeli government, and he flew commercially to Israel by way of Athens. I returned to my room to wait for the Bushes to arrive at the hotel. The phone rang and it was the head of the Israeli "company"—the Mossad.

"I thought you were going to meet the Bushes at the airport?" he asked testily.

"I *was*, but . . ." I stumbled.

"But you weren't there!" he declared.

"How do you know?" I asked.

"It's my business to know, Gordy," he responded heatedly. "Now, let me tell you something. This guy was one of the best friends Israel ever had when he was head of the CIA. We had the most productive, cooperative relationship with him that we've had with any CIA director that we've ever dealt with." Nahum's point was crystal clear. The Mossad's respect for George Bush was enormous.

Ultimately the Bushes and I joined up, and we had three and a half marvelous days. The Israelis and I worked the Bushes eighteen hours a day. We did everything we set out to do, and the government of Israel was terrific. We had the helicopters. We had the opportunity to see most of the critical places and meet with most of the key leadership of the country. George Bush really got a sense of the country and the land and the people. He and Barbara fell in love with Israel and the Israelis. The Friday night dinner between the two "company" heads took place at Chez Simone. There were three tables in the backroom of this intimate restaurant. The Bushes, the head of the Mossad, and I sat in the corner table. The two other tables in front were filled with Mossad agents. This was 1979, and the entire conversation at dinner was about Iran. The shah had fallen in January of that year. Bush posed a number of questions: What did the Mossad know about the fall of the shah? When did they know it? What information did they relay to the U.S.? To whom did they transmit it and what response did they get?

The bottom line was that the Israelis predicted the fall of the shah. Part of the foreign aid that the U.S. had given the shah was funneled by him as financial incentives to the mullahs and the *bazaaris*. Unless the mullahs and the small merchants in the bazaars were backed in this way, the Mossad was certain the shah would fall. Israel knew this back in mid-1977! Carter accused the shah of human rights violations and maintained the U.S. aid was funding abuses by the Savak, the shah's secret police. The CIA's intelligence had concluded the shah was in solid shape. As far as the U.S. was concerned, there was no problem in Iran. The situation was even worse: Israel's view was known by the CIA and ignored. Bush was surprised at the CIA's arrogance and impressed with what he learned about the thoroughness of Israeli intelligence.

On the return flight to the States, we were all exhausted. Halfway over the ocean, George woke up from a nap and said, "Gordy, this is the most exciting and wonderful trip we have ever had. I just can't thank you enough." Of all the places that he'd visited in the world, George found Israel to be a magical and incredibly positive experience. Barbara shared his enthusiasm. They had been overwhelmed by the vitality, the energy, the optimism, and the sense of dynamic growth in Israel, as well as the sense of people helping people. And, of course, they were deeply moved by the visits to the Christian holy sites and the respect the Israelis showed for all religions.

It was an intriguing paradox. At the CIA, George Bush didn't really know anything about Israel and he was still one of their greatest friends. And yet these realities are reconcilable, because they're both true. While he had no real knowledge, he had great sympathy for Israel as a democracy, as a country with shared values, and as a haven for the refugees that were created by the Holocaust.

Then, on board this return flight, came the second invitation: "Gordy, I now really hope you're ready to come on board and take a major position in my campaign."

"George," I said, "I can't do it yet."

"What do I have to do next?" he asked somewhat puzzled.

"I have bombarded you with information and with emotional stimuli," I said. "What you really need to do is to sort out your thoughts and your position on the Middle East and on Israel. Once you have formulated your position, I can then relate to it or not relate to it. I can support you or not support you based on how comfortable I am with where you are. However, before I can support you, I need to understand your position fully. Unless I do, how could I be comfortable representing you to the Jewish-American constituency?"

"Will you help me formulate that position?" Bush asked.

That was something to which I readily agreed. During July and August, I spent weekends with him. In Kennebunkport or Indianapolis or Chicago. Wherever he was, we would find two hours here or five hours there. After a period of six weeks, he developed a forty-page document that represented his position on the Middle East, including Israel. It remains a dynamite paper still today. On all the critical issues, Bush had positions that I could support.

"Now, dammit, Gordy, are you ready to come on board?" Bush asked me once more.

"George, you have to do one more thing."

"What's that?!"

"You need to go before a national body of U.S. Jewish leaders and you have to tell them your positions and follow that up with a press conference. You have to communicate your Middle East platform to the *New York Times*."

"Set it up, Gordy."

And, I did, even though I had to leave shortly for a business trip to China.

The American Jewish Committee hosted a seminar for the leaders of the national Jewish organizations at the AJC headquarters in New York. About 250 people came and then the committee organized a press conference for both the Jewish and the non-Jewish press at which Bush appeared.

After China, I was on my way to Florida to chair a conference. I changed planes in San Francisco. I called Bert Gold, the Executive Director for the American Jewish Committee.

"How did Bush do?" I asked.

"The man was fabulous! He was great at the assembly with the leadership group. He was great at the press conference. He got wild reviews." I was very pleased with the news, but I was racing to catch a flight to Miami. I felt like I had been on an airplane forever. I didn't even know what day or time of day it was. After checking into the

Fontainebleau Hotel, the phone rang. I picked it up and Bush was on the other end.

He said just one word.

"Well?!"

"George," I answered, "you own me."

With that, I became the Vice Chairman of George Bush's National Finance Committee and the Deputy Chairman of his National Political Committee. I traveled to over thirty-five cities raising money and votes for his candidacy. At the end of his presidency, George Bush grasped the details of the Israeli-Arab relationship and the Arab-Arab, Shia/Sunni and East/West aspects of the Middle East.

After he lost in his bid for the presidential nomination, how did George Bush become the Republican vice presidential nominee? Dick Allen gave me this account: The 1980 Republican Convention took place at the Renaissance Center in downtown Detroit—built to reinvigorate that city after the 1967 riots. Ronald Reagan was in his suite in the adjacent hotel with Dick, who was then his national security and foreign policy adviser. The remainder of Reagan's inner circle, including Mike Deaver and Ed Meese, were visiting Max Fisher at his suburban Detroit home. The group was attempting to negotiate with former President Gerald Ford's team to persuade him to accept the vice presidential nomination under Reagan. The negotiations with Ford collapsed, and the Reagan team telephoned to say they were heading back to the Renaissance Center. Dick has told me Reagan turned to him and asked, "Dick, what do I do next?"

"What about Bush?" Allen asked.

"It won't fly," Reagan answered, "he's not absolutely pro-life."

It was true that Bush was not dogmatic on that matter, which Reagan was.

Allen picked up a copy of the Republican platform sitting on the coffee-table of Reagan's suite, which included a plank on abortion.

"If Bush would embrace the Republican platform in its entirety as the basis for the campaign, is that acceptable to you?"

"Yes, it would be," Reagan answered.

"Why not call and ask Bush if he does?" Allen suggested.

Dick Allen, who was the only one with Bush's phone number, called Bush, who was not expecting a call from the Reagan camp. Dick put Reagan on the line.

"If I ask you to run on the Republican ticket as the vice presidential candidate, could you embrace the Republican platform as a basis on which to campaign?" Reagan asked.

"Governor, I would be honored," was Bush's answer.

Here is what George Bush says about the matter in his book, *All the Best*:

> I went to the Republican convention in Detroit knowing the vice presidency was a possibility, but I did not expect it. Rumors were flying that Reagan would ask President Ford to join the ticket, and in fact the two did discuss it in Detroit, but could not reach an agreement. No one was more surprised than I was when I answered the phone in my hotel suite and Ronald Reagan was on the other end of the line.

ONE KEY THING I LEARNED FROM MY FIRST ENCOUNTERS WITH GEORGE BUSH IS:

Be honest with yourself. Know what you know and don't know.

Be willing to learn. Know yourself. Know your strengths and weaknesses. A leader must be honest with him- or herself. George Bush already had the character, leadership, and moral authority when I met him in 1978. He also had incredible credentials and skills. He possessed confidence in himself, and he had a strong sense of who he was. George Bush knew both his strengths and weaknesses. He was eager to receive constructive criticism. When I characterized his knowledge of Middle East affairs as insufficient, he accepted the input constructively. He dug in with determination and acquired an authority of competence on Israel and the Middle East. Bush's position paper on the Middle East became a road map that broadly defined the decisions he took as president. And his travels to Israel also gave him a profound emotional grasp of the mind and the heart of Israel and the Israeli people.

Henry "Scoop" Jackson

Henry "Scoop" Jackson was born in Everett, Washington, in 1912. There was once a clever newspaper reporter in the comics whose name was "Scoop" and had an ability to get other people to do his work for him. One of Henry Jackson's sisters felt this description fit her brother to a tee. Throughout his illustrious career, Jackson was a masterful delegator. He began his forty-five years of public service as a prosecutor chasing down bootleggers. Jackson was elected to the U.S. House of Representatives in 1940, and to the Senate in 1952.

Scoop Jackson spent a total of forty-three years in Congress in both the House and the Senate and was a towering figure in the Democratic Party during his career. He was one of the greatest authorities on national defense ever to sit in Congress. No surprise. Seattle-based Boeing is the second largest national defense contractor in the United States. Jackson was a legendary hawk. Soviet Ambassador Anatoly Dobrynin considered Jackson to be the U.S.'s "number one cold warrior." Neither Jackson nor his wife, Helen, were Jewish. What is surprising is that Jackson was one of Israel's best friends ever in the U.S. Senate. There were only 43,000 Jews in the state of Washington in 2001 (0.7%) and probably far fewer during Jackson's time! What was behind his commitment? Jackson served as an enlisted man during World War II. After his return, Presi-

dent Roosevelt sent him as an observer to Buchenwald after its liberation. The horrors he saw firsthand in the Camp impacted him forever. Jackson campaigned unsuccessfully for the Democratic presidential nomination both in 1972 and 1976. He died in office as a senator in 1981.

The Jackson-Vanik Amendment

The Soviet "education tax" was enacted in mid-1972. The ostensible reason: to repay the Soviet Union for the cost of educating the emigrants who were leaving. The real one: to erect an insurmountable barrier to emigration. This rankled Henry Jackson to the bone, who once told Israeli Prime Minister Yitzhak Rabin that if Norway had had the same policies as the Soviets, Jackson's father would never have been able to leave Europe and come to America. Jackson's thinking coalesced into what was to become an amendment to the 1974 Trade Act. The bill's co-sponsor was an Ohio Democratic congressman named Charles Vanik. The measure was simply designed and denied "unconditional normal trade relations" to those countries that refused to allow their citizens to emigrate to other lands. The amendment in effect attached a tangible trade penalty for those nations which ignored the Universal Declaration of Human Rights sanctioned decades before by the United Nations. On October 4, 1972, Scoop Jackson formally introduced the legislation that would become Jackson-Vanik in the Senate. In his astute and comprehensive biography of Jackson, which this chapter cites often, Robert Kaufman observes: "The Jackson-Vanik Amendment to the U.S. Trade Act combined Jackson's commitment to the political well-being of the state of Israel with his antipathy toward the Soviet Union."

In 1972, Jackson spoke before the National Conference on Soviet Jewry. He urged a proud and defiant attitude toward the Soviets. The conference voted to support the Jackson-Vanik Amendment. The Nixon White House, especially Secretary of State Henry Kissinger, vigorously opposed Jackson-Vanik. It was seen as completely contrary to the spirit of détente, which the Nixon administration was attempting to build with the essentially totalitarian regimes of countries like the Soviet Union and China. Jackson would not be intimidated. When the U.S. was headed down a seemingly unstoppable path toward détente, which Reagan would later reverse, Jackson seized a defining moment to stand his ground and fight for the principles of human rights within the Soviet Union. He tied improvement in economic relations with the United States to improving human rights conditions for Soviet citizens. A far broader expectation: Our policy should be driven not just on how nation-states behave toward other nations, but also on how a state behaves with regard to its own people. This was not only a defining moment for Scoop Jackson, it was also a milestone for America and for the cause of human rights throughout the world.

In response to the bill, Nixon enlisted Max Fisher to quietly lead a campaign against Jackson-Vanik within the American Jewish community. Nixon saw that he could not prevail against Jackson in the Senate but was certain he could win in the House. Nixon was sure he had locked up the Ways and Means Committee of the House through its powerful chairman, Congressman Wilbur Mills. Jackson waged an ingenious lobbying campaign to change Mills's vote and got a footwear maker named David Hermann to lobby Mills. According to Robert Kaufman, Hermann said to Mills, "during the Hitler period, we stood by... This may be another case. We have to get these people out." In December 1973, the House passed Jackson-Vanik by a margin of 388 to 44. On the same day, the Senate approved the measure by a vote of 77 to 4. Changing Wilbur Mills's vote was the key to victory in the lower chamber. After the administration got whipped in Congress, it tried a different gambit. Henry Kissinger managed to roadblock implementation of the amendment by creating a de facto committee with himself, Jackson, and Soviet Ambassador Dobrynin. The intent was clear: to stalemate Jackson-Vanik, because Kissinger saw it at odds with his own grand plan of détente. Although Jackson-Vanik passed the Congress, Nixon never signed the bill. He had resigned in 1974, while the haggling with Kissinger continued. It was Gerald Ford who ultimately signed the amended Trade Bill with Jackson-Vanik attached on January 3, 1975.

Earlier I have described how crucial Jackson-Vanik was viewed by the refuseniks with whom I met in Moscow in July 1974. Andrei Sakharov esteemed Scoop Jackson as the "champion" of the Soviet human rights movement. One of Scoop Jackson's greatest admirers was, and is, Natan Sharansky. In 1975, it was Jackson who took it upon himself to host another Soviet dissident Alexander Solzhenitsyn before a group of other U.S. Senators. Again, in the spirit of détente, President Gerald Ford had declined to meet with Solzhenitsyn.

A November 2001, White House Web site posting (during the first administration of George W. Bush) praised the success of Jackson-Vanik in the following way:

> Jackson-Vanik has been an extraordinary success in securing freedom of emigration in the Soviet Union and its successor states.

Earlier I described the high drama of Israeli resupply during the Yom Kippur War of 1973. Scoop Jackson played a crucial role in the resupply of Israel in visiting President Nixon on October 11, 1973, and calling for the president to support Israel. Jackson's visit to Nixon came just two months before the decisive showdown in Congress on the Jackson-Vanik Amendment. Nixon had vilified Jackson as "irresponsible" in a White House meeting claiming that Jackson's position was "sacrificing disarmament and cooperation." It took a person of great character and courage—and Jackson was one such person—to rise above the fray of the trade amendment. He refused to ignore the moment and showed up in the Oval Office to plead Israel's case. Nor did he bargain away Jackson-Vanik to get Nixon's backing for Israel.

Later Jackson pinpointed the side effects of détente as the very causes of the Yom Kippur War in the first place. "Without Soviet support and material encouragement, without Soviet training and equipment, without Soviet diplomatic and political backing, the war would never have been started," Jackson asserted. "And yet Dr. Kissinger... comes before the American people to say that Soviet behavior had been moderate and not irresponsible. I cannot agree."

Early in 1976, Jackson flew to Columbus, Ohio, with a full agenda. During his visit, Jackson and I met in the library of my brother's restaurant, the Lindenhof. Jackson wanted to enlist me for a prominent role as a fund-raiser in his bid for the Democratic presidential nomination in that year. At the time, I was a Republican supporting Gerald Ford. Jacob Javits was a moderate Republican from New York state who was also a staunch supporter of Israel. I could just as easily been a "Jacob Javits Republican" as a "Scoop Jackson Democrat." Their progressive positions on human rights coupled with their uncompromising backing for Israel and a strong U.S. defense posture were almost indistinguishable stances.

At the dinner, I told Jackson about the enthusiasm with which the refuseniks in the Soviet Union greeted the Jackson-Vanik Amendment in 1974, and the cult hero status he had attained among a very discerning group of leaders there. One on one, Jackson was a compelling person. What he said stood out for me:

> "My parents both came from Norwegian stock. My father immigrated here. They were both Christians. But, my mother had empathy for the Jews and what they had suffered, even before the Holocaust. She believed in a strong Judaism."

In 1956, Jackson took a trip all across the Soviet Union and got to know the country on the ground. He told me about the details of the trip and how that visit became a cornerstone for his carefully reasoned stand on the Soviets. That really impressed me. He painted an image that he later used in his speeches in which he compared the Soviets to night-time burglars in a hotel. "They work their way down the hallways and see which doors are unlocked. Then they sneak in." The point was the Soviets didn't go in with fanfare. They just quietly infiltrated new countries, extending their base of power.

In 1956, Jackson made a visit to the eight-year-old state of Israel. He recounted a conversation he had with an Israeli officer: "You know, Senator Jackson," the officer told him, "Israel has a secret weapon... The Arabs don't understand how powerful it is. Every Israeli soldier—or a member of his family—has seen the inside of a German concentration camp."

Scoop Jackson was persuasive. I went to Max Fisher and asked for advice. Since I was in the process of making the transition from fundraising for Jewish causes to Jewish political action, he counseled me not to engage in "aisle crossing." It would only damage my credibility and my ability to get things done. I told Jackson I couldn't play a role in his campaign, but he was, and he remains, one of my heroes. My respect for his character, his moral courage, and his wisdom has only increased with time. He was a great American leader.

Jackson was frequently at odds with fellow Democrat Jimmy Carter when Carter was president. Jackson believed in human rights, but he opposed Carter's selective advocacy on human rights against right-wing governments like the shah of Iran and its acceptance of the very same violations among left-wing regimes.

In 1977, Jackson fought with Carter, opposing a reconvened Geneva Middle East peace conference. According to Kaufman, Jackson argued to "encourage rather than discourage a separate Egyptian-Israeli deal that deferred the resolution of issues surrounding the West Bank for subsequent negotiations among the affected parties." It was simply a matter of pragmatism. Jackson thought the Egyptian-Israeli conflict could be solved immediately. The Israeli-Palestinian standoff could take decades to settle. How right he was.

The AWACS Sale to Saudi Arabia

In 1978, under President Jimmy Carter, the United States sold highly advanced F-15 fighter planes to the Saudis. Prior to the U.S. presidential election in 1980, the Carter administration made a deal that would make Saudi military might even more sophisticated, despite Jackson's vehement opposition as chairman of the Senate Armed Services Committee. Carter's people agreed to sell F-15 fighter plane enhancements including Sidewinder missiles to the Saudis. This was a secret transaction that had not yet received Congressional approval.

Following Ronald Reagan's victory over Carter in the 1980 presidential election, the Carter administration offered the Reagan transition team three options. One, the Reagan team could reject the plan and take the heat for *not* doing it. Two, the plan would go forward, but the Carter White House would announce it and take the heat for the decision. Reagan would fulfill the deal but simply carry out already formulated U.S. policy. Or, three, the Carter policy could be adopted and announced by the Reagan administration. Dick Allen, later National Security Adviser, was asked by the president-elect to evaluate these options and to make a recommendation to him.

One week after the Reagan victory in the November 1980 election, Dick Allen called me to Washington and confided in me the terms of the arms sale and what the options were. "The president hadn't made up his mind yet," Dick Allen said. "We've got [Secretary of Defense-designate] Weinberger, Haig, and the whole military supply industry in support of this deal." At that time, Secretary of State-designate Alexander Haig had a vision of a grand alliance of the moderate pro-Western states with Israel in opposition to the Soviet Union and its allies. Haig's vision called for Saudi Arabia to be part of the Western alliance.

Dick Allen asked me to go to Israel on a secret mission as a private citizen and to feel out Israeli attitudes toward the sale. I was to play no official government role whatsoever. My assignment was to find out under what conditions, if any, the Israeli government would be willing to accept the sale of F-15 enhancements, including Sidewinder missiles, without a fight. In December 1980, I flew to Tel Aviv and met with everybody who could possibly have an impact on the decision. That included both sides of the political spectrum and the top military, intelligence, and finance officials—the entire gamut, from Prime Minister Begin and his Foreign Minister Moshe Dayan on down. I came back in early January 1981 and reported to Allen that—under certain conditions—Israel would agree *not* to oppose the sale. However, Israel needed reaffirmation of its special and strategic relationship with the United States. Israel wanted to institutionalize that strategic relationship through joint military exercises with the United States.

At the time, Israel also needed loan relief. The Israelis wanted to stretch out $3.5 billion worth of outstanding indebtedness over a longer period of time and at lower interest rates. By the spring of 1981, the prime interest rate had skyrocketed to 20%! In addition, the Israelis wanted to make stipulations on the equipment sale itself. The deal, they said, should be restricted to F-15 enhancements and Sidewinder missiles and should not include fuel pods, which would increase the range of this aircraft. Israel felt that it could then prevail against the Saudi F-15 add-ons and would be able to maintain the qualitative edge in equipment and personnel. I reported my findings back to Dick. He coordinated the negotiations with the Israelis and then sold the terms of the Israeli package first to Haig, then to Weinberger, and ultimately President-elect Reagan. It was on this basis that the Reagan transition team accepted the third option of the Carter people—to inherit the F-15 enhancement sale and to announce it as their own.

Some Jewish leaders—most notably Max Fisher—didn't really oppose the sale of the F-15 enhancements to the Saudis. However, most of the American leadership strongly opposed the sale. In mid-March, the executive committee of the Republican Jewish Coalition met with President Reagan to express opposition to the sale of the F-15 enhancements. The evening before the presidential meeting took place, the executive committee—all Reagan-Bush supporters most of whom felt betrayed by the very idea of this sale—gathered in the Hay-Adams Hotel in Washington, to develop a carefully worded statement that would be read in President Reagan's presence the next day. Max read the finalized text to the group. Max's own position was to express the group's feelings while not antagonizing the president with inflammatory language.

The meeting with the president took place in the Cabinet Room of the White House. Max read the policy statement, but he tempered some of the language, so that "deeply disturbed by" became "a little bit disturbed by" and the words "opposed to" were dropped altogether. Over my years as a political activist, I have attended perhaps twenty-five meetings of groups with the president. I can recall none like this one. Individuals in the coalition were the nucleus of the group that delivered Ronald Reagan a remarkable forty-two percent of the Jewish vote in 1980. Feeling betrayed by the statement that was actually read, some of the committee members stood up and voiced their objections. They made it clear in unequivocal terms that they were prepared to stop at nothing to block the enhancements, if these jeopardized the security of Israel. President Reagan carefully and quietly listened to the input. He then made a straightforward and convincing statement. He said that he understood the anxiety of the group. However, this decision had to be seen in the context of a broader picture. The United States was fully committed to maintaining Israel's viability and qualitative military edge. While the president's comments didn't fully resolve the concerns, they at least served to quell some of the apprehension.

The attempted assassination of Ronald Reagan occurred on March 30, 1981. The next day, the arms sale to Saudi Arabia was on the agenda of the National Security Council. A new wrinkle emerged. Defense Secretary Weinberger advocated selling AWACS (airborne warning and control system) *in addition to* F-15 enhancements and the Sidewinder missiles to the Saudis. At the time, there were four American

AWACS-equipped planes in Saudi Arabia being flown by American pilots. The AWACS is a military control system with incredible electronic gear—especially radar and sensing systems. For example, while hovering thousands of feet in the air, an AWACS-equipped airplane is able to identify what kind of a vehicle is traveling on a road 200 miles away. It can spot enemy aircraft in the sky and determine which plane is the most vulnerable to attack, which squadron should attack them, and even what missiles to use...instantly! Today, a rudimentary computer game has some of the same wherewithal. Back then, the AWACS's technology was an awesome strategic advantage. At that time, AWACS was among the most highly sophisticated military equipment in the world. Weinberger won out in his recommendation to sell AWACS to the Saudis at the National Security Council meeting. This was a massive change in the arms sale deal that Dick Allen had asked me to explore. I immediately called Dick and two points became clear: Dick felt that Weinberger had taken advantage of Reagan's condition after the assassination attempt. And, as far as Dick was concerned, the combined sale represented a completely different package. It was clear that the previous understanding with the Israelis was off the table, and the administration would need to start new negotiations with the Israelis.

The Conference of Presidents of Jewish Organizations met on March 31. Although I knew about the proposed AWACS sale to the Saudis, the conference members did not. The meeting was called to draft a strong letter opposing the F-15 enhancement sale package to the Saudis. Because of the assassination attempt, the conference members concluded it was inappropriate to send President Reagan a letter of opposition. Instead they sent a letter praying for his recovery. Four days after the shooting, the president was still under medical care. Weinberger visited the Reagan suite in the hospital and persuaded the president to sign off on the executive order that added AWACS to the F-15 enhancements package and authorized the Executive Branch to proceed with the sale of AWACS to Saudi Arabia.

The Jewish community and much of the national Jewish leadership in the Republican Party went ballistic. So did Henry Jackson. Scoop Jackson and I both came to be intensely involved with the AWACS issue, although I must make it clear that we did not work in tandem on this initiative. From a distance, I admired his moral courage, his dedication, and his integrity in taking the stand he did.

The Defense Department, I should note, had a commercial consideration in mind. It wanted to sell AWACS-equipped aircraft to the Saudis because the Boeing production line that made them was coming to an end of its run and was to be closed down. (Two to three years are needed to restart that kind of production line.) Secondly, if the United States government could sell more AWACS-equipped planes to foreign governments, it would help defray the development cost, and reduce the cost of AWACS to the United States government. Thirdly, the U.S. had a serious trade deficit, and the Treasury Department had told Defense it wanted to bolster our trade balance.

Scoop Jackson was opposing a bread-and-butter project for Boeing, the state of Washington's number one employer. Jackson genuinely believed that Boeing made the best military aircraft in the world. Despite all of this, Jackson still regarded the sale of AWACS to the Saudis as unconscionable. He thought giving the Saudis AWACS would antagonize the Egyptians. He distrusted the Saudis for their covert funding of the PLO. Astutely aware of Saudi Arabia's fragile internal stability, he was concerned by the possibility of a sophisticated weapons system like AWACS falling into the wrong hands. The officials at Boeing didn't even *try* to stop Scoop Jackson. When it came to defense decisions, he followed his own drumbeat. If the uninformed accused him of being the "Senator from Boeing," even rivals and foes among his colleagues would bristle at the thought and deny it. Jackson's integrity was that deeply respected within the Senate.

*   *   *

On April 15, 1981, the Conference of Presidents of Major Jewish Organizations asked me to chair a national coordinating committee. Its purpose was to block the sale of AWACS to Saudi Arabia through Congressional action. Before I accepted the chairmanship, I wanted to see Vice President Bush because this assignment would put me on a collision course with the administration. I felt that I and the Israelis had been misled by the White House. I believed Israeli national security was horribly threatened by the sale AWACS to Saudi Arabia.

I met with the vice president and told him what I intended to do.

"Gordy, do you really know what an AWACS is?" he asked.

I confessed I didn't.

"Before you become a political kamikaze pilot for this cause, you need more information. I know the Israelis feel very threatened that this will upset the balance of power in the region. I want to arrange a briefing for you at the State Department and at the Defense Department to explain the whys and wherefores of this sale." I agreed to this. That put a series of meetings into motion. At the State Department, I was briefed by Walter Stoessel, the number three person at State, along with Nick Veliotes, who was the Deputy Under Secretary in charge of the Middle East and the Middle East staff. At Defense, I was also briefed by Colonel Oliver North, a future member of the National Security Council Staff, and Bing West, Assistant Secretary of Defense for International Security Affairs.

In these sessions, I was told exactly what an AWACS is and what it could and couldn't do. The briefing also outlined the U.S.'s grand strategy regarding Saudi Arabia. That included our need for access to Middle East oil, and our strategic relationship with King Saud, who had come to power through the assassination of his cousin. The king was pro-Western but there were cousins of his who wanted to be king who were pro-Soviet.

Sixty percent of the world's proven oil reserves were in the Persian Gulf at the time. Virtually all of Japan's oil, most of Europe's oil, and much of our oil came from the Gulf states. The U.S. needed oil from the Middle East, friendly hands in control of that oil, and assured access to and egress from the Gulf. The U.S. was very concerned about instability in the region and how it might impact the Saudi monarchy. Would there be an invasion by Iran or Iraq? What about an insurrection inside Saudi Arabia? Iran was in the hands of Islamic fundamentalists who were hostile to America. How could we protect our vital interests in the region, especially our passage through the Straits of Hormuz—perhaps the most valuable piece of real estate in the entire world? Would a land-based U.S. presence in the Middle East be possible? The Saudis rejected U.S. land bases for two reasons. First, perceived catering to the Americans might provoke radical elements inside Saudi Arabia to stage an insurrection. An internal upheaval might also invite an invasion by one of their neighbors. Second, they didn't trust us, because we had already abandoned a close ally— another monarch—the Shah of Iran.

If there could be no U.S. bases, how about prepositioning our equipment as the Soviets were already doing in South Yemen? The Saudis said the difference between bases and prepositioning equipment wasn't sufficient enough to warrant the risk. Prepositioning equipment is placing military hardware such as planes or weapons in a foreign country with the understanding that the materiel would be available for use. Prepositioning does not require the host country to provide real estate for a base or to allow the continuing presence of foreign troops.

The third best option—and the only available one according to the Department of Defense—was to sell the Saudis sophisticated equipment compatible with our own. The Saudi equipment would be maintained at their expense. In the event a threat arose and we needed to use the equipment, the U.S. would fly its rapid deployment forces from the U.S. to Saudi Arabia. This option would be virtually the same as prepositioning. And, the Department of Defense contended, although we would sell the Saudis AWACS, we would *not* sell them top-of-the-line technology, for fear someone might steal it. If we ever needed to actually use these aircraft in a confrontation, we would bring our own "black-boxes" with the latest technology in them. In addition, Saudi Arabia agreed to provide the U.S. oil at "reasonable prices."

These briefings took two days. After the sessions, whatever anxiety I had with respect to the threat to Israel's security posed by the AWACS sale evaporated like mist under bright sunlight. The briefings explained how Saudi ownership of AWACS was not a fundamental risk to Israel. In fact, the idea of an existential threat to the nation was absolutely absurd. If the Israelis felt vulnerable, Dick Allen was the first to point out to me that Israel would just blow the planes out of the sky or destroy them on the ground. AWACS-equipped aircraft are vulnerable and can be knocked out by a single missile. There might be casualties, but it would not affect the existence of the state.

My next step was to visit again with Vice President George Bush. I asked him directly if he had received the same AWACS briefings I had. The answer was no. "*Promise me* you'll have the briefings," I said, "because what I learned scares the living daylights out of me as an American. Put aside the fact that I am a friend of Israel. Israel will take care of itself and will destroy these planes if they pose a problem. The real issues are these: First, for the U.S. to rely on Saudi Arabia to defend America's vital national strategic interest in the Gulf is the height of absurdity. Second, to take our most sophisticated technology and to put it at risk in an unstable area of the world without adequate measures to protect it from falling into hostile hands is unbelievable."

I advised the vice president that I still intended to chair the national fight against AWACS: "Despite its military arsenal, Saudi Arabia was, and is, weak, impotent, and essentially defenseless. Saudi Arabia could easily be taken over by any of its enemies, and this great technology, I argued, could end up in the hands of any determined enemy who might want it. We would be well served to learn from a precedent. We had ships in the Persian Gulf that were struck by Harpoon missiles we had sold to Iran before the fall of the shah. Mr. Vice President, as an American, I am appalled at this policy. President Reagan is prepared to confront the Soviet Union on the issue of world peace, and it seems he is unwilling to confront the Saudis on the need for a base in the Middle East to protect our strategic interests there. The policy is flawed, and, because of the briefings, I'm going to accept the chairmanship of the Jewish community's coalition against AWACS. I'm opposing this decision because I think it's bad for the United States of America."

George Bush accepted my decision to oppose the AWACS sale and understood my motivations. Being the kind of person he is, he knew the AWACS campaign was a matter of principle for me. And, George Bush understands and respects matters of principle better than any person I have ever met. Dick Allen was chosen by President Reagan to lead the campaign for Congressional approval of the sale. The AWACS controversy put me on a collision course with friends and mentors in the administration. To my astonishment, this adversarial role didn't harm my relationships with George Bush and Dick Allen. I honestly believe it was because I was dealing with individuals who had such strongly defined moral principles. Their commitment to democracy included respect for honest disagreements.

In my opinion, the proper long-term solution was having a U.S. base in Saudi Arabia, not selling the Saudis AWACS technology. The great threat in Saudi Arabia was, and is, internal insurrection. It doesn't take much to kill a king. The Wahhabi fundamentalism of Saudi Arabia is an ominous threat to America and democratic countries throughout the world. If radical fundamentalists gain control of Saudi Arabia, we are in danger of losing access to the oil in the region. We shouldn't be in a position where that could possibly threaten us, and yet we are. Consider that it took us from August 2, 1990 until January 1991 to position 500,000 troops and the equipment needed to mount Operation Desert Storm and drive Iraq from Kuwait. Were there a coup within Saudi Arabia, how long would it take us to have troops on the ground to control the situation? What, for example, could threaten the oil protection and delivery system before troops and matériel from across the oceans could be positioned to defend it? To assure the supply of oil, the U.S. should either unilaterally or in conjunction with Europe and Japan, permanently station ground, air, and naval forces in the region. This was, of course, before the American offensive in Iraq in 2003.

Once I decided to accept the coalition's leadership, I wanted to have the benefit of Richard Nixon's thinking and advice on how he thought we should proceed with efforts to block the AWACS sale. Nixon had been disgraced and ousted from office. But, he remained a hero of mine. He had saved Israel in 1973 by authorizing the biggest military resupply in the history of America, and he was a brilliant authority on international affairs. In this domain, he was a voice whom Ronald Reagan truly trusted. Not knowing Nixon, I called Max Fisher to see if he would arrange a meeting.

At 7:00 A.M. one morning in late April 1981, Max and I went to the Federal Building in Manhattan's financial district. This was the site of the ousted president's official office. It was cold and pitch-dark. His one aide announced our arrival. In the farthest corner of this huge, dimly lit room, Nixon sat in an easy chair, his profile illuminated by a reading lamp. When Max and I entered, Nixon got out of the chair, and wordlessly walked toward us with his shoes squeaking in the high-ceilinged room. Nixon's handshake was the most lifeless I had ever experienced.

Limp handshake or not, after a few pleasantries between Max and Nixon, I sat at the feet of the master for three hours. He gave us a comprehensive assessment of Israel's strategic options regarding AWACS. This included the consequences of an entire chessboard of power shifts. Nixon knew every leader of every country in the Middle East and whether they were Shia or Sunni, rational or volatile, trustworthy or suspect. He knew how long they were in power and how long they would likely stay there. One by one, Nixon rattled off the metrics of the nation's economic and military might, and the tensions that existed with their neighbors. Nixon executed a geo-political tour de force. When the meeting was over, my head was spinning. His bottom-line: The U.S.–Israel relationship was more important than the individual issue of AWACS. "The one thing I would advise,"

Nixon emphasized, "is this: There is only one United States. It's the only friend Israel has that can come to its aid when it's needed. Be careful that you don't ask for more than it is possible for America to deliver without compromising essential American interests. Advise the Israelis never to stretch the relationship to the point of breaking on a non-existential issue. And, AWACS is not an existential issue." Nixon understood the principles of national self-interest and real-politik. As for protecting America's strategic interests in the region, he supported the Administration's policy and the sale of AWACS to Saudi Arabia. Nixon's position on AWACS was clearly at odds with Scoop Jackson's but it was nonetheless eminently well-reasoned.

To me at the time, the AWACS sale represented a flawed strategy to protect U.S. vital interests in this region. What *was* the real issue? It's not what we sell to the Arabs, but how to maintain Israel's qualitative edge. How do you maintain such an overwhelming balance of power in Israel's favor that Israel either can win or successfully deter aggression because it is *perceived* she would win a war? How do you assure that Israel can maintain the military qualitative edge—real and perceived—against belligerent Arab states? That in turn will advance the peace process. George Bush understood this tactic. If "even-handed" treatment meant abandoning a qualitative strategic edge for Israel, what then? Israel was finished and so was stability in the region. War would be inevitable.

Sometimes, there is victory in defeat. The pro-Israeli community had to lose in order to win. One result of the administration winning the AWACS fight was that President Reagan was able to project the strong leadership required to confront the former Soviet Union and to help bring about the accelerated collapse of that system. It was essential for the pro-Israel community to wage the AWACS battle for Israel to maintain its qualitative edge. However, if the pro-Israel community had won the AWACS battle, the great paradox is that Israel would have been seriously weakened because America's position as a world leader would have been compromised.

The AWACS controversy was fraught with complexity. Was it a mistake for me to lead this initiative against AWACS? Based on hindsight, I believe I did the right thing in a narrow sense. The controversy made Washington very careful about selling weapons systems to the Arabs. One by-product of opposing AWACS was enormously valuable. In the past quarter century, there hasn't been a single arms sale to the Arab nations that could upset Israel's qualitative edge. But both the American Jewish community and I were wrong in a greater and more important way. President Reagan had to win the AWACS contest to demonstrate his leadership strength—strength that was decisive to winning the Cold War. Winning that war redefined the geo-political landscape of the Middle East and was of enormous long-term strategic benefit to Israel.

In September 1981, it was Jackson who led the Senate fight against AWACS. He was willing to bring the Saudis under the umbrella of AWACS protection, but recoiled at the thought of them holding onto the umbrella's handle. Dick Allen brought several senators to the Oval Office to meet with President Reagan. Among them were Iowa Senator Roger Jepson and Maine Senator William Cohen (later Secretary of Defense in the Clinton Administration). With his inimitable combination of charm and forcefulness, the president said to the Republican senators essentially the following:

> Without your help, I could never have been elected. You are planning to vote against the sale of AWACS to the Saudis. Do you want it on your conscience that you contributed to the failure of the Reagan presidency? Is AWACS more important than following the mandate that the American people have given to us?

Jepson and Cohen were persuaded by the president's argument and changed their minds. Then came the vote. I was in the Senate Gallery on October 28, 1981. The atmosphere was electrifying.

Reagan won, 52–48. And, in the long run, Israel did, too.

SEVERAL KEY THINGS I LEARNED FROM SCOOP JACKSON ARE:

Have the courage to follow your moral compass especially if it runs in the face of commonly accepted beliefs.

Scoop Jackson's attitudes and assumptions regarding the Soviets were completely congruent with Reagan's, just as the two were of the same mind in defending Israel's future. Dying in 1983, Jackson never had the satisfaction of seeing the wisdom of the policies he long recommended in leading to the downfall of the Soviet Union. It's no surprise that Jackson's most important staff aide, Richard Perle, went on to become Assistant Secretary of Defense between 1981 and 1987 during the Reagan administration. Perle was an important architect on the Reagan team in helping to bring down the Evil Empire.

Never risk publicly rupturing a relationship with a strategic ally on a non-existential issue.

You always have to ask yourself the question, especially in the middle of a crisis: Are we facing an existential, life-threatening issue? Never squander goodwill for the sake of personal pride or short-term ideological goals. If I can't have the outcome I would *prefer* to have, what will be the consequences? If they aren't truly devastating, how forcefully do I want to press my case? This is a lesson I learned from Nixon in the context of the AWACS battle, not something I learned from Jackson, but I'm sure that Jackson embraced the same view.

Scoop Jackson was not Jewish, but he was always the advocate of Israel. In fact, Jackson never shirked from demanding what he felt the world owed the Jewish State of Israel. He could never understand why American Jews would vote solidly for defense spending to back Israel, while many would shun or even oppose strong defense spending for the United States itself. They didn't seem to understand that the very foundation of a strong Israel was a militarily strong America.

There is nothing more formidable than a person of conscience.

Scoop Jackson passionately believed in both an invincible America and a strong, viable State of Israel. He simply felt a compelling moral responsibility for not letting anything like the Holocaust happen ever again. He failed in his 1972 and 1976 runs at the presidential nomination. But, senatorial colleagues polled informally said he was the best-qualified senator to become president. Eulogizing him, Senate Majority Leader Howard Baker called Jackson "a man of majestic stature, of strength and conviction . . ." Four times, I saw Jackson exercise strength of conscience and moral courage in moments when others would easily cower: the crafting of the Jackson-Vanik amendment in 1972–1974, the resupply of Israel in 1973, his advocacy of bilateral Egyptian-Israeli negotiations in 1977, and the AWACS confrontation in 1981. Scoop Jackson was one of those truly principled leader who could courageously translate matters of conscience into pragmatic acts. One of Jackson's favorite quotes, according to Robert Kaufman, came from the theologian Reinhold Niebuhr:

> If the democratic nations fail, their failure must be partly attributed to the faulty strategy of idealists who have too many illusions when they face realists who have too little conscience.

George Bush and Yitzhak Shamir

Yitzhak Shamir was born in Poland in 1915. He studied law both at Warsaw University, after he emigrated to Palestine in 1935, and Hebrew University. A founding member of the "Stern Gang" that mounted an armed insurrection against British rule, Shamir has always been seen as a street fighter and a man with outspoken views. When Stern was reorganized into the successor organization Lechi—he was one of the three governing members. During his involvement with Lechi, the organization was responsible for the assassination of Lord Moyne, the British Minister of State in the Middle East and the UN representative in the Middle East, Folke Bernadotte. The British arrested and exiled Shamir. Ultimately France gave him asylum. Shamir served in the Mossad from 1955 to 1965. He did not become a member of the Knesset until 1973. He served as foreign minister from 1980 to 1983. Between 1984 and 1990, Shamir rotated in and out as prime minister within a National Unity Government. In 1990, the rotation of the top spot within the National Unity government ended, and Shamir served as Likud prime minister until 1992.

During the period from January 1989 to June 1992, I had the opportunity to observe one of the most fascinating relationships I have ever witnessed in my life—that of U.S. President George H. W. Bush and Israeli Prime Minister Yitzhak Shamir. This three-and-a-half-year period began with Bush's inauguration in January 1989. At the time, Shamir was the Likud prime minister in a National Unity government with Shimon Peres of Labor as foreign minister. That government collapsed in 1990, and Shamir continued as prime minister heading a Likud-based coalition with a razor-thin majority in the Knesset, until that government fell in June 1992.

What made the relationship between George Bush and Yitzhak Shamir so intriguing (and at times so volatile!) was that both men were totally passionate about service to their country and to their people. Those were passions that I fully understood. In a sense, I also shared them—with perhaps one caveat. I always viewed myself as an American citizen, and my Jewish loyalties were always somewhat more focused toward the Jewish people than to the Jewish state.

While Bush and Shamir had passions they could both appreciate, it is hard to imagine two political personalities cut of more different cloth. Bush believes in relationship diplomacy and in relationship politics. The loyal and trusted friends and colleagues with whom he forged both his business and political success are central to George Bush. Relationships are an important factor in his whole lifestyle and in his successes. He grew up in privilege, to be sure. But, it was also a model of privilege with an austere expectation of service and results. "To whom much is given, much is expected." On the other hand, Yitzhak Shamir knew the hard street fighting world of the ghetto. He is very much a loner—mistrustful and inclined to be cynical. Both were warriors, but with different scripts—Bush as the youngest pilot in the history of the Navy in World War II—dashing, decorated, and glamorous—and Shamir as a guerrilla mounting a rebellion—rough-hewn and calculating.

If it sounds like Shamir's repertory was confined to the dark world of violence, that is not at all the case. He has a grueling appetite for detail. While in office, he read everything that the Mossad sent him, not just the summaries. He has a highly intelligent and analytical mind. George Bush is a natural leader. In social or personal diplomacy, his sense of human detail is both impeccable and awesome. He is a master of such niceties as the acknowledgment and the thank-you note. Yitzhak Shamir had a way of coming across as dismissive, condescending. He could leave Bush steaming for not having called or written to clear up a glitch in communications from Israel on an important point. Yet, Shamir was not oblivious to Bush's expectations. I remember a call of appreciation from Shamir to Bush, for example, regarding Bush's help on Ethiopian Jewry. And, there was an apologetic call for the timing of settlement expansion by then Housing Minister Ariel Sharon but, the "pardon me" was long in coming.

Shamir never trusted Bush because Bush came from affluence, from the Eastern establishment and later from Texas oil. Shamir believed you couldn't trust anyone deep into oil. Also, Bush never showed Shamir emotional involvement and attachment to Israel. During the eight years that Bush was vice president, William Safire of the *New York Times* intimated that Bush was sympathetic to or at least even-handed with the Arabs. This inaccurate stereotype was one Shamir readily accepted.

If George Bush showed no visceral passion for Israel in their meetings—despite what he certainly believed down deep—Shamir was cool, unemotional and skeptical in one-on-one encounters. No U.S. president I have ever met is more gifted in creating a genuine atmosphere of warmth and trust one-on-one than George Bush. Bush masterfully built the coalition that fought the first Gulf War one world leader after another, but he was unable to communicate with Shamir. When they were together, Bush instinctively would launch into a conversation by reaching out. Shamir's response was not to trust the warmth. The chemistry was bad. It's just that simple. The two were like oil and water. No matter what happened, it got worse, not better.

Shamir is a very difficult man to get to know, and he can be testy. It's hard to have a conversation with him, if you don't know him and if he hasn't known you for a long time. Shamir is a tough guy who lived through the Holocaust. He is mistrustful and cynical. He lost his family in Poland to the Nazi death camps. He starts with the presumption that Israel has to defend itself. It can't rely on anybody. Bush is just another one of those people for whom he has no trust.

During my ongoing work with both men, there were a series of mis-communications. For Shamir, he may have seen those cases as being driven by tactical necessity. On the other hand, as I'll describe, Shamir trusted Bush in ways that were totally out of character for Shamir—first in the case of not retaliating against Iraq in the 1991 Gulf War and second in the Madrid Peace Conference, which experts contend in an ironic way, may have toppled his government.

There is one fact George Bush may not have fully appreciated. Among Bush's aides, there were a lot of people in the bowels of the State Department, the Defense Department, and even in the White House who wanted to embarrass Israel. At times, they were rejoicing at the strained relationship between Shamir and Bush. In State, for example, there are doubtless more careerists and professionals who are pro-Arab than who are pro-Israel. Why would that be so? There are some twenty different Arab desks and there's one Israel desk. There are more opportunities for somebody who learns Arabic to get positions than for those who have learned Hebrew. This is not about sinister cabals. This is about the mathematics of opportunity and advancement.

The cavernous rift in matters of style made it all the harder to bridge issues of substance. Between 1989 and 1990, there were three major personal incidents that created a great deal of stress and tension between Bush and Shamir—settlements and loan guarantees, the ab-duction of Sheik Obeid, and Jerusalem. George Bush was President of the United States and leader of the free world. He constantly con-sulted his own moral compass and steered his course in the context of the best interest of the American people. While he was always com-mitted to a militarily strong and independent Jewish State of Israel, is-sues were bound to arise that would cause him to take a much broader view than the consequences for Israel and the Middle East. The only compass that mattered to Shamir was the continuing, rightful existence of Israel. The different vantage points were bound to create substan-tive conflict between the two leaders.

George Bush, to his credit, separated Bush/Shamir from America/Israel. On the America/Israel equation, there was steadfastness in the commitment of Bush toward Israel, both in terms of financial aid and military assistance and in all the critical dimensions that were necessary to Israel's well being. Strategic cooperation expanded under the Bush Administration to new heights. Indeed, U.S. foreign aid to Israel remained intact, and Israel's qualitative edge militarily was sustained. Strategic cooperation grew in both the military and political arenas. Under George Bush, the U.S. never attempted to impose a settlement on the Middle East. That the U.S.–Israel relationship remained so strong is particularly striking given the personal tensions between him and Yitzhak Shamir—two heads of state who were ill-starred to cooperate.

To understand the nature of my observations, it will help the reader to know the following: In 1988, I was National Chairman of the Bush for President National Jewish Campaign Committee, Co-chairman of the National Finance Committee, and Co-chairman of the Campaign's Middle East Advisory Committee.

Throughout this period, as often in the past, I played multiple roles in the American-Israeli relationship: sounding board, clarifier, and back-channeler among them. When I visited the Israelis, I made it absolutely clear, I was not authorized to speak for anybody. I was not a member of the government. The president didn't ask me to come. Of course, they knew I had just seen the president. And, they knew I would see the president when I went back. Still, I was a free agent and not an agent of the president. George Bush used me with the hopes of getting certain things done or made easier on his behalf. I was not, nor would I permit myself to become, a messenger. Israel and America already had ambassadors to deliver a message. My foremost goal during this period was to help further the peace process. Why did the top officials in Israel see me? Because they knew I saw the president of the United States and he trusted me.

What transpired over the three-and-a-half years of the Bush-Shamir relationship? I measure it by a series of seven key milestones or topics:

Bush and Shamir's first meeting.

The capture (abduction) of Sheik Obeid.

Jerusalem.

Settlements and Loan Guarantees before the 1991 Gulf War.

The 1991 Gulf War.

Loan Guarantees after the War.

The Madrid Peace Conference.

Shamir had his first meeting with Bush as president on Wednesday, April 6, 1989. The topics were: U.S.–Israeli strategic cooperation, military prepositioning and joint exercises, and U.S. foreign aid to Israel. Bush assured Shamir that he was committed to Israel's security and supportive of a bilateral peace process. Shamir tried to reassure Bush that Israel genuinely wanted peace. The meeting couldn't have been better. When it ended, Bush mentioned to Shamir that he would like his cooperation, as he pursued the possibility for advancing peace in the region during the beginning of his presidency. Bush commented that he wanted time to advance the peace process and that the expansion of settlements by Israel on the West Bank was a particular sticking point with Arabs. Out of consideration for that fact, Bush requested that Shamir defer settlement activities for several months. Bush wanted a chance to see what he can do to advance the peace process first.

Since Shamir had had a great meeting, he didn't want to spoil the closing moments. He decided not to say anything, rather than to challenge Bush and debate him about settlements. Bush interpreted Shamir's silence as acquiescence. Shamir thought very differently— he *hadn't* pledged his agreement, because he didn't say anything at all. That's exactly what each thought because that's what each told me in private conversations. In reality, they misread each other.

On the Sunday following the Wednesday meeting, Bush was at Camp David. In the Sunday *New York Times,* he read that the Israeli Cabinet had approved three new settlements. Bush understandably went ballistic. His chief of staff, John Sununu, called me at the Denver airport. (Sununu, who is of Lebanese descent, has also has been misread by the community and was viewed as a hostile, unfriendly Arabist. Nothing could have been further from the truth.) Sununu told me the big problem was no longer settlements. The issue was trust. Shamir didn't have the courtesy to pick up the telephone and let Bush know in advance what he was doing. Even if Shamir was going to expand the settlements, and he felt that he had no choice but to do so, he should have at least called in advance. Respect from an ally demanded it. The president shouldn't learn about this in the newspaper.

Bush had both a substantive disagreement and a style disagreement as well. I called the Israeli ambassador and told him the issue is no longer "settlements, no settlements." The issue had become the confidence and the trust of the President of the United States in the Prime Minister of Israel. Bush felt abused and betrayed. "My advice to you," I said, "is to have Prime Minister Shamir pick up the phone now, call the president and apologize for any misunderstanding that occurred. I suggest he assure President Bush that he, Shamir, did not deliberately undermine a commitment made to the president of the United States. The prime minister should explain what his silence meant and admit that he should have called the president in advance of this news appearing in the press. In short, Prime Minister Shamir should apologize."

Shamir couldn't bring himself to call Bush and apologize. It was just alien to Shamir. From April to June, there was a chill between Washington and Jerusalem. Anybody and everybody in the know tried to get a message back to Shamir to phone, to write, to do something. Shamir then decided to craft an eight-page letter. Then the chill plunged into a deep freeze! Instead of appeasing and calming Bush, Shamir's letter provoked him further. Instead of discussing issues of respect and process, the letter laid out Likud's justification for Israeli settlements. This rubbed salt in the wound for Bush and made him even madder.

*   *   *

In February 1988, U.S. Colonel William Higgins of the NATO peace-keeping force in Lebanon had been kidnapped by Hizbollah. For a year and a half, nothing more was heard about Higgins. He was presumed to be in custody somewhere in Lebanon. In July 1989, I visited Israel in the spirit of furthering the Middle East peace process and the U.S.–Israel relationship during Bush's first year as president. Coincidental with my visit, on July 28, the Israelis entered Lebanon and captured Sheik Obeid, a Lebanese terrorist and kidnapper. The Israeli government had seized Sheik Obeid in the hopes of exchanging him for an Israeli Air Force navigator, Ron Arad. Arad was shot down in a mission over a Palestinian refugee camp in 1986. Although no Arab state confirmed that Arad was still alive, Israeli intelligence believed him to be alive at the time of the Obeid incident. Obeid remains imprisoned in Israel as of this writing in 2006.

The Israeli press was elated that their government had captured Sheik Obeid in an operation that must have been approved by Prime Minister Shamir. On July 31, 1989, Hizbollah released gruesome pictures of Colonel Higgins hanged in his cell. On world television, Higgins was reported as having either hanged himself or been hanged. If the latter, was his death a direct retaliation for the Sheik Obeid capture?

Immediately following the capture, President Bush publicly condemned the taking of hostages under any set of circumstances, and he equated the capture with a kidnapping for ransom. Bush's view inflamed the Israelis and Shamir who felt there was no symmetry between seizing Sheik Obeid, who is a murderous terrorist responsible for planning and bringing about the deaths of hundreds of innocent people, with the taking of an innocent individual as a hostage. Fueling the debate further, Senator Robert Dole made harsh comments against the action of the Israelis, especially when it appeared that a consequence of the Sheik Obeid capture was the death of Colonel Higgins. At the time, Robert Dole was taking an uncharacteristic stance for a conservative Republican, but his views may have meshed with declining public sentiment toward Israel. His coolness toward Israel continued. In February 1990, he wrote an op-ed piece in the *New York Times* urging diversion of some of Israel's $3 billion in foreign aid to rebuild-ing a democratic Russia and other new East European democracies.

When I returned from Israel, I met with the president on August 10, intending to share with him what I had learned on my trip, especially on furthering the peace process and moving the American-Israel rela-tionship back on course. When I entered the Oval Office, the president was not to be seen. This meeting was to be held—I quickly concluded—in the inner sanctum. A concealed panel in the Oval Office is actually a door that leads into a working office for the president as well as a pri-vate dining room. The president was alone in the working office, and he was livid. The Sheik Obeid incident overshadowed all other as-pects of the American-Israeli relationship on that day.

"Gordon, I'm very troubled," he said "I am the president of the United States. My policies must always be what's best for our country. Our policy differs from Israel's policy with respect to hostages. We do not take hostages to barter for hostages. We capture terrorists and put them on trial, as we tried to do with the kidnappers on the *Achille Lauro*. We do not negotiate with terrorists and we do not pay ransom to terrorists. Israel does. With respect to settlements, we believe that they are an obstacle to peace and they are not advancing the peace process. The feelings that Dole has expressed represent the feelings of many Americans when they saw Higgins swinging from that rope."

"Mr. President," I said, "the Israelis believe that Higgins was killed some time earlier."

"If they have proof, I'd like to see it," the president responded. "Also if they knew earlier that Higgins was dead and they did not tell us, that's terrible. That's no way to treat a friend. I will continue to speak out against kidnapping, because that's what it is. I hope Israel doesn't do anything precipitous that results in the death of another American hostage. That could create a very serious reversal in Amer-ican public opinion and cause relationship problems between us." In truth, George Bush would have been opposed to taking Obeid hostage even if there had been *no* American hostages in Beirut. Kidnapping was a clear matter of principle for him.

We talked about Robert Dole's comments. I characterized Dole as a Lone Ranger in the very negative way he was speaking out about Israel. The president was silent. He did not repudiate Dole's statement. He said that Dole was angry and frustrated and that he spoke for many people. "The U.S. and Israel have a special, strategic relationship. They are a strategic ally, but Israel has a responsibility to deal with us as partners and not to go off on their own and do what they think is in their own interest," the president said. "They should not recklessly risk American lives with my finding out about it after the fact. What's more, this is on top of all the other stuff that has been going on with Shamir." Bush said he got a phone call from Shamir after the Higgins matter became public. It was a cordial exchange, but Bush still did not know why the Israelis had captured Obeid and what, if any, consideration they gave to the consequences to the American hostages in Lebanon before taking action.

"Mr. President," I asked, "what would you want Israel to have done in this situation: Communicate in advance? Communicate simultaneously? Coordinate with us? What would you have had them do? Mr. President, do you want Israel to advise us in advance or simultaneously, when they are going to take actions that imperil the lives of Americans? It's important that the relationship rules are clear. On the one hand, if they coordinate with you, the implication is clear." I didn't have to spell it out to him. His eyes told me that he understood it immediately. "If you want them to coordinate with you," I elaborated anyway, "that implicates America in the act. If they carry it out and we jointly plan it, we're guilty of doing it. We're an accessory or we are partners in the execution."

"Well, hell no," he answered, "I don't want Israel to coordinate."

"Then what do you want them to do, do you want them to get your approval or do you want to be informed in advance? This would have put at risk an operation which was very dangerous for the Israelis to undertake," I explained. "They sent Israeli commandos inside Lebanon, into the camps of the terrorists, and they plucked Obeid out of his home. One false slip and those kids were all dead." Bush understood that from his CIA days. "When you deal in advance," I continued, "there's a risk of a leak that can cost people their lives."

Then he said he wanted the Israelis to keep the U.S. posted simultaneously as the action is taking place. A crucial nuance had to be resolved. "When is it simultaneous, Mr. President? To me, simultaneous means that the forces have completed their mission, they're in the air, the helicopters have departed Lebanese territory, and they're about to land safely in Israel. That would be a simultaneous communication." And, I believed that helped establish some important groundrules going forward. I could see the conversation was coming to a close. Perhaps some progress had been made on future ground rules, but the Bush-Shamir relationship had taken another clear step backward.

"Nothing is going to persuade me that it's not kidnapping," the president summed up, "It's kidnapping. I know that you don't want to hear me say it, but it is and I will continue to speak out against it. They didn't capture Obeid to bring him to trial, they kidnapped him for ransom and they intend to use him to exchange for other hostages. They didn't inform me in advance and I understand why and I wouldn't want to know. But why the hell didn't they tell me simultaneously? And I still want to know if they showed consideration for the consequences of their actions to the American hostages that are held in Lebanon beforehand."

The issue of Jerusalem entered the Bush-Shamir relationship in March 1990, and was never really cleared up. In the spring, President Bush was in California at Walter Annenberg's estate, meeting with the prime minister of Japan. At the press conference with the Japanese prime minister, the president committed a gaffe as to the status of Jerusalem.

In response to an unexpected question about the Middle East, he defined Jerusalem as technically being "occupied territory." He was not properly prepared to answer the question, as he expected to be talking about Japan. When the journalist asked the question, Bush stated what has been official U.S. policy since 1967. It may be official, but it is never spoken—certainly never by the president of the

United States. The "public" formulation is that Jerusalem should remain united, and it should continue to be open to people of all religions. One can say its sovereignty should be determined later. U.S. policy is also clear that the U.S. embassy in Israel won't be moved from Tel Aviv until the final status of Jerusalem is established within the framework of a peace treaty.

Why then is the policy of Jerusalem being occupied territory "on the books?" Here was the American position regarding Jerusalem: We do not want to recognize the annexation of East Jerusalem. We do not recognize that any of the "neighborhoods" in Jerusalem are simply neighborhoods. The United States considers these areas settlements on occupied territory. Therefore you can't spend American foreign aid dollars to support them. Technically U.S. diplomats don't go to East Jerusalem, even though there's a consulate over there. Predictably, the comment in California set off a hew and cry in the Jewish community in Israel and in the U.S. When I next met with the president, I told him he made a mistake that was politically unwise. Even though what he said was technically right, he would be better off getting the matter behind him. He wished he hadn't said it at all.

Prime Minster Shamir took Bush's comment on Jerusalem at face value, rather than as a speaking error. President Bush looked particularly clumsy because President Reagan had already pledged the U.S. would move its embassy to Jerusalem, even though that never came to pass. Referencing East Jerusalem as occupied territory worsened the relationship even further. Shamir's confidence in Bush was eroded, and it was not very high to begin with.

A complex maze of factors determined the relationship between George Bush and Yitzhak Shamir between the years 1989 and 1992. The three primary elements were Israeli settlements in the occupied territories of the West Bank and Gaza, U.S. loan guarantees, and the 1991 Gulf War. Understating the intricacies of these elements and their interconnection, while essential to grasping the relationship between Bush and Shamir, is also a lengthy digression that is not directly on the topic of character, courage, and leadership in the defining moments of life. For that reason, I have included this aspect of the Bush-Shamir relationship as an appendix titled: "Settlements, Loan Guarantees and the 1991 Gulf War." While I think readers may learn valuable background from this more extended discussion, the main points of that appendix are summarized in the following paragraphs.

Even back in 1979, George Bush felt settlements on the West Bank and in Gaza were an obstacle to peace. In 1989, Israel faced a dramatic wave of immigration from Eastern Europe. In that same year, the Israelis were pressing for loan guarantees from the United States that would earn the country a financial advantage on the international bond market. George Bush, now president, opposed the guarantees, viewing them as indirect financing of settlement expansion. The American Jewish community was sympathetic to Israel on the loan guarantee matter and felt it had enough support in Congress to pressure the president to implement the loan guarantees without Israel having to make concessions on settlements.

In August 1990, Iraq invaded Kuwait. The U.S. responded decisively. Its response was not just aimed at Iraq's illegal, imperialistic, and unprovoked invasion of Kuwait. It was also about oil and the United States' strategic reliance on the oil reserves of the Persian Gulf. As one U.S. senator put it, "If they grew bananas in Kuwait, do you think we would have been in Kuwait? If they grew bananas in the Persian Gulf region, would we have sent 500,000 kids to free Kuwait?"

To build an effective coalition against Iraq, the United States needed to rally support among friendly Arab nations. Settlements and loan guarantees to Israel were an obstacle to the Arabs. The Bush administration persuaded Israel to postpone the discussion of loan guarantees until after the imminent hostilities with Iraq were concluded. In December 1990, through a frank and decisive meeting, President Bush convinced Prime Minister Shamir that the United States and the Coalition were going to war against Iraq. If Israel involved itself preemptively, President Bush explained, it could jeopardize the very groundwork of the Coalition. He said that the U.S. military would immediately identify and destroy Iraqi Scud missile launchers and that there was no need for a preemptive strike by Israel against Iraq and would provide Israel with additional Patriot anti-missiles for its own defense. The prime minister gave the president his word that Israel would not make such a strike. Then the president requested that Israel not retaliate if some conventional Scud attacks occurred. While the prime minister had rejected such a suggestion out of hand in the past, he now agreed to reconsider his position. This was a defining moment in U.S.–Israeli relations and was of fundamental importance in the U.S. being able to create a broad-based Coalition against Iraq.

The Coalition launched the 1991 Gulf War on January 16, 1991. Among the earliest Coalition actions were airstrikes against Scud launchers in western Iraq. During the war, Iraq launched Scud missiles with conventional warheads into Tel Aviv and the Israelis did not retaliate. Prime Minister Shamir exercised strong leadership in restraining Israel from retaliating. As a result of some forty Scud missiles attacks, five Israelis died, a few more were injured, and property damage was inflicted. When the war ended, the entire geo-political landscape of the Middle East had changed compared with 1991. Iraq was no longer a military threat in the Middle East, and the Soviet Union was in the process of self-destructing. George Bush and the United States felt that Israel owed the U.S. and the Coalition a debt of gratitude for bringing about these changes as well as for the American lives lost in the 1991 Gulf War. Israel felt differently. It believed that the United States owed Israel gratitude for not retaliating when attacked by Iraq and for not pressing the U.S. on the loan guarantee issue. As the Israelis saw it, it was time for the U.S. to recognize Israel's restraint through approving the loan guarantees.

The administration just wanted the matter of loan guarantees to go away. Secretary of State Baker's Middle East objective was to lay the groundwork for the next Middle East peace conference. In July 1991, I visited with Prime Minister Shamir in Israel. He believed that the Americans were siding with the Arabs and that this would undermine bilateral negotiations. Shamir told me that the Camp David approach worked because both sides met without preconditions and they negotiated. He thought the Arabs would bide their time and wait for the Americans to impose their land-for-peace bias on Israel. Shamir basically told me he *personally* wouldn't and couldn't give up an inch of land. He didn't think Israel should give up an inch, **but** Israel is a democracy. You don't know who is going to be the next prime minister, he said. You don't know who is going to be sitting at the negotiating table, because you don't know how long this conflict could last. We've been at war for forty some years, the negotiations could go on for another ten, fifteen, twenty years. Get it started, he felt. Get the process underway and give it a chance. Prime Minister Shamir felt that he could sell his point of view to the Arabs. He believed a bilateral, direct process would ultimately prevail. But, he knew he couldn't control his longevity in office.

The administration was able to persuade Shamir to again postpone addressing the issue of loan guarantees. The Madrid Conference ultimately convened, but the meeting was brief. Those peace discussions were supplanted by behind-the-scenes negotiations later in Oslo. Madrid resulted in face-to-face negotiations between the Arabs and Israel for the first time since Camp David. George Bush said there would be no imposed settlement, that the participants would have to work out the solution themselves. In the end, the Madrid Conference lasted three days. On October 31, 1991, Yitzhak Shamir made Israel's opening statement at the conference.

After the Madrid Conference, the following resulted:

1. The loan guarantee issue was never resolved during Shamir's tenure.
2. Shamir was ousted from office seven months later largely because of his apparent openness to negotiate.
3. The Madrid Conference *did* lead to some Arab state and superpower recognition (e.g., China) of Israel, which had positive economic gains.

4. The open forum of the Madrid Conference was not continued. It was replaced by the secret negotiations in Oslo and a fruitless sidetracking of the peace process fixated on Yasser Arafat and the PLO.

The American Jewish community's call for loan guarantees ultimately prevailed. The loan guarantees were approved, but that took place after Israel's voters had ousted Shamir from office and he was replaced by Yitzhak Rabin. Shamir's willingness to participate in the Madrid Conference may have added to his defeat at the polls. George Bush's dogged opposition to the loan guarantees over a period of years tarnished his image within the American Jewish community. In the end, the loan guarantees themselves proved to be of negligible value.

SOME KEY THINGS I LEARNED FROM GEORGE BUSH'S RELATIONSHIP WITH YITZHAK SHAMIR ARE:

You have not effectively communicated until the other party shows they have understood what you intended to say.

All of us have different filters. In every important instance, ask people to please play back what they thought they heard. Significant differences in understanding can happen in the same home, just as easily as across oceans.

A great leader subordinates his personal feelings to his organization's interest and goals.

Bush separated his feelings about Shamir from his feelings for Israel. The American-Israeli relationship was maintained despite the mutual dislike and mistrust between Bush and Shamir. There was never a threat to withhold or cut financial aid, halt the flow of military equipment, or to slow down the many bilateral activities to strengthen strategic cooperation between Israel and the U.S.

Don't jeopardize a strategic partnership for less than an existential threat.

Loan guarantees became a huge emotional issue. In retrospect, Israel's pursuit of them was sheer nonsense. To my knowledge, the loan guarantees have never delivered any significant economic benefit to Israel. Even at the time they were sought, the gains of having the loan guarantees would have been trivial and on a relative basis did not make sense.

Even in the most strained relationships, it is possible to generate trust in crisis.

Yitzhak Shamir and George Bush truly mistrusted each other. Their feelings about each other as people never changed and their emotions were so strong they could have paralyzed the ability of the United States and Israel to act. Nonetheless, each had an unwavering dedication to the well-being of their respective nations. Once this was understood, it was possible to transcend personal feelings.

When President Bush convinced Shamir that the U.S. and the Coalition were going to war against Iraq, the two individuals arrived at an understanding regarding Israel's posture on foregoing an Israeli preemptive attack on Iraqi missile launchers. This breakthrough was of fundamental importance in creating the necessary coalition against Iraq and was also a dramatic, defining moment in the relationship of the two countries.

Visionary Leadership

To grasp and hold a vision, that is the very essence of successful leadership.

— Ronald Reagan

Vision is the art of seeing what is invisible to others.

—Jonathan Swift

No arsenal, or no weapon in the arsenals of the world, is so formidable as the will and moral courage of free men and women. It is a weapon our adversaries in today's world do not have.

—Ronald Reagan

History teaches that wars begin when governments believe the price of aggression is cheap.

—Ronald Reagan

Ronald Reagan

Projecting Strength and the Power of Focus

*My first real encounter with Ronald Reagan came at a
Young Presidents Organization "university" in Acapulco
in 1975. One of the programs was designed to give young
business leaders access and exposure to the major decision
makers in business and public life. Reagan was challenging
Gerald Ford, the incumbent president from his own party,
for the nomination. Reagan appeared before a panel of YPO
members. The session was organized in the style of* Meet
the Press. *I was one of the three interviewers, and you
could classify me as a hostile one. At this point I didn't know
Bush or Reagan, and I was supporting Ford. Based on what
I knew of Reagan from the media, my regard for him wasn't
high. I was out to give Ronald Reagan a bruising. The first
question I asked Reagan was, "What assumptions do you
make about the nature of man?" His answer danced around
the question. In fact it was a non-answer. Still, the question-
ing moved along to the other two interviewers and then
circled back to me. Then I said, "Governor, I'm not sure I
understood your answer to my first question." Reagan shot
back, "Well that's fine, because I know I didn't understand
your question." The crowd roared with laughter. He killed
me on the spot and took the sting out of all the subsequent
questions I asked him. That was the first lesson I learned
from Ronald Reagan: the power of humor.*

Ronald Reagan had been a Chicago Cubs sportscaster and Hollywood actor. He had been a Roosevelt Democrat. Ultimately, Reagan redefined the important issues for the well-being of the nation he loved so deeply. It took years of preparation for Reagan to develop his beliefs and principles of leadership, linking courage, faith in freedom, faith in his own people, and our ability to triumph over Soviet totalitarianism.

In 1976 I was supporting President Ford's reelection bid and I was the president's guest in his box at the Republican National Convention in the Kemper Arena in Kansas City. A stranger was seated next to me. Ronald Reagan's name was placed into nomination and the arena erupted into thunderous applause and shouts.

After twenty minutes of irrepressible applause, I turned to the stranger next to me and said "Enough is enough!" He turned to me and said, "Young man, that's the trouble with you Americans. You don't really appreciate democracy. Let me tell you who I am and why I'm here. My name is Ardeshir Zahedi and I'm the Iranian Ambassador to the United States. I have just flown to Kansas City from Geneva, Switzerland. Despite the fact I have terrible back pain, I flew all night across the Atlantic lying on the floor of my private plane just to come to this convention. I brought my entire staff. Look up at the highest rafter and you will see them," he continued, pointing to his people. "I brought them here so they could see democracy in action. Look at what's going on down there?! Where else in the world could a sitting president of a country—President Nixon—be unseated *without a gun being fired*? Where else could a sitting non-elected vice president, Gerald Ford, succeed the president *without a gun being fired*? And now, the sitting non-elected president is being challenged on the floor by a California governor who wants to deny him the right to be the nominee of that party *without a gun being fired*. That's democracy! I'm here to study it and to learn from that experience and to hope that someday we can bring that back to Iran." Zahedi's comment made a deep impact on me. Unfortunately the rise of the Ayatollah Khomeni denied that dream to the Iranian people.

From 1979 forward, as I have described, I was an active supporter of George Bush as candidate for the Republican Party's nomination for the presidency of the United States. I played a leadership role as both a policy advisor and a fund-raiser for Bush in the campaign. Once again Ronald Reagan was the adversary. When Reagan won the nomination, I threw in the towel. Then, Reagan offered Bush the vice presidential slot. Bush accepted, and I was suddenly back in action. In fact, the stakes had become far more serious because Reagan had real prospects of winning.

How did the Jewish community regard Ronald Reagan in 1980? First, I would emphasize that looking back at Reagan today is to view him through a colored glass. In retrospect—and with the possible exception of Bitburg, when he could have been better informed— President Reagan left office in January 1989, with a sterling reputation among the Jewish community. In 1980, however, there was a great deal of skepticism about Reagan. True there was Jewish support for Reagan, but it was mostly a vote *against* Carter rather than a vote *for* Reagan. In 1980, Jews both backed Reagan *and* were mistrustful of him. He got 42 percent of the Jewish vote.

Dick Allen, Reagan's first national security adviser, was, and remains, a close friend of mine. (As I have commented, Dick was the key in arranging the Avital Sharansky meeting in the Oval Office with Reagan.) I want to emphasize that the following is really Dick's story. I can only vouch for it's accuracy and emphasize that it's so instructive I can't resist including it in this book. Dick was given the task of preparing the transition on national security matters before Ronald Reagan took office in January 1981. In a discussion we once had, Dick recalled the enormous frustrations he felt at the time. He couldn't get through to Reagan, who was on his ranch near Santa Barbara. Dick couldn't get him to focus on national security issues for two minutes over the phone. Dick was very concerned. These matters of national security had to be dealt with before the inauguration. It was terribly challenging for Dick. Until he saw the president-elect in person, matters couldn't go forward. These decisions were too important for Dick to make in Reagan's stead. Finally, Reagan called him out to the ranch. Dick had been working twenty-hour days, seven days a week. His eyes were red. He looked exhausted.

Reagan had been out riding horses and cutting brush. He looked like a million bucks. When they sat down to chat, a tanned and relaxed Reagan asked, "Dick, what would you like to talk about?"

"First of all, Governor, we have to set up a schedule to go over these issues. They just keep building up. And—" Dick said as he handed Reagan a stack of papers, reports and proposals.

"Wait a minute," Reagan cut him off, paused and leaned back, "Let me tell you something, Dick. It's important that I *be* healthy and that I *look* healthy when I'm inaugurated on January 20. The people have to look at me and feel comfortable that I have the vitality, the energy, and the health to handle this job. I have to *feel* exactly that way too. It's been a tough campaign. So, I'm renewing myself. Secondly, the most important thing I have to work on is my inaugural speech. In it, I have to outline my vision for this country and the priorities of my administration. These are the priorities against which I expect to be judged by history and by my peers. Now, you just hold on to all this stuff. We'll deal with it in good time."

With that, Reagan took the huge mound of paper and handed it back to Dick. On inauguration day, Reagan did exactly what he said he would do. His instincts were a hundred percent right. For him to deliver that speech looking tired and exhausted would have been catastrophic. Delivering it in the way he did set the agenda for one of the most successful presidencies in American history. Ronald Reagan recognized the importance of projecting himself as the President of the United States of America. He successfully transitioned from having been a Hollywood figure, a governor, and a campaigner. President Reagan seized the defining moment of his inauguration to transform the American agenda.

Right after the inauguration, Dick went to see President Reagan to organize the presidential briefing program on national security. Dick entered the president's working office and said, "Mr. President, we'll start our formal security and intelligence briefings tomorrow morning at 8 A.M. That will be the daily schedule."

"That's very nice, Dick," Reagan said, "I hope you enjoy being there, because I won't be available until nine." Reagan had recruited a host of very bright and competent people to whom he would delegate. That's exactly what he intended to do while he focused on his very limited list of priorities. In those things he really cared about, Reagan controlled the decision making.

I knew and worked with five sitting presidents—Ford, Carter, Reagan, Bush, and Clinton. I learned from all of them, but I learned the most about leadership from Ronald Reagan. Reagan's belief in the checks and balances of our constitutional government acknowledged the reality of Evil and evil people. Reagan coupled an understanding of global differences with a firm belief in America. Jimmy Carter whined about the hypocrisy of American values, especially abroad. Reagan's message was: What a great country! What a great people! He took the country off psychological life support. He was determined to rekindle faith of Americans in America. The destiny of America was to preserve and extend freedom in the World. That was in his soul when he came to office. He did not acquire that conviction after he was elected. American presidents seldom acquire their convictions in office. They are too busy manning the controls. The weak presidents come with poorly formulated or ill-founded convictions. Reagan's were clear and cast in stone.

Peace through strength was a core value for Reagan. He felt that every war ever fought was waged because one side thought they were stronger than the other and took advantage of perceived weakness to attack. He was going to drive up the cost for the Soviets to compete with America to the point where they would say, "Enough!" Reagan saw the Strategic Defense Initiative as a doable and necessary undertaking. He was at variance with a lot of people who were afraid that merely going down that road would provoke a third world war. His message to the Soviet Union was: We'll outspend you in national security! And by the way, we can afford it and you can't.

Contrary to a commonly held opinion, Ronald Reagan was highly intelligent and extremely knowledgeable about the issues that he cared about. He had an underlying faith and trust in the readiness and willingness of the American people to sacrifice in order to protect their freedom. Reagan had a compelling vision of how to extend freedom in the world. He had the conviction that America was challenged by an Evil Empire. He walked away from the summit table with Gorbachev at Reykjavik to prove that he would not accept conciliation with a foundering Soviet Union. It wasn't about détente, it was about victory. This was not about a compromising arrangement where we both co-exist. The other system had to go. And, it did.

One evening, I was President Reagan's guest at a private White House dinner. He was a most gracious, charming, and witty dinner companion. His positive, optimistic, outgoing nature was infectious. He had great stories and he told them well. If I met Ronald Reagan once, I met him twenty times. On the twentieth visit, he *still* didn't remember who I was. This was long before the ravages of Alzheimer's. Not being recognized didn't bother me in the slightest. It's just that Reagan's mind wasn't programmed in that way. He was totally focused on his goals, the foremost of which was securing the future of an America he loved deeply. He also cherished Israel. Richard Nixon told Max Fisher that Ronald Reagan had the highest level of commitment to the State of Israel of any U.S. president.

Ronald Reagan was also determined to reignite economic growth. And, he lit a fireball in the economy. It wasn't that he caused this to happen. He simply directed his people to unfetter the marketplace, and the free market did the rest on its own. He was unhappy with the air traffic controllers when they struck. But, this was not—as has been often contended—first and foremost an economic policy issue for Reagan. Transportation Secretary Drew Lewis recommended that the controllers be fired outright. The issue wasn't if their union, PATCO, was right or wrong. It was if those strikers had the right to put the nation at peril. President Reagan said they didn't. Everyone expected chaos overnight. It didn't happen. The president wouldn't have even gone into the air controllers' matter if it hadn't had national security implications.

Without a doubt, I learned more about leadership from Ronald Reagan than any other leader with whom I have had the pleasure and honor of working.

SOME KEY THINGS I LEARNED FROM RONALD REAGAN ARE:

Leaders need clarity of vision.

Know where you want to go. Know what critical few results you want to accomplish and against which you want to be judged in advancing toward your vision.

Courageous leadership has the tenacity to determine if and when a difference will be made.

Ronald Reagan's passion was to defeat the most significant threat to world freedom at that time, which was totalitarian Communism. Unlike Nixon and Kissinger, Reagan didn't see détente, which he considered an accommodation with Evil, as the best attainable outcome for U.S. foreign policy. Reagan's defining moment, in my opinion, was his courageous leadership in not backing down at the Reykjavik Summit with Gorbachev in 1986. Reagan's objective was to **win.** Which he did, and the world is better for it. If you believe that one person can make a difference, you will take risks. Even when odds are they won't pan out, there are good reasons to take risks. Take them for the sake of the causes of credibility and of integrity.

Prioritize and focus.

Internalize your vision and your goals before you embark on a new role or course of action. You won't have time to develop one while you are on the job. Leaders need to build a strong team and to empower its members. You'll never get everything done that you want to, so decide early what critical few goals you want to achieve. Don't let your ego lure you into believing you are indispensable in every initiative you need done.

Radiate hope and optimism.

Hope and optimism are magnetic traits that attract people to your orbit. They also energize people needed to achieve the agenda you are advancing for them. No matter how dire things might be painted to be, the glass is always half full, not half empty.

How you look and feel *does* matter.

Reagan was a leader who understood public relations. Because of his age, he was being judged by his appearance, he needed to project energy, strength, and presence. A leader needs to be healthy, and to appear to be healthy, to gain confidence from supporters. This is especially so for someone entering a new role when they are older or recovering from recent illnesses—situations where observers might doubt the person's stamina or energy. Paying attention to how you look and feel is not just public relations, it's the essence of managing personal energy, and it is crucial.

Build a strong team—delegate and empower.

Reagan emphasized talent not credit. "It's amazing how much you can get done when you don't worry about who gets credit." This sign originally attributed to Harry Truman was also displayed on

Reagan's desk and a fixture of his philosophy. It was the mentality that allowed so many things to be accomplished in the Reagan administration. This philosophy never has traction unless the leader sets the tone. There is perhaps no better example of a strong, gifted team player in the Reagan Administration than Secretary of State George Shultz. With his multiple Cabinet roles over the years and remarkable academic and business experience, Shultz was a towering figure. Henry Kissinger has said that Shultz was the best qualified person in the country to be the president of the United States.

Your identity should come from within.

Your sense of self-worth should come from within. You are not the jobs you fill. You are who you are inside. Reagan never viewed himself as President of the United States. He was temporarily entrusted with the responsibilities of the presidency. He showed the office of the president tremendous respect. He never walked into the Oval Office without a coat and tie. Reagan made a definite and constant distinction between himself and the role that he played. He was not the president. He was Ronald Reagan. He never took press attacks on the president personally, that is why he was called the Teflon president. The only attacks that troubled him were assaults on his wife, Nancy. He was as dedicated to her as she was to him.

Withdraw with grace.

When his term of office was over, Ronald Reagan receded from the landscape with unimaginable grace. He went back to chopping wood, riding his horse into the sunset, and enjoying life with Nancy. With uncanny skill, Reagan could distinguish between the purposeful achievement of his legacy as president, a role that he left behind him, and being the son of an Irish immigrant shoe salesman who had the great good fortune to be an American citizen.

Leaders Lead!

In my opinion, Ronald Reagan was not a *good* president. He was a **great** president and he accelerated the collapse of the former Soviet Union. Reagan made the world a better and safer place in a dramatic way. He was able to do so because he believed in the American people, in liberty, and in the power of the American way of life. The stakes were high. The risks were enormous. The costs of being wrong—horrendous. Ronald Reagan had the character and courage to act on his beliefs and to accept the risk of failure.

Communicate, communicate, communicate!

Epilogue

Write Your Own Obituary!

Ozymandias
—Percy Bysshe Shelley (1792–1822)

I met a traveller from an antique land,
Who said—"Two vast and trunkless legs of stone
Stand in the desert.... Near them, on the sand,
Half sunk a shattered visage lies, whose frown,
And wrinkled lip, and sneer of cold command,
Tell that its sculptor well those passions read
Which yet survive, stamped on those lifeless things,
The hand that mocked them, and the heart that fed;
And on the pedestal, these words appear:
'My name is Ozymandias, King of Kings,
Look on my Works, ye Mighty, and despair!'
Nothing beside remains. Round the decay
Of that colossal Wreck, boundless and bare
The lone and level sands stretch far away."

Alfred Nobel is esteemed today as the benefactor of the Nobel Prizes.
Most of his life, Nobel was an armaments engineer and chemist.
He invented dynamite in 1866, when he was still in his early thirties.
Later he formulated smokeless gunpowder. Then he founded a sprawling and diversified armaments business. Nobel became immensely wealthy.

Alfred Nobel had a brother named Ludwig. Ludwig was an enormous financial success in his own right. A Swedish immigrant to Russia, he built the foundations of the Russian oil industry and became known as the Oil King of Baku. According to historian Daniel Yergin in his book *The Prize,* Ludwig "died of a heart attack while vacationing on the French Riviera. Some of the European newspapers confused the Nobel brothers and instead reported the death of Alfred. Reading his own premature obituaries, Alfred was distressed to find himself condemned as a munitions maker, the 'dynamite king,' a merchant of death who made a huge fortune by finding news ways to maim and kill. He brooded over these obituaries and their condemnations, and eventually rewrote his will, leaving his money for the establishment of the prizes..."

Alfred did not live a particularly long life. He died in his early sixties, but he *did* confront a defining moment before his end which motivated him to choose a new pathway. He had the character and courage to undertake a dramatic transition in the purpose of his life. Not that what he had done earlier was intrinsically evil—for example, dynamite stabilized the use of nitroglycerin and probably saved the lives of millions of miners. Nonetheless, Alfred Nobel was determined to be remembered for leadership that would make a positive difference to the human experience: The Nobel Prizes.

Most of us, I am convinced, have a deep-seated conviction that we want our lives to make a difference. Most of us also have an inkling of the contribution we *could* make, if we only energized the passion dormant in our souls and asserted the leadership to do it. Some of us have had both the determination and the good fortune to discover and follow that passion—be it as a surgeon or a soldier, a politician or a parent, a musician or a mathematics professor. For the rest of us, passion is something we postpone. Most people—it is sad to say— live unfulfilled lives. Unfulfilled, yet seemingly without a moment to spare, because they don't grasp and accept the priorities of living. If you don't have a passion in life, this book will probably not have awakened it. Nor can it provide you with a passion. *No one can deliver you with a ready-made passion, no matter what they claim.* Discovering your passion and the pathway to realizing it is something only you can do.

For those of you who are postponing pursuing the passion in your life, I have a question for you: *Have you checked your contract lately?* You know, the contract that governs the terms of your life. Most people confidently believe they can postpone the big issues in their life until some time in the future. You have a deal, you may believe. You can delay living your passion and fulfilling your life until you've made your bundle or until the kids are through college or until whatever milestone you name. Well, if you've glanced at your contract recently, you'll note that you are **not** in control of the timing. The termination date is ominously blank. Never forget that the actuarial tables on life expectancy are averages.

Alfred Nobel may have been motivated by getting his obituary or his tombstone right. That fueled his drive to make a difference. If that motivation helps, use it. I have. But, what's really important? It's not being remembered. It's making a difference.

One of the most extraordinary people I have ever known is my friend Les Wexner, founder and CEO of Limited Brands, which operates blockbuster businesses like Victoria's Secret. One day about twenty-five years ago, Les had the beginning of an epiphany. He had bought a home in Vail, Colorado. At the time, Les was about forty, a multimillionaire bachelor who didn't even ski—yet. He ended up going to Vail as often in the summer as in the winters. He found it a good place to reflect and plan. The second or third summer he was there, Les decided he was going to do something memorable, at least for him. He was going to climb Vail Mountain, which means going from an altitude of 8,000 feet to 12,000 feet. To get in shape, he did runs of five to twelve miles for ten days.

On the day he decided to make his climb, Les was wearing a pair of shorts and a T-shirt. He didn't bother with a backpack or a water bottle or letting anyone know that he was doing this. He just parked his car and started scaling the mountain. When he got to about

10,000 feet, a sudden electrical storm brewed up. There was lightning, thunder, and sheets of rain. Les just figured he'd keep on chugging up the mountain. When he arrived at the peak, he was soaking wet and totally alone, but he felt the rush of victory. He said he felt just like Rocky on the steps of the Philadelphia Museum of Art. So Les started down the mountain and wondered how he would reward himself. Would he buy an ice cream cone or a beer?

Then a second thunderstorm struck—I call it the thunderstorm of the soul. Beer or ice cream? What was he thinking about?! He realized he had just danced with Death itself. What would have happened if he had been hit by lightning, or if he broken his ankle and been exposed to hypothermia? Les said it was the first time he ever really confronted his own mortality. His first thoughts were about the Limited. The business was doing very well, but it was still in its infancy, and people really depended on him as the driving force. That led to another thought. What would people say about him when he was gone? He wrestled with that idea for a couple of years.

Then another even more engaging realization enveloped him:

> What people say about you when you're gone doesn't matter much. What matters is what you say about yourself in the here and now. I wasn't happy. Yes, I had done a little community work. Still, when I was confronted with appraising what I would say about myself in the here and now, I wasn't happy. The business had grown very successfully. I made an enormous amount of money. I could have clearly retired at the age of forty and lived very comfortably. But I wasn't happy.

Les Wexner was resolving a defining moment in his life. Les decided that he did indeed believe in God. Les also decided that his local community in Columbus, Ohio, and Ohio State University were significant for him. He realized that the Jewish people and Israel were very important to him. This epiphany changed his priorities and his life. The rest is a personal history of involvement and leadership rarely matched in our time. When I began this book, I wrote about the courage and character of Avital Sharansky and recalled that great wisdom: "When you walk atop the mountain, you never see it." You see beyond it. Tackling your own mortality *in what you do today* may be the most empowering decision in your life. It can be *your* defining moment.

Your Obituary

This exercise may help you to find your passion, live your purpose, and make the world a better place:

> Assume you have just passed away. In less than a hundred words, write your own obituary. Be honest and be tough. Talk about what you dreamt of doing and never did.

> > Which defining moments did you face successfully and which did you fail to seize?

> > Did you achieve your dreams and goals? What are you most proud of achieving in your life to date?

> > What were the three most serious mistakes and what did you learn from them?

> Examine your life today:

> > What is your passion in life?

> > Are you following it? If not, why not?

> > What specific obstacles are standing in your way?

> > What sacrifices would you need to make to follow your passion and live your purpose?

> > Would it really be so painful to make them?

> > Would the pain be worth the gain?

Who—in the entire world—is living the life you would most like to live?

What do you most admire about this person?

How would you go about meeting and learning from him or her?

What would you ask this person?

Assume you are granted another thirty years to live.

How would you like your obituary to read then?

How will you have made the world a better place?

What attitudes, skills, networks, and opportunities will you require to make this different set of achievements possible?

How will you need to change your top three priorities in order for this second obituary to be written?

What benchmarks will you use to measure how well you are doing?

What does this exercise tell you about your greatest strengths and your greatest weaknesses?

Keep in mind what management guru Peter Drucker said about strengths and weaknesses: Too much time and energy are wasted trying to overcome our weaknesses as opposed to sharpening and leveraging our strengths.

Meier was a wise old Rabbi who lived in a little shtetl in the middle of the nineteenth century. There was a young boy called Beryl who heard about the wisdom of Meier but doubted he was as wise as his reputation suggested. The youngster decided to challenge the old man's wisdom. Beryl caught a live butterfly and brought it to Meier, hiding it behind his back.

"Old man," he asked, "what do I have in my hand?"

Immediately Meier said it was a butterfly.

"Is it alive or dead?" Beryl asked. If he says it's dead, the boy reasoned, I'll let it fly away. If he says it's alive, I'll crush it to death in my hand. In either case, Meier will be proven wrong.

"Beryl," Meier said, "you have the destiny of that butterfly in your hand. It's in your power to give it life and freedom or to crush and destroy it. What do you choose to do?"

The fate of the world is in each of our hands.

What do **you** choose to do?

APPENDIXES

Settlements, Loan Guarantees
and the 1991 Gulf War

EVEN BACK IN 1979, George Bush felt settlements on the West Bank and in Gaza were an obstacle to peace. He believed the issues of the West Bank and sovereignty over Jerusalem needed to be resolved within the framework of the existing U.N. Resolutions 242 and 338. At that time, Bush opposed an independent Palestinian state, but favored Israel ceding territory for peace within the framework of these two resolutions. He advocated direct, bilateral negotiations between Israel and the Arabs, leading to some sort of Palestinian entity in a confederation with Jordan. While he was president, George Bush did not change his position on an independent Palestinian state, although he ultimately accepted the concept. When President Clinton embraced the position of a two-state solution, George Bush did not publicly oppose it.

In 1989, loan guarantees were a pressing international issue for Prime Minister Yitzhak Shamir but not for President George Bush. The Soviet Union still existed. The Berlin Wall hadn't collapsed. There were tensions in the Gulf. Secretary of State James Baker was still trying to make progress in the Middle East, but this wasn't a front-burner matter. President Bush supported $3 billion in foreign aid grants to Israel because he believed it was essential for Israel to maintain its qualitative military edge against the combined military might in the belligerent Arab states. Simultaneously, he saw an ironclad linkage between loan guarantees and the financing of settlement expansion. He believed that these settlements jeopardized the peace process, and it was against U.S. national interest to encourage them. Bush wanted stability in the Middle East because it brought avoidance of war and assured U.S.

access to oil. He was more focused on doing the right thing that would be a lasting, crowning achievement for his legacy. The settlements issue and his relationship with Shamir were more of an irritant.

During 1989, the relationship between Bush and Shamir worsened after the Berlin Wall came down and democratization began to sweep across Eastern Europe. Suddenly there was a massive influx of immigration to Israel. In the eyes of the Likud government, the perfect home for the new immigrants was the West Bank. In 1990, prior to Desert Storm, the loan guarantees issue heated up as Israel began to pursue these guarantees aggressively. This backing would pledge that the U.S. government would pay both the principal and interest on $10 billion of bonds issued by the Israeli government if Israel defaulted on paying the bondholders. Israel had never defaulted on bonds in the past and didn't expect to in the future. However, having the U.S. guarantees would allow Israel to pay bondholders a lower rate of interest. President Bush was concerned that the loan guarantees would translate into de facto financing of the settlements in the occupied territories and would permanently undermine the peace process. In Bush's mind, that created a clear linkage between settlement expansion and U.S. loan guarantees.[1]

President Bush wouldn't change his position on loan guarantees absent a serious halt to Israel building settlements. In short, no loan guarantees. Shamir was absolutely adamant on the settlements issue, and refused to consider exchanging settlements and the land they were on for peace. Neither would he accept linking loan guarantees to a halt in building settlements. He viewed Bush as a threat to the position that he and Likud held with respect to settlements. As the tide of immigration to Israel swelled, there was growing support for the settlements among many members of the American Jewish community. They believed they could use Congressional pressure to force President Bush to grant the loan guarantees. The American Jewish community determined they had enough votes on Capitol Hill to secure Congressional approval of the loan guarantees.

*   *   *

It wasn't until December 1991, that the Soviet Union was officially dissolved, but it was already clear in mid-1990 that the Soviets would no longer be a decisive factor in the Middle East balance of power. Determined to reconfigure the region's internal Arab power structure on his own terms, Saddam struck. On August 2, 1990, Iraq invaded oil-rich Kuwait. Shamir raised the issues of loan guarantees in mid-1990 during mobilization of a U.N.-mandated Coalition of more than thirty nations to oppose Iraq. President Bush asked that the issue of loan guarantees be deferred until it could be focused on properly. He also felt the U.S. acceding to loan guarantees would disrupt building the Coalition against Iraq. The Israelis and the American Jewish leadership went along with Bush in the full belief that Congress would support the loan guarantees. But, they also knew it would be hard to put together the anti-Iraq Coalition. The loan guarantees would inevitably raise the high-profile matter of settlements and that could jeopardize the ability to put the Coalition together. For the present, creating and sustaining the Coalition against Iraq became the highest priority.

Israel was sizing up the impact of a potential war with Iraq on Israel. Before Desert Storm, Shamir doubted that Bush would go to war and destroy Iraq. In general, he did not trust Bush to go to war against the Arabs. Shamir didn't believe that Bush had the courage to do that. When Iraq invaded Kuwait, Shamir was concerned about Iraq also attacking Israel through Jordan. He feared Iraq might provoke a war with Israel, and he needed to defend the security of his nation. Leading up to the 1991 Gulf War, Saddam was sending out signals that he would be prepared to get out of Kuwait, if Israel exited the occupied territories. George Bush rejected that option absolutely, and the U.S. position was communicated to other Arab states.

In September 1990, Israeli Defense Minister Moshe Ahrens was in the U.S. to assess America's intentions in the Gulf. That's when Israel got its first cue to stay on the sidelines in the confrontation brewing between Iraq and the Coalition. National Security Adviser Brent Scowcroft told Ahrens that Israel should think twice about retaliating if attacked. If Israel retaliated, Scowcroft contended, this would play right into the hands of the Iraqis. Israel's military involvement would bring about the destruction of the Coalition, making it more, not less difficult, for the U.S. to deal with the threat from Iraq. Consider absorbing the blow, Scowcroft recommended. Ahrens was aghast. How could you even ask that of us? he demanded. How could you ask a friendly nation to absorb an attack and not defend itself? It's out of the question. Ahrens asked me if this was President Bush's thinking. "Misha," I told him, "this is the first time I have heard such a position. I'm shocked the same way you are. Let me find out more." I talked to President Bush, and he said that Scowcroft had acted independently. The president said he appreciated Ahrens' response and that the issue deserved to be discussed.

As to whether Israel should absorb the hit, I told President Bush it was an outrageous thing to ask. You couldn't ask Israel to compromise itself on the altar of building a coalition that's being created for the purpose of saving the ass of the Kuwaitis and the Saudis. You couldn't humiliate Israel in this way. When I met with the Israelis, I told them they had to decide for themselves whether that was something they could or could not do. "It's not for me, living in the safety of Columbus, Ohio, to tell you," I remember saying, "but I'm not detached about this issue on a personal level. I've got a daughter who is living in Jerusalem." When I went to Israel, I learned the entire cabinet was totally opposed to accepting the American request. They were absolutely united and adamant on this position, especially Sharon and Shamir—who was the most passionate opponent of restraint.

We were asking the Israelis to accommodate us in two ways: (1) If attacked, don't respond, and (2) Don't disrupt the atmospherics right now by raising the issue of loan guarantees. Concerned about Israel's ability to survive an Iraqi onslaught, Shamir asked to meet with Bush in December 1990 to gauge how serious, and to what extent the Americans were about using force. Five years earlier, no one would have believed America would have put a half million troops on the ground to defend Kuwait from Iraq. Their meeting persuaded Shamir that Bush was really going to make war, and just not go in and dabble. While the Americans were there to protect America's interest, Bush asserted he also wanted to serve the cause of peace in the Middle East by destroying the capacity of Iraq to make war. With the collapse of the Soviet Union, these two factors would change the equation on the Arab-Israel front to such an extent that there would be a new reality in the Middle East. I saw Shamir after he met with the President. Shamir looked me straight in the eye, and said he trusted the president to do what he said he will do. On December 28, 1990, Shamir promised Bush that Israel would not launch a preemptive strike against Iraq. In my opinion, this courageous decision on the part of Shamir was a defining moment in U.S.–Israeli relations.

Desert Storm began on January 16, 1991. We didn't go into Kuwait to save Kuwait. We did not go to war in the Persian Gulf, in my belief, because we wanted to enforce the principle of non-aggression or to maintain Kuwait's national sovereignty. We needed and need a stable, reliable access to the region's oil. International law may speak to the sovereign boundaries of nations. Sometimes they are upheld. Other times they're not. Kuwait was a case of Big Oil. Boundaries mattered. As one U.S. senator said, if they grew bananas in Kuwait, do you think we would have been in Kuwait? If they grew bananas in the Persian Gulf, would we have sent 500,000 kids to free Kuwait? Brent Scowcroft holds a different view. "We were trying to build a new world order following the collapse of the Soviet Union," he has told me, "We were trying to set up rules that would outlaw unprovoked aggression by one nation state against another." There is probably truth to both positions.

During the war, Iraq launched Scuds with conventional warheads into Tel Aviv, and the Israelis did not retaliate.[2] Shamir reined in Israel. When I met with him in June 1990, he had been the most outspoken opponent of America's suggestion. When the War began less than a year later, he persuaded the Israeli Cabinet that Israel should do nothing to destroy the Coalition. And, Shamir held absolutely true to his word. The important consequence of the 1991 Gulf War in terms of the Bush-Shamir relationship was Shamir's willingness to reverse positions and support Bush. Shamir's courageous leadership recognized that the overarching concern for Israel was not the Scuds but the Coalition's success in destroying Iraq's capacity to make war. That achievement would create a huge change in the Mideast's geopolitical landscape. The question remained: Would it provide the basis for a substantive turnaround in Bush/Shamir relations?

What were the consequences of Israeli non-retaliation? Absorbing forty some Scuds that killed five people, injured a few others, and inflicted some property damage. In every war Israel has ever fought, the casualties were very high, and they would have been higher if Israel had joined the fray with Iraq. The Americans believed that Israel had gained enormously from a more stable and peaceful Middle East as a consequence of Desert Storm. The Labor opposition—Shimon Peres and Yitzhak Rabin—as well as Shamir and Sharon knew that Israel had benefited from Iraq's offensive capability being destroyed. They assumed that the Americans were intent on cleaning up the Iraq threat posed by weapons of mass destruction (WMDs). They expected the U.S. would enforce the U.N. resolution inspections, and the cause of peace in the region would be served and the avoidance of war would be very high. They felt that a whole new era had begun.

At the same time, the Israelis in general believed that they had done the Americans two favors: incurring the personal pain and losses from the Scud attacks, and putting off the loan guarantees. The prospect of hundreds of thousands of Jews either coming or potentially coming out of the former Soviet Union raised the urgency of the loan guarantees to the Israelis. The humanitarian need to absorb these immigrants was great, and Israel believed that the loan guarantees were fundamental to providing the necessary financial support.

Immediately following the successful completion of the Desert Storm operation, Moshe Ahrens came to the U.S., and met with all the top officials. He heard the American position: American kids were sent to war and many died. We absorbed the costs, together with our Coalition allies, of breaking and destroying the offensive capability of Iraq, driving Iraq out of Kuwait, and stabilizing the Gulf. While it was not America's motivation, a very obvious consequence of our action was a greater security and stability for the people of Israel and, for the first time, a lesser likelihood of war and the possibility of peace. The

U.S. was looking for gratitude. It expected the Israelis to appreciate what the Americans had done and the costs incurred, but the Israeli attitude was very different.

When the short-lived ground war in Kuwait ended victoriously with a ceasefire on February 27, 1991, Prime Minister Shamir believed it was payoff time to reward the Israelis for their restraint during the conflict. Israel calculated the unrecoverable economic losses of the war—including disruption of tourism—to be about $6.5 billion. It renewed its request for loan guarantees, reasoning that this was not a linkage issue tied to settlement expansion. This was a matter of humanitarian support for an influx of immigrants. Israel reasoned the Americans had just forgiven something like $6 billion worth of outstanding Egyptian debt. And, the Egyptian role in the 1991 Gulf War was a token gesture, although hugely important on a diplomatic scale as seen by the White House. On May 5, Zalman Shoval, Israel's ambassador to the U.S., publicly reasserted Israel's stance that it would be seeking $10 billion in loan guarantees from the U.S..

Rather than being a reward for supporting the Coalition in the 1991 Gulf War, the White House wanted the matter of loan guarantees just to go away. Their focus was on bringing about the next step in the peace process—what was to become the Madrid Peace Conference. President Bush wanted to open the door to bilateral negotiations between Israel and the Arabs with the U.S. acting as an evenhanded broker. Bush felt if the Israelis read the loan guarantees as a license to settle and for the U.S. to finance more settlements on the West Bank, the peace process would be poisoned.

President Bush and Secretary of State Baker had created a goal of launching a peace process that would build on the peace agreement already reached between Israel and Egypt. Baker started his shuttle diplomacy to the Middle East in the spring of 1991 to lay the groundwork of the next Middle East peace conference. These negotiations would bring together Israel and the remaining Arab countries—Jordan, Lebanon, Syria and the Palestinians. The PLO would not sit at the table, but be part of a joint Palestinian-Jordanian delegation. The U.S. and the Soviet Union would attend as sponsors.

On July 5, 1991, during a visit to Israel, Prime Minister Shamir and I talked about loan guarantees, settlements, and the peace process. In his view, the American contention of "linkage" sent the wrong signal. He believed that the Americans were siding with the Arabs and that this would undermine bilateral negotiations. Shamir told me that the Camp David approach worked because both sides met without preconditions and they negotiated.

Shamir wanted the U.S. just to be an honest broker, and not to impose a viewpoint. By advancing land for peace, Shamir thought that the U.S. had adopted the Arab position and lessened the Arab motivation to negotiate with an open mind. He thought the Arabs would bide their time and wait for the Americans to impose their land-for-peace bias on Israel. But, Shamir knew he was speaking only for himself. He said he didn't know who the prime minister would be representing Israel at further Middle East peace negotiations, nor how long they would take, but that he—Shamir—was ready to enter the process. In the search for peace, he would risk an outcome other than the one he wanted.

This July 5th encounter with Prime Minister Shamir was the most profound single meeting that I ever had with an Israeli head of state. Shamir basically told me he *personally* wouldn't and couldn't give up an inch of land. He didn't think Israel should give up an inch, **but** Israel is a democracy. You don't know who is going to be the next prime minister, he said. You don't know who is going to be sitting at the negotiating table, because you don't know how long this conflict could last. We've been at war for forty some years, the negotiations could go on for another ten, fifteen, twenty years. Get it started, he felt. Get the process underway and give it a chance. Prime Minister Shamir felt that he could sell his point of view to the Arabs. He believed a bilateral, direct process would ultimately prevail. But, he knew he couldn't control his longevity in office.

During the July 5 meeting, Shamir asked me: "Gordy, is the U.S. intending to expel Israel from the Territories? I'm very worried about

U.S. intentions. We're back to this loan guarantee issue. A freeze on settlements is being linked to Israel getting loan guarantees." Israeli intelligence had told him: The U.S. had committed to the Arabs that the U.S. would side with the Arabs to force Israel to the bargaining table, to push Israel out of the West Bank Territories, and to compel Israel to accept an independent Palestinian state. Shamir wouldn't support these steps because he believed it put Israel's future security at risk. The Americans were, Shamir concluded, prematurely focused on a final outcome, rather than keeping true to the spirit of Camp David, which called for confidence to be built over time.

Prime Minister Shamir's amazing openness on long-term peace negotiation strategy was matched by his obstinacy in confronting President Bush on the linkage question. Shamir told me he knew there was sufficient support in the Congress to override the president's will. Through domestic pressure in the U.S., Israel would be able to get the loan guarantees without having to make a concession on settlements. I told the prime minister that I thought he was getting bad information.

A confrontation was brewing. On July 1, President Bush had declared, "We're [the U.S.] not giving one inch on the settlements question." The very next day Housing Minister Ariel Sharon announced that Israel would continue settlement expansion. On July 19, five Arab nations—Saudi Arabia, Egypt, Jordan, Lebanon, and Syria—publicly agreed to the U.S. peace conference proposal. In the latter part of August, Secretary of State James Baker was about to return from a vacation in Wyoming, and to plunge back into his drive for a new Middle East peace conference. Bush and Brent Scowcroft supported Baker's initiative but feared that Israel and the U.S. would be on a confrontation course over settlements and loan guarantees. This would be a no-win situation for everyone.

On Saturday, August 31, I flew to Kennebunkport, Maine, to meet with the president and Scowcroft to discuss the issue of loan guarantees in the context of the peace process. In a meeting on Sunday, I emphasized the key elements of Shamir's position: The peace process will have a life of its own, Israel is a democracy, and no one can predict who will conclude the negotiation nor how. I told the president that I was now persuaded that Shamir had a genuine desire to pursue peace. At the same time, I said, "Publicly he's not going to give one inch and that's equally understandable." The president was surprised, and positively inclined toward the broad-gauged attitude Shamir was taking toward achieving peace. I cautioned President Bush that the appearance of pressure on Israel regarding the settlements would now set the tone for what could happen at a peace conference. It could create a siege mentality in Israel, and move Israel further to the right, and a unique opportunity to advance the peace process would be lost.

In our discussion, Brent Scowcroft introduced an important new theme. He said the settlements were declared illegal.

"If so," I responded, "that's new policy. They haven't been under either President Reagan or President Bush. The policy has been that settlements were unwise . . . but not illegal."

"Under Carter," Scowcroft reminded me, "settlements *were declared* illegal, but you're right. They aren't considered to be now." Despite that acknowledgment, it was clear to me that President Bush would stand firm on his settlements-loan guarantees position.

When I came back from the meeting, I was convinced that the president was not playing games. These were matters of principle for him: Settlements were an obstacle to peace. And, settlements and loan guarantees were irreconcilable. The Israelis had to choose one or the other. I decided to call Prime Minister Shamir immediately on my return to Columbus. My message amplified what I had already told Shamir on July 5. Shamir's information, and his belief that he could defeat Bush through a Congressional vote was, in my judgment, just plain wrong. I recounted what I had learned in Kennebunkport word for word, but Shamir wouldn't budge. My advice to Prime Minister Shamir was that the president was adamant: either loan guarantees *or* settlements, and it was my judgment that Bush's position would prevail in Congress. The president was not about to waver. "Gordy, if I back down now," Shamir said, "the Arabs will be dancing on their rooftops that America has shifted away from its strategic support for Israel. This will be seen as a sign of weakness in the American-Israeli alliance, and it will be an invitation to war."

On Thursday, September 5, I went to the Conference of Presidents of major Jewish organizations in the United States. This body was responsible for charting the best political course for the organized American Jewish community to take in support of Israel. I told them what the president of the United States was contemplating. They thought he was trying to use me to create alarm within the community, so they would weaken in their resolve to support loan guarantees. I told them that the president and the secretary of state did not believe there would be sufficient Congressional votes to override the administration on this. The White House had decided that linkage did indeed exist, i.e., the settlements would be financed by the loan guarantees, therefore no loan guarantees.

All hell was about to break loose. Shamir had agreed to keep the public pressure low on the loan guarantees until September 6. Baker pressed him for a further deferral of the matter until after the peace conference took place, and Shamir dismissed that idea. Spontaneously, President Bush called the press into the Oval Office and said he wanted a 120-day delay on the issue of loan guarantees. "We don't need an acrimonious debate just as we're about to get this peace conference convened," he maintained.

The response of the American Jewish community was thunderous. On September 12, one thousand Jews converged on Capitol Hill. Their purpose was to lobby Congress in support of loan guarantees. The president gathered the press together on the same day to address the issue again in less than a week, saying: "We're up against very strong and effective . . . groups that go up to the Hill. I heard today there were something like a thousand lobbyists on the Hill working the other side of the question. We've got one lonely little guy [namely me, President Bush] down here doing it." He reiterated his call for a 120-day delay and vowed he would veto Congressional support for loan guarantees should the Congress pass a measure earlier than that.

Consider the arithmetic. First, this was not a grant. It was only a guarantee. Israel has been in the debt market ever since its founding in 1948. Over those fifty-seven years, it has never defaulted on either the interest or principal payments it owed. Let's assume that Israel went to market for $10 billion worth of bonds. The U.S. government guarantee would have yielded perhaps a two point advantage in interest rates.[3] That's $200 million a year. Over the 10 year duration of the bonds, that amounts to $2 billion. However, since you have to start to make payments during the life of the bonds, the net advantage over ten years would be more in the neighborhood of $1 billion. The bottom line: Israel was seriously aggravating, and testing its relationship with its greatest ally by far, for the sake of a billion dollars. And, based on history and the strength of its economy within the region, the likelihood that Israel might default was statistically insignificant. There was no existential threat involved here. A billion dollar financial advantage over ten years at the price of alienating the only ally who could—and who had—rescued Israel from genuine threats to its very existence was, in my opinion, a very unwise tradeoff.

Between September 12 and October 2, James Baker saved the day. He was able to persuade the Israelis to postpone the request for loan guarantees. Baker softened the atmospherics and avoided what would have been a disaster. On October 2, the Senate—knowing that the heat was now off—agreed to defer the loan guarantees issue per President Bush's request. On October 20, the Israeli cabinet agreed to have Israel participate in a peace conference in Madrid.[4]

Prime Minister Shamir did not expect Yitzhak Rabin to beat him in the Israeli national elections in June 1992, which he of course did. Shamir was convinced Labor's course would result in national suicide. Shamir's views were his deepest commitments of principle, to what he believed was necessary for the security of the State of Israel. Still he was willing to put those views on the table and expose them to risk, in order to pursue the possibility of peace without preconditions, in a direct, bilateral negotiation. He wanted to put the settlements issue aside. He also expected the loan guarantees to be forthcoming without linkage to the settlements or the peace process. He expected the U.S. to approve the loan guarantees needed to absorb the people coming out of the former Soviet Union strictly on humanitarian grounds.

Did Shamir really want peace? I believe he did and that he genuinely wanted to make a deal with the Arabs. Shamir felt autonomy for the Palestinians was the appropriate next step. He was willing to go five years to conclude a deal with the Palestinians and the Syrians. In fact, he had a state of no war both with Jordan and Syria.[5] Following the collapse of the Soviet Union and without an Iraq capable of making war, he felt he could preserve the state of no war and that was okay with him. Shamir didn't care about making peace with Syria. What *did* he care about? Resolving the regional instability that was destructive to the growth of the Israeli economy, settling the Soviet Jews, and addressing the issues of tension between America and Israel. But Shamir wasn't prepared to give up an inch. He didn't feel he had to.

1 The loan guarantees were finally secured in 1992, after years of negotiation with the United States. The formally stated purpose of these guarantees was to support "Israel's extraordinary humanitarian effort to resettle and absorb immigrants from the republics of the former Soviet Union, Ethiopia, and other countries."

2 The U.S. supplied Patriot Anti-Missile Missiles to Israel to combat the Scuds. The supply included U.S. training to operate this defense system, but the Israelis themselves actually manned the launchings. The effectiveness of the defense system remains questionable and may have been a consequence of either less than ideal intercept rates by the Patriots or a tendency of the Scuds to self-destruct . . . or both.

3 As a benchmark, the prime rate in September 1991 was 8%.

4 That the Soviet Union attended the conference had its amusing side. A coup against Gorbachev had been attempted just two months before the conference opened. Less than two months after the conference was convened, the USSR was dissolved!

5 In certain situations, a lasting peace may take generations to attain or may never be achievable. In those cases, 'no war' or the commitment to defer war may be the only practical option.

Suggested Readings and Resources

Histories of the Jewish People and of Israel

Dimont, Max I., *Jews, God and History,* 2nd ed. New York: New American Library, 1994. If you are looking for a book or source that reveals how Jews and Judaism have contributed to civilization, this is it. What's more, Dimont's account is a remarkably straightforward and breezy read.

Eban, Abba Solomon, *Heritage: Civilization and the Jews,* New York: Simon & Schuster, 1984. "This is the story of a small people with a large place in the destiny of mankind," as Eban himself writes. A breathtaking exploration by one of the most learned and engaging people I was ever privileged to meet.

Johnson, Paul, *A History of the Jews,* New York: Harper & Row, 1987. Johnson is a consummate history writer, and his treatment is as rich in anecdotes as it is thoughtful in its overall viewpoint.

Konner, Melvin, *Unsettled: An Anthropology of the Jews,* London and New York: Penguin Books, 2004. An intriguing treatment of Jewish history seen as a series of cultural epochs in the context of civilization generally.

The Long Way Home, Koch Lorber Films, 1997. This is a powerful account of the Jewish experience after the nightmare of the Holocaust—between the end of World War II and the creation of the state of Israel in 1948. It tells the story of survivors, scattered in displaced persons camps and denied entry to Palestine, and their journey to become nation-builders in a new land.

Sachar, Howard M., *A History of Israel: From the Rise of Zionism to Our Time,* New York: Alfred A. Knopf, 1976, 1996. An indispensable and authoritative guidebook tracing the evolution of the State of Israel and the defining moments in its history.

Sachar, Howard M., *A History of the Jews in the Modern World*, New York: Alfred A. Knopf, 2005. A great companion to Sachar's *A History of Israel*. The storytelling is so vibrant you never notice the masterful scholarship behind it.

Sachar, Howard M., *Farewell España*, New York: Vintage, 1995. The tragic and compelling story of the Sephardic Jews and their departure from Spain after the Inquisition.

Biographies and Autobiographies of Leaders

Bar-Zohar, Michael, *Ben-Gurion: The Armed Prophet*, Upper Saddle River, New Jersey: Prentice-Hall, 1968. An insightful account of the life of Israel's founding father and first prime minister.

Begin, Menachem, *The Revolt*, New York: Nash Publishing, 1977. This book is presently available in at least two different editions. The trials and triumphs in founding the state of Israel by one of the great leaders in that struggle, and how character and courage were constantly tested.

Cooke, Robert, *Dr. Folkman's War: Angiogenesis and the Struggle to Defeat Cancer*, New York: Random House, 2001. A compelling account of one of our time's great scientists, courageously engaged in one of history's most monumental scientific challenges.

Friedman, Rabbi Herbert A., *Roots of the Future*, Jerusalem and New York: Gefen Publishing House, 2001. A charismatic leader who has led an electrifying life. One of the few remaining heroes who participated in founding the Israeli state. Courageous and determined in rescue missions, he has earned the highest honor Israel can confer.

Golden, Peter, *Quiet Diplomat: Max M. Fisher*, New York: Cornwall Books, 1992. This authoritative chronicle captures countless details of Max Fisher's remarkable life and how he became a titan among leaders within the American Jewish community.

Herzog, Chaim, *Heroes of Israel: Profiles of Jewish Courage*, Boston: Little Brown, 1971. A thoughtfully crafted account of Jewish leaders and the courage that allowed them to help shape Jewish history.

Hurwitz, Zvi Harry, *Menachem Begin,* Jerusalem: Gefen, 2004. The firsthand story of one of Israel's founding fathers by the head of the Menachem Begin Heritage Center in Israel.

Kampelman, Max M., *Entering New Worlds,* New York: Random House, 1992. This book is currently unavailable, but if you can find a copy at your public library or buy it used, then don't pass up the chance. It's the remarkable saga of a World War II pacifist who was later to become Ronald Reagan's chief arms negotiator!

Kasich, John, *Courage is Courageous: Ordinary People Doing Extraordinary Things to Change the Face of America,* New York: Doubleday, 1998. Inspirational to say the least, this book is a chronicle of everyday folks reaching out to take command of their defining moments.

Meir, Golda, *My Life,* New York: Putnam, 1975. A prime minister's personal account of a remarkable life, and an insight into the extraordinary contributions she made to the young state of Israel. Although currently unavailable, Meir's version of her own life is the best, and may be obtainable through your library.

Sharansky, Natan, *Fear No Evil: The Classic Memoir of One Man's Triumph Over a Police State,* New York: Public Affairs, 1988, 1998. The subtitle says it all. This is must reading: for inspiration and to understand the struggle between good and evil and democracy and tyranny in the modern world.

Wiesel, Elie, *Night,* New York: Farrar Straus & Giroux, 2006. One of the great personal documents of all time. A journey through evil in Auschwitz and Buchenwald by a survivor and Nobel Prize winner.

Jewish and Israeli History Illuminated through Maps

Gilbert, Sir Martin, *The Arab-Israeli Conflict: Its History in Maps,* UK/USA: Routledge, 2005. The history of Israel has hinged on its geographic relationship with its neighbors. Gilbert's book reveals the essence and the relevant detail involved.

Gilbert, Sir Martin, *The Routledge Atlas of Jewish History,* London and New York: Routledge, 2003. The geographic odyssey of the Jews over history captured in 140 insightful maps.

Jewish Thinkers and Judaism

Freedman, Shalom, *Living in the Image of God: Jewish Teachings to Perfect the World (Conversations with Rabbi Irving Greenberg)*, Northvale, New Jersey and Jerusalem: Jason Aronson, Inc. 1998. A top Jewish thinker tackles matters of great relevance in the modern world.

Hartman, David, *A Living Covenant: The Innovative Spirit in Traditional Judaism*, Woodstock, Vermont: Jewish Lights Publishing, 1998. A brilliant and independent interpretation of Judaism and reflections on life.

Heschel, Rabbi Abraham Joshua, *God in Search of Man: A Philosophy of Judaism*, New York: Farar Straus & Giroux, 1976. An extraordinary scholar whom I was blessed to know and learn from personally. Readers will find his linkage of God and humanity compelling and remarkably accessible.

Kaufman, Robert G., *Henry M. Jackson: A Life in Politics*, Seattle, Washington: University of Washington Press, 2000. A meticulous and engaging exploration into the career of one of America's most independent, effective and courageous political leaders.

Mendelssohn, Moses, *Jerusalem or on Religious Power and Judaism*, Waltham, Massachusetts: Brandeis University Press, 1983. The eighteenth-century Jewish philosopher Moses Mendelssohn was a titan of the Enlightenment. This classic outlines the religious foundation of Judaism.

Sharansky, Natan (with Ron Dermer), *The Case for Democracy: The Power of Freedom to Overcome Tyranny and Terror,* New York: Public Affairs, 2004. A totally current analysis of the political struggle that is the centerpiece of international relations today.

Telushkin, Rabbi Joseph, *Jewish Literacy*, New York: HarperCollins, 1991. In this collection of more than three-hundred brief chapters, Rabbi Telushkin documents the essence of Jewish thought and wisdom.

Washofsky, Mark, *Jewish Living: A Guide to Contemporary Reform Practices,* New York: UAHC Press, 1997. Reform Jewish practice as explained by a leading teacher with an emphasis on application in everyday life.

Fictional Accounts of the Jewish Experience
Based on Historical Realities

Michener, James A., *The* Source, New York: Fawcett, 1986. An eminently readable history of the Jewish people traced as a genealogy of fictional individuals, and written by a gifted expert in epics.

Uris, Leon, *Exodus,* New York: Bantam, 1983 (paperback reissue). The epic fictional account of the founding of Israel with an uncanny grasp of the drama and feelings of a momentous epoch.

Uris, Leon, *Mila 18, New York: Bantam,* 1983 (paperback reissue). You won't forget this account of World War II and the Holocaust, but you will forget it is fictionalized in an instant. The treatment of the Warsaw Ghetto is a masterpiece.

Leadership, Motivation and Networking

Bennis, Warren and Bert Nanus, *Leaders: The Strategies for Taking Charge,* New York: Harper Perennial Library, 1985. Leadership's most respected guru outlines the principles of leadership in straightforward terms.

Giuliani, Rudolph W. with Ken Kurson, *Leadership,* New York: Hyperion, 2002. A remarkable leader who turned around the fortunes of New York City, and admirably led the city in one of America's darkest moments in 2001.

Hoffer, Eric, *The True Believer: Thoughts on the Nature of Mass Movements,* New York: Harper Perennial Modern Classics, 2002. Hoffer's vintage study rings as true today as when it was initially published in 1951. This crisply written account of mass movements is a must for understanding the workings of modern global politics.

Mackay, Harvey, *Dig Your Well Before You're Thirsty,* New York: Doubleday: 1997. Acknowledged as the most practical and authoritative guide to networking written by a master networker and opinion leader.

Riordan, William L., *Plunkitt of Tammany Hall,* New York: Signet Classic, 1995. Just for fun! This chestnut is a century old and is a textbook not in leadership, but in wily political survival.

Miscellaneous, but significant

Taneva, Albena and Ivanka Gezenko (editors), *The Power of Civil Society in a Time of Genocide: Proceedings of the Holy Synod of the Bulgarian*

Orthodox Church on the Rescue of the Jews in Bulgaria 1940–1944,
The Sofia University Center for Jewish Studies and Sofia University
Press, St. Kliment Ohridski, 2005. Illuminating source documents tracing the Bulgarian Orthodox Church's remarkable role in defying Nazi-
inspired evil.

Yergin, Daniel, *The Prize: The Epic Quest for Oil, Money & Power,* New
York: The Free Press, reissue, 1993. Probably the most authoritative
single work on how oil has affected the world's power structure and—
very directly—the fate of Israel in our age.

NOTE: Quotes and references to Senator Henry Jackson appearing on
pages: 168, 186–191, and 205 are drawn from Robert G. Kaufman's book *Henry M. Jackson: A Life in Politics,* (Seattle, Washington: University of Washington Press, 2000).

Web Sites

There are a number of excellent Web sites with information about Jewish
affairs and Israel. Readers may find the following particularly useful.

www.chabad.org: This colorful Web site includes extensive personal background on the Rebbe and captures the passion and enthusiasm of the
Lubavitchter movement.

www.jafi.org.il/education/jafi75/index.html: If you're looking for a time-
line of defining moments in Israel's history from independence to the
present day, you'll find none better.

www.jewishfamily.com: A wonderful guide to contemporary Jewish parent-
hood and family life.

www.jta.org: An authoritative source for breaking Jewish news around the
world.

www.jewishvirtuallibrary.org: A rich resource with an excellent glossary
and an outstanding collection of overview biographies.

www.jnf.com: This is the Web site of the Jewish National Fund—a leading
force in the physical development of the land of Israel and the education of Jews worldwide. Learn about the exciting goals of Blueprint
Negev. A forthcoming Web site is under construction that will be
linked to the JNF Web site to keep readers of *Defining Moments*
posted on current information related to this book.

A Chronology of Defining Moments

January 1933	Hitler comes to power as chancellor of Germany.
1935	The viciously anti-Semitic Nuremberg Laws articulating Nazi racist principles and guidelines against the Jews and other minorities are enacted.
September 1938	The Munich Conference is held in which the the European Allies agree to try to appease Nazi Germany and allow its annexation of the Sudetenland from Czechoslovakia in the vain hope of preventing World War II.
1939–1945	World War II, and 50 million people are killed, including 6 million Jews who are murdered simply for the crime of being born.
June 21, 1941	Germany invades the Soviet Union, terminating the non-aggression pact between the two countries.
February 1943	The battle for Stalingrad (today Volgograd) ends after being waged for most of a year. It is the bloodiest single battle in human history with nearly two million military and civilian casualties. Hitler's defeat at Stalingrad marks the turning point for the Eastern Front of Europe in World War II.
January 1944	Hitler's siege of Leningrad, which had begun in September 1941, ends in defeat for Germany and the Axis powers.
January 1944	The War Refugee Board is formed in the United States and headed by Treasury Secretary Henry Morgenthau. This is the first direct U.S. initiative to save victims of

the Holocaust. A shamefully late and pitifully small effort, it nonetheless provided funding to finance Raoul Wallenberg's efforts to rescue Hungarian Jews.

March 1944	Germany invades Hungary, its one-time World War II ally.
May–July 1944	Approximately 550,000 Hungarian Jews are transported to the Nazi death camps and murdered.
June 6, 1944	The D-Day invasion at Normandy marks the turning point of World War II on the western front of Europe.
August 25, 1944	The Soviets "liberate" Romania.
September 1944	Germany withdraws from Bulgaria.
January 1945	The Soviets "liberate" Hungary.
January 26, 1945	Auschwitz is liberated.
November 29, 1947	The United Nations votes to partition Palestine into an Israeli state and a Palestinian state. The Arabs reject the partition.
May 14, 1948	The state of Israel is declared independent. A hundred million Arabs declare war on 600,000 Jews, who survive and prevail, but at the cost of 6,000 Israeli dead and thousands more wounded.
January 1950	Israel declares Jerusalem its capital.
1956	The Suez War in which France, Great Britain, and Israel overrun Egypt after Egypt nationalizes the Suez Canal. The United States demands all three nations withdraw from their positions. The canal is reopened, but remains closed to Israel between 1948 and 1975.
June 5, 1967	The Six-Day War: Israel responds to Egyptian provocations. East Jerusalem, the West Bank of the Jordan River, the Golan Heights, Gaza, and the Sinai Peninsula come under Israeli control.
1969	Golda Meir becomes prime minister and remains in office until 1974.
September 1970	Egyptian President General Nasser dies. Anwar Sadat becomes Egyptian president.
September 1970	Black September: Civil War breaks out in Jordan with a Palestinian attempt to overthrow King Hussein. The

Soviets are supplying Syria, and 300 Syrian tanks are poised on the Jordanian border waiting to invade Jordan. The U.S. prevails on Israel to be willing to become an ally of Jordan and resist the invasion, even though Israel is technically at war with Jordan. On the show of Israeli counterforce, the Syrian tanks are withdrawn. The PLO is ousted from Jordan and settles in Lebanon via Syria.

August 1972

The Soviet Union imposes the so-called "Diploma Taxes," which demand an exorbitant exit fee on any well-educated person wishing to emigrate. The measure is aimed at Soviet Jews.

January 30, 1973

Two former Nixon aides are convicted of charges relating to the Watergate incident.

May 18, 1973

The nationally televised Congressional hearings regarding the Watergate break-in begin in the United States.

October 6–26, 1973

Yom Kippur War: Egypt, Syria, Jordan and Iraq lead Arab nations in a surprise attack against Israel. Israel's survival is in peril, but the war is ultimately won with massive U.S. resupply. It becomes clear to the pro-Israeli community in the United States the center stage for protecting Israel's interests has shifted from the financial to the political arena.

October 10, 1973

Vice President Spiro Agnew resigns. Additionally, the White House continues to be embroiled in the Watergate controversy.

December 1, 1973

David Ben-Gurion dies at the age of 87.

April 11, 1974

Golda Meir resigns as Israeli prime minister after domestic criticism for Israel's lack of preparation preceding the Yom Kippur War. She is succeeded by Yitzhak Rabin.

October 1974

King Hussein renounces Jordanian claims to the West Bank to open the way for the PLO to establish a Palestinian state there.

August 8, 1974

Richard Nixon resigns as U.S. president; Gerald Ford replaces him.

January 3, 1975	The Jackson-Vanik Amendment goes into effect to eliminate trade benefits to any country with discriminatory emigration and human rights policies.
1975	King Faisal, who had ruled Saudi Arabia since 1962, is assassinated. He is succeeded by King Khalid.
July 4, 1976	Israel stages a successful commando raid in Entebbe, Uganda, to liberate remaining passengers of a Palestinian-hijacked Air France jetliner. The Athens-to-Paris flight initially had about 250 passengers. All but a hundred had been released. Those one hundred were either Jews and/or Israelis.
January 1977	Jimmy Carter becomes U.S. president.
April 7, 1977	Prime Minister Yitzhak Rabin withdraws as a candidate in national elections in Israel.
May 17, 1977	The Likud Party receives the largest number of votes in the Israeli general election, paving the way for Menachem Begin to become the first non-Labor prime minister.
November 20, 1977	In a historic visit to Jerusalem, Egyptian President Anwar Sadat addresses the Israeli Knesset.
September 17, 1978	Begin and Sadat sign Camp David Accords.
1978	Golda Meir dies.
1978	Natan Sharansky is imprisoned.
January 16, 1979	The Shah of Iran surrenders his office at the request of Prime Minister Shapour Bakhtiar, and departs for Egypt.
March 26, 1979	Israel and Egypt sign a peace treaty. Jordan opposes it.
July 1979	George H. W. and Barbara Bush make their first trip to Israel and meet with Avital Sharansky.
July 16, 1980	Ronald Reagan is nominated as the Republican presidential candidate.
November 4, 1980	Reagan wins election as U.S. president with an electoral college landslide of 489–49.
January 1981	Ronald Reagan inaugurated president with George H. W. Bush as his vice president. Alexander Haig is named Secretary of State.

1981	Israel annexes the Golan Heights.
March 30, 1981	Attempted assassination of Ronald Reagan.
April 3, 1981	President Reagan signs the AWACS executive order on his hospital bed.
May 28, 1981	Avital Sharansky meets with President Reagan in the Oval Office, and the president makes his pledge about the priorities of Soviet Jewry and Natan in the context of U.S.–Soviet relations.
June 7, 1981	Israeli Prime Minister Menachem Begin directs the Israeli Air Force to destroy the Osirak nuclear reactor near Baghdad, a reactor which had been built with French technology.
June 30, 1981	Menachem Begin is reelected as Israeli prime minister, defeating Shimon Peres.
October 1981	Egyptian President Anwar Sadat is assassinated.
July 16, 1982	George Shultz replaces Alexander Haig as U.S. Secretary of State.
1982	Fahd succeeds Khalid as king of Saudi Arabia.
June 6, 1982	Twelve-year Israeli incursion into Lebanon begins to drive Syrians and PLO terrorists from Israel's northern border.
November 12, 1982	Andrei Andropov becomes Soviet leader.
March 8, 1983	President Reagan makes "Evil Empire" speech.
April 18, 1983	Terrorist bombing of U.S. Embassy in Beirut kills thirty-two.
September 1983	Menachem Begin resigns as Israeli prime minister and is replaced by Yitzhak Shamir. Thereafter Begin lives a reclusive life until his death in 1992.
October 23, 1983	Terrorists blow up Marine barracks in Beirut, killing 241.
January 1984	The Shamir government in Israel falls.
February 1984	Konstantin Chernenko becomes Soviet leader on death of Andrei Andropov.
September 1984	After elections, a National Unity government is formed in Israel with Shimon Peres as prime minister. Yitzhak

Rabin rejoins the Israeli government and serves as defense minister.

November 6, 1984   President Ronald Reagan reelected in a second electoral college landslide, 525–13.

January 8, 1985   Donald Regan becomes White House chief of staff and James Baker becomes secretary of the treasury.

March 7, 1985   Vice President George H. W. Bush meets in Sudan with President Numeiry and Vice President Omar Tayeb, the head of the Sudanese Secret Police.

March 11, 1985   Mikhail Gorbachev becomes Soviet leader upon death of Konstantin Chernenko.

March 22, 1985   U.S. C5-As evacuate Ethiopian Jews from the Sudan in Operation Sheba.

May 8, 1985   President Reagan visits Bitburg and Bergen-Belsen.

October 7, 1985   The Italian cruise ship *Achille Lauro* is hijacked by the Palestinian Liberation Front to gain the release of Palestinians in Israeli prisons. A passenger is murdered because he is Jewish.

November 16, 1985 Geneva Summit meeting of Ronald Reagan and Mikhail Gorbachev.

October 1986   Roles reverse in Israel's National Unity government with Yitzhak Shamir becoming prime minister and Shimon Peres foreign minister.

February 11, 1986 Natan Sharansky is released from Soviet custody and crosses the East-West border in Berlin.

May 1986   The rally for Soviet Jewry takes place in New York. Natan Sharansky addresses the crowd of approximately 100,000.

August 1986   Natan and Avital Sharansky meet in Jerusalem with Vice President Bush.

October 11, 1986   Reykjavik Summit with Ronald Reagan and Mikhail Gorbachev. In a defining moment for the Cold War, President Reagan stands firm and a breakthough is reached in controlling intermediate-range nuclear weapons.

February 17, 1987	Howard Baker replaces Donald Regan as White House chief of staff.
December 1987	The First *Intifada* begins.
December 6, 1987	Vice President George Bush addresses the "Let My People Go" Rally on the Mall in Washington, D.C. An estimated 250,000 people attend Solidarity Sunday, including half of the members of Congress. The plight of Soviet Jews is given a high profile as Soviet leader Mikhail Gorbachev is in Washington to sign the INF intermediate arms treaty with President Reagan on December 8.
May 11, 1988	President Ronald Reagan endorses Vice President Bush's candidacy for U.S. presidential nomination.
January 1989	George H. W. Bush becomes U.S. President and Dan Quayle is vice president. James Baker becomes secretary of state.
December 1989	Andrei Sakharov dies in Moscow.
January 1990	Nathan Sharansky meets with President Bush in the Oval Office and discusses Sakharov's final message and the fate of Soviet Jewry.
March 12, 1990	Israel's National Unity government collapses. Yitzhak Shamir continues as prime minister. Yitzhak Rabin exits as defense minister.
May 1990	Boris Yeltsin becomes president of the Russian Republic.
August 2, 1990	Saddam Hussein invades Kuwait.
June 1991	Boris Yeltsin is democratically elected as the president of the Russian Federation.
January 15, 1991	Operation Desert Storm starts the Gulf War as the United States begins the ouster of Iraq from Kuwait.
August 1991	Attempted coup against Mikhail Gorbachev in the Soviet Union.
June 23, 1992	Yitzhak Rabin elected prime minister of Israel.
November 1992	Bill Clinton is elected president of the United States. After he assumes office, Warren Christopher becomes secretary of state.

September 13, 1993	Yitzhak Rabin and Yasser Arafat sign the Declaration of Principles in a ceremony hosted by President Bill Clinton on the White House lawn. This declaration marks the culmination of the Oslo Peace Talks and calls for a Palestinian commitment to recognize Israel and end terrorism. In exchange, Israel agrees to recognize the PLO.
1994	The Israeli Gaza Strip security barrier is erected.
April 22, 1994	Richard Nixon dies.
December 10, 1994	Shimon Peres, Yitzhak Rabin, and Yasser Arafat receive the Nobel Peace Prize.
October 26, 1994	Israel-Jordan peace treaty signed in Arava.
November 4, 1995	Israeli Prime Minister Yitzhak Rabin is assassinated. Shimon Peres becomes prime minister of Israel.
June 5, 1996	Benjamin Netanyahu elected Israeli prime minister and serves until 1999.
February 8, 1999	King Hussein of Jordan dies.
May 1999	Ehud Barak becomes Israeli prime minister.
December 1999	Russian President Boris Yeltsin resigns unexpectedly and is replaced by Prime Minister Vladimir Putin.
June 10, 2000	President Hafiz Assad of Syria dies.
March 2000	Vladimir Putin is elected president of the Russian Federation.
January 2001	George W. Bush becomes U.S. president. Dick Cheney is vice president. Colin Powell is appointed secretary of state.
September 2000	The Second *Intifada* begins.
February 6, 2001	Ariel Sharon is elected Israeli prime minister.
September 11, 2001	New York's World Trade Center destroyed, the Pentagon attacked, and a commercial jetliner crashed in Pennsylvania en route to an attack on the Capitol. The attack is perpetrated by nineteen Al-Qaeda homicidal terrorist hijackers, with a total of 2,948 confirmed dead and twenty-four missing.
Late 2002	Construction begins on the Israeli West Bank security barrier.

March 14, 2004	Vladimir Putin is reelected president of the Russian Federation.
June 2004	Ronald Reagan dies.
November 2004	George W. Bush is re-elected U.S. president. Ohio is the critical state providing the electoral margin of victory.
November 11, 2004	PLO leader Yasser Arafat dies in Paris.
November 2005	Ariel Sharon leaves the Likud Party and forms a new centrist party called Kadima.
January 4, 2006	Israeli Prime Minister Ariel Sharon suffers a massive stroke on his ranch in the Negev.
March 28, 2006	Acting Prime Minister Ehud Olmert leads the Kadima Party, receiving the largest number of votes in the Israeli general election.

Note: There are several dates included here on which there is no clear consensus. In some cases, dates include only the month and the year. The important objective has been to outline the flow of events.

Glossary

AIPAC—The acronym for the America Israel Public Affairs Committee, formed by Cy Kennan in the 1950s. This is a pro-Israel advocacy group that supports strengthening the America-Israel relationship. It is not a political action committee.

aliyah—The return of Jews from all over the world to the Jewish homeland of Israel.

Altalena—An Irgun-owned and commanded ship, loaded with much needed armament and ammunition, that was nonetheless attacked and destroyed by the armed forces of Israel on Prime Minister David Ben-Gurion's direction in June 1948. The attack took place during a temporary ceasefire in the War of Independence. This defining moment established the infant nation of Israel would have only one army.

American Jewish Joint Distribution Committee—(JDF, "Joint") Founded in the early twentieth century, the JDC was established to provide on the spot relief to Jews in the "pale of settlement" of Eastern Europe and continues to provide on-site relief to Jews worldwide to this day.

AWACS—An acronym for a highly sophisticated air command-and-control surveillance and intelligence system. Working over long distances, AWACS is capable of both identifying enemy aircraft and directing their destruction by means of friendly aircraft and weaponry.

Balfour Declaration—A 1917 British foreign policy statement advocating the creation of "a Jewish national home in Palestine."

Bar-Lev Line—A fortification system built on the eastern bank of the Suez Canal after Israel occupied the Sinai in the 1967 Six-Day War and intended as a first-line of defense against future attacks from Egypt.

Betar—A Palestinian-based Jewish youth movement founded in the early 1920s by Vladimir Jabotinsky. Betar is a Hebrew acronym for the

"League of Joseph Trumpeldor" and is named for a colleague of and co-fighter with Jabotinsky.

Bitburg—A city in Germany near the border with Luxembourg. Its cemetery was the site of a visit by U.S. President Ronald Reagan and German Chancellor Helmut Kohl on April 11, 1985. The visit was intended to be a show of final reconciliation between the U.S. and Germany following World War II, but the cemetery included the remains of more than forty members of the hated Nazi SS, and President Reagan's presence at this state ceremony led to an outcry on the part of the American Jewish community.

Black September—The unsuccessful attempt by the Palestinian Liberation Front (PLF), a faction of the PLO, to overthrow King Hussein in Jordan in September 1970 that led to the ouster of the PLF, first to Syria and then to Lebanon.

Chabad—A member of the Hasidic, Lubavitchter movement of Judaism, which began in Russia in the latter part of the eighteenth century.

Conference of Presidents of Major American Jewish Organizations—This body was established in 1954 to help coordinate initiatives within the American Jewish community and includes the heads of fifty-two autonomous Jewish organizations.

Council of Jewish Federations and Welfare Funds—A national organization that provided advisory and best-practices guidance to its members, which totaled approximately 170 Jewish communities (federations). The Council was merged into the United Jewish Communities in 1999.

Diaspora—Literally "scattering" in ancient Greek. The first use of Diaspora refers to the expulsion of the Jews from Biblical Israel to Babylonia in the 6th century BCE. The far more relevant use of the term Diaspora describes the dispersal of Jews by the Romans after the destruction of the Second Temple in 70 A.D. and the Roman attempt to force assimilation of the Jews throughout the Roman Empire by denying them a homeland.

Etzel—*See* Irgun.

Evian Conference—The Evian Conference, involving thirty-two countries, took place in July 1938 in Evian, France, to discuss the fate of European Jews. The conference wasn't even able to reach sufficient consensus to pass a resolution condemning Nazi Germany's systematic program of terrorization against the Jews. The only country to make a serious offer of refuge for the Jews was the Dominican Republic.

Gachal (also Gahal)—An Israeli political party established in 1965, and a cornerstone for what was later to become Likud.

Green Line—Boundaries defined by the armistice after the 1967 War reflecting territories captured and occupied in that conflict. Of those territories, East Jerusalem, the Golan Heights, and Gaza were immediately annexed by Israel. The permanent status of the West Bank was not established, and Israel ultimately exited Gaza in 2005. The United States prohibits the use of any U.S. taxpayer dollars to fund Israel's development of land beyond Israel's 1948 boundaries.

Haganah—A Jewish self-defense organization in Palestine operating under the direction of the Jewish Agency and formed during British rule of Palestine. The Haganah later became the basis of the present-day Israeli Defense Forces.

Hasidic—Most recently in Jewish history, describing Orthodox Jews who follow precepts originating in Eastern Europe in the early 18th century. *See also Chabad.*

Intifada—Two eras of Palestinian terrorist activity, beginning in 1987 and 2000 respectively, directed at Israel and characterized by rioting and other acts of destruction against human life and property.

Irgun (Zvai Leumi)—An underground Jewish military organization operating in Palestine between 1931 and 1948. Its most important leader was Menachem Begin. Also known by the term Etzel.

Jackson-Vanik Amendment—Legislation denying U.S. trade benefits to any country with discriminatory emigration and human rights policies. The bill was cosponsored by Washington Senator Henry Jackson and Ohio Congressman Charles Vanik. It became law on January 3, 1975. The Amendment also gives the President the option to sign annual waivers to its provisions to selected countries. The People's Republic of China was one country that received such waivers in the past.

Jewish Agency—Founded in 1923, the Jewish Agency was originally designed to represent the interests of Jews living in Palestine. It grew to become a government of Jews in exile in anticipation of the founding of a Jewish state.

Jewish National Fund (JNF)—Founded in 1901 by the World Zionist Organization, the original purpose of the JNF was to raise money to acquire land in Palestine from Arabs prior to the establishment of the state of Israel in 1948. To this day, the JNF remains the largest landowner of real estate in Israel after the Israel Land Authority. Over time, the JNF's mission has changed. After Israel's establishment, the JNF's next goal was the development of water systems, forestry, and soil-protection programs within Israel. Today the JNF is the main bridge linking the Jews of the United States and Israel on social and economic issues. The JNF is active in leadership development and education and pro-democracy advocacy in U.S. high schools and colleges. The JNF's leading current priority is to increase the population of the Negev desert by a quarter million Jews in the next five years.

Jewish Brigade—Made up of Jews native to the Middle East and European Jews who had resettled in Palestine, the Jewish Brigade was a unit of the British army formed in September 1944.

Jewish Legion—A military organization that was founded by Vladimir Jabotinsky and which fought with the British against the Turks in Palestine during World War I. Participation in the Jewish Legion, and later the Jewish Brigade, gave Jews the opportunity to learn military skills, discipline, and organization which were invaluable in conducting Israel's War of Independence.

Knesset—The Israeli Parliament. The Parliament currently has 120 seats. Regular parliamentary elections occur every four years.

Kristallnacht—A German word meaning "crystal night." It has come to mean "the night of broken glass." Kristallnacht occurred in Germany and Austria during the dark hours of November 9–10, 1938. The crystal in synagogues was destroyed, and many Jewish religious and secular buildings were set afire. Brutal and widespread devastation of human life and property took place. This Nazi campaign also resulted in the flagrant, unjustified arrests of Jews, and the destruction of Jewish homes and businesses.

Ladino—A language that is a mixture of medieval Spanish and Hebrew. It is used primarily by the Sephardic Jews of Eastern Europe.

Lebanon—This country was the site of the most recent of the six wars in which Israel has been engaged in the Middle East. In 1982, Israel advised the United States it would wage an offensive reaching 22 kilometers into Lebanon intended to disable Palestinian rocket attacks. The resulting engagement, which during one phase extended as far as Beirut, enmeshed Israel for eighteen years.

Lechi—A faction of the Irgun that separated itself in 1940 as an anti-British underground group in Palestine. Yitzhak Shamir, later Israeli Prime Minister, was Lechi's most prominent member. Also known as Lehi.

Likud—A coalition of conservative factions that was first organized in 1973 in opposition to the ruling Labor Party, and which scored its first national victory in elections in 1977 under Menachem Begin.

Loan guarantees—In 1989, Israel faced a dramatic surge in immigration from the Soviet Union. As a result, Israel sought loan guarantees from the United States that would earn Israel a financial advantage in its borrowing of $10 billion on the international bond market.

Lubavitscher—*See Chabad.*

Madrid Peace Conference—Convened after the Gulf War in October 1991, this was the first official direct meeting of Israel with Arab states other than Egypt. The most lasting outcome of the Madrid Conference was that it laid the groundwork for a peace treaty between Israel and Jordan, signed in July 1994.

minyan—A quorum of ten adult Jews needed to create a Jewish community in which Jewish practices and rites can be conducted. Traditionally, and for Orthodox Jews yet today, all members of a *minyan* must be male.

Mossad—The Israeli equivalent of the U.S. Central Intelligence Agency.

Munich Conference—The international meeting that led to an agreement made on September 10, 1938 between Britain, France, Germany and England that ceded the Sudetenland portion of Czechoslovakia in a misguided effort to avert a second world war beginning in Europe. This act of appeasement to Hitler was brutally breeched when Hitler staged his unprovoked invasion of Poland on September 1, 1939.

National Unity Government—During several periods in Israel's history, the nation has been governed by a coalition of what have historically been the two leading parties—Labor and Likud.

Nuremberg Laws—These were enacted at the national convention of the Nazi party in September 1935. In them, all German Jews were stripped of their citizenship in a demeaning ultimatum. Other measures in the Laws deprived Jews of basic human rights and freedoms and any form of legal protection. Under the Laws, a Jew was defined as any person who was of at least one-eighth Jewish ancestry.

Operation Moses—This Israeli airlift of 7,800 Ethiopian Jews from Sudan used Israeli planes and took place between November 1984 and January 1985. It resulted in the evacuation of 7,800 Ethiopian Jews to Israel.

Operation Sheba—Also known as Operation Joshua, began on March 28, 1985, and was a U.S. mission that utilized U.S. Air Force planes to airlift 494 imperiled Ethiopian Jews from Sudan to refuge in Israel.

Operation Solomon—This Israeli-organized evacuation of 14,324 Jews from Ethiopia's capital took place on May 24, 1991, utilizing Israeli El Al jets and U.S. Air Force transports. The rescued Jews were resettled in Israel.

Oslo Peace Talks—Secret talks held in 1993 between Israel and the Palestinian Liberation Organization that ultimately led to the signing of an agreement of mutual recognition between Israel and the Palestinians on the White House lawn in September 1993. Since Oslo, the effectiveness of this diplomatic initiative has been viewed with significant skepticism given Palestinian unwillingness to live up to agreements entered into with Israel.

Pale of Settlement—From 1835 to 1917, the twenty-five provinces in tsarist Russia where Jews were permitted to live. The Pale (which means boundary line) circumscribed portions of what was then western Russia and today includes parts of Russia, Ukraine, Poland, Belarus, and Lithuania. Jews in the Pale were subject to brutal conditions and pogroms that resulted in the deaths of thousands. Once the home to five million Jews, the Pale held the largest Jewish population in the world and was the home of most of the 2.5 million Jews who ultimately emigrated to the United States between 1875 and 1917.

Palestine Liberation Organization (PLO)—Formed in 1964, a coalition of various Palestinian nationalist organizations that became autonomous in 1967, and was headed by Yasser Arafat between 1969 and his death in 2004.

Palmach—Established in 1941, an elite combat and Jewish leadership unit within the Haganah.

payos—These are the traditional locks worn as a hairstyle by traditionally observant Orthodox men.

Rebbe—Spiritual leader of a Hasidic community. The title is generally dynastic, but not always.

refuseniks—Soviet Jews barred in their effort to emigrate to Israel, especially those in the 1970s and 1980s.

Righteous Among the Nations—These are non-Jews who rescued Jews from Nazi persecution during World War II at personal risk to themselves and/or their families. Their heroic deeds are memorialized at the Yad

Vashem Holocaust Memorial outside of Jerusalem. Also known as the Righteous Gentiles.

Roadmap (for Peace)—A plan for the peaceful co-existence of Israel with its Arab neighbors first articulated by President George W. Bush in June 2002. The oversight of the Roadmap has been entrusted to the so-called "Quartet" comprised of the United States, Russia, the European Union, and the United Nations.

Sabra—A native-born Israeli, as well as a Jew born in Palestine before Israeli statehood in 1948.

Scud—A Soviet-designed tactical ballistic missile widely exported around the world including to Arab nations in the Middle East.

Shabbat (shabbas)—Hebrew for Sabbath or day of rest, extending from sundown Friday night to sundown Saturday night.

Six-Day War—In 1967, Israel's masterful military response to Arab provocations that resulted in Israel's gaining control of East Jerusalem, the West Bank, the Golan Heights, Gaza, and the Sinai. The trigger point of the Six-Day War was Egypt's illegal sealing off of the Straits of Tiran for shipping to and from the Israeli port of Eilat.

Stern Gang—*See* Lechi.

Straits of Tiran—This three-mile wide sea passage joining the Red Sea and the Gulf of Aqaba controls oceangoing access to Eilat, Israel's only southern seaport, and Aqaba, Jordan's only seaport.

Suez War—The 1956 war waged by Great Britain, France, and Israel after Egypt nationalized the Suez Canal. As an end to hostilities, the United States forced the withdrawal of Britain, France, and Israel from Egypt and the restoration of the canal's control to Egypt.

United Jewish Appeal (UJA)—Founded in 1939 to raise money in the United States to assist Jews in need throughout the world. After Israel came into being in 1948, the UJA's focus shifted to support Jews in distress who are living abroad and to fund their relocation to and absorption in free societies, primarily Israel, as well as providing on-the-spot humanitarian relief to be administered by the American Jewish Joint Distribution Committee for Jews living in Israel and elsewhere.

United Jewish Communities—Founded in 1999 when the United Jewish Appeal, the United Israel Appeal, and the Council of Jewish Federations and Welfare Funds merged to help formulate a national agenda for the American Jewish community. Included under this one umbrella in North America are more than 150 Jewish federations and 400 independent Jewish communities.

United Nations General Assembly Resolution 242—Adopted in 1967, the resolution calls for Israeli withdrawal from land occupied in the Six-Day War, but it insists that Arab states must recognize Israel's "right to live in peace within secure and recognized boundaries." The Resolution establishes that harmony between Israel and its neighbors will result from the transfer of land for peace, but it does not specify how much or which specific land will be exchanged, only that it will be agreed to by direct bilateral negotiation. In addition, the resolution addresses refugee issues and waterway access.

United Nations General Assembly Resolution 338—Adopted in 1973, the resolution was framed to bring about a ceasefire to the Yom Kippur War, and to call for the implementation of resolution 242.

War of Attrition—A conflict initiated by Egypt in 1968 to attempt to regain the Sinai, which it had lost to Israel in the Six-Day War of 1967. The hostilities ended in 1970 with a cease-fire and no change in Israel's and Egypt's relative positions vis-à-vis 1967.

War of Independence—Begun in 1947, before Israel was established as an independent state in 1948, and concluded in 1949. This was the initial conflict with Israel's Arab neighbors that accompanied the nation's creation, and Israeli victory astonished the world when 600,000 ill-equipped and militarily inexperienced Jews were able to defeat the collective might of 100 million Arabs.

War Refugee Board—A U.S. government agency created in January, 1944. It was headed by Treasury Secretary Henry Morgenthau to rescue Holocaust victims and focused particularly on the Jews of Hungary.

West Bank—The Biblical territories of Samaria and Judea west of the Jordan River captured from Jordan in the 1967 Six-Day War. Its outer perimeter is an element of the Green Line. The area is home to about 1.3 million Palestinians and 230,000 Jews.

weapon of mass destruction (WMD)—First used in 1937, the term has come to mean such non-conventional weaponry as nuclear, chemical, or biological devices that can inflict enormous loss of human life in a single attack.

Yamit—An Israeli settlement on the Sinai Peninsula created after Israel occupied the Sinai in the Six-Day War and exited in 1982, when Israel returned the Sinai to Egypt as a result of the Israel-Egypt Peace Treaty signed at Camp David.

yeshivah—The system of schools, often residential, which teach the Torah, Mishnah, and Talmud—the principles of Judaism—to young people.

Yom Kippur War—An Arab-Israeli War fought in October 1973, that began with a surprise attack by the Arab nations against Israel on the high holy day of Yom Kippur. Israel almost lost the war, and was saved only through the massive resupply efforts of the United States. The war ended after about three weeks with a ceasefire brokered by the United States and the Soviet Union.

Young Leadership Cabinet—(of the UJA) Founded in 1961, the purpose of the Young Leadership Cabinet has been to develop succeeding generations of leaders for Jewish organizations in the United States through, according to founder Herb Friedman: "raising people by strengthening their individual Jewish identities, linking their hearts and souls to the land of Israel and the worldwide people of Israel, [and] influencing their children's attitudes in their same direction."

Further definitions of terms about Judaism, Israel, and the Middle East can be found at an excellent Web site—the Glossary component of the Jewish Virtual Library. Its address is:

www.jewishvirtuallibrary.org/jsource/gloss.html

Acknowledgments

In 1981, shortly after the Reagan administration took office, my dear friend Norm Traeger paid me a visit. He brought me a tape recorder as a gift and said to me, "Gordy, you are going to have the opportunity to be involved in some extraordinary events in the coming years. You owe it to the Jewish people to make a record of your experiences, and some day you should write a book about them." I never used the tape recorder, but Norm was right about the book. The fact that I collected eighteen file drawers of notes over the next two decades was my response to Norm's suggestion. Without this documentation, I could not have written this book.

There are so many people to thank for their help and encouragement to me in my writing.

My good friend Harvey Mackay has written six bestsellers and sold over ten million books. Without Harvey's guidance and encouragement, this book would not have been written. He has mentored me throughout the entire process, and all I can say is thank you.

Harvey's most important contribution was recommending Ron Beyma as my collaborator. Ron is a consummate professional writer, researcher, organizer, and has become my friend. Without Ron this book could not have been written.

Harvey also introduced me to Arthur Klebanoff, my agent, who has guided me through the complexities of publishing and brought me together with Beaufort Books and Midpoint Trade Books. This was the perfect marriage for a new-to-market author.

Beaufort's principals—David Nelson, Eric Kampmann and Gail Kump—have over eighty years of experience in trade book publishing, sales, and distribution and have generated excellent distribution for this book. Susan Hayes did an outstanding job of editing. At Beaufort, I would like to thank Ian Kimmich for his coordination of book promotion and communications support. I also want to thank Amy King for her work on book jacket design.

Harvey also introduced me to David Hahn of Ruder-Finn's Planned Television Arts. He and PTA's Deborah Kohan developed and managed the public relations and publicity for the book.

Russell Robinson, the Executive Vice President and CEO of the Jewish National Fund, had the vision to see the value to the Jewish people and to the JNF of organizing and sponsoring my national book tour. In partnership with Sharon Tzur, President of Media Watch, under the capable leadership of Rabbi Zelig Chinitz, they are implementing a twenty-city tour. Zelig has also coordinated the overall launch plan for this book and helped in numerous logistical matters, ranging from confirming selected facts in the book to coordinating and integrating the activities of JNF, Media Watch, Beaufort Books, and PTA. Supporting Zelig in communications and logistics, Nora Marcus made an important contribution, especially in helping with the design of the book's Web site.

A special thank you to my daughter, Cathy Zacks Gildenhorn, who spent untold hours going through eighteen file drawers of backup material to help develop the documentation for the stories in this book. She was also a significant advisor in helping me to resolve how to match the book's tone with its targeted readership.

Some of the individuals profiled in the book were also of great help to me in reviewing their chapters of the book itself. These include Dr. Judah Folkman, Rabbi Herb Friedman, Annette Lantos, Natan and Avital Sharansky, and Elie Wiesel.

Thanks also to those who helped me in verification and vetting various chapters in the book: Richard V. Allen, former National Security Advisor to President Ronald Reagan; Jean Becker, Chief of Staff to former President George H. W. Bush; Arnauld de Borchgrave, Director for International Threats at the Center for Strategic and International Studies in Washington, D.C.; Jorge Diener, Shoni Pomerantz and Julia Dandalova of JDC operations in Bulgaria; Marjorie Fisher; Francine Friedman; Alan Gill, Executive Director of International Relations of the American Jewish Joint Distribution Committee; Don Gregg, former Ambassador to Korea and National Security Advisor to Vice President George Bush; Harry Hurwitz, Director of the Begin Institute in Jerusalem; Rabbi Areyah Kaltmann; Phyllis Kaminski; Richard Krieger, Associate U.S. Coordinator for Refugee Affairs in the Reagan Administration; Larry Moses, President of the Wexner Foundation; General Brent Scowcroft, National Security Advisor to Presidents Gerald Ford and George H. W. Bush; The George H. W. Bush Presidential Library; the Ronald Reagan Presidential Library; and the Yad Vashem Archives in Jerusalem.

Thanks as well to Amanda Piergiovanni; Jackie Gardner; Janice Beyma, Ron's wife and partner; Greg Bailey of Harvey Mackay's staff; and Annette Evdos—all of whom put forth extra special effort and administrative support to bring this book to market.

I want to also thank the sixty readers who gave me invaluable feedback to help make the book better and my appreciation to Tom Blumberg critiquing and improving the marketing plan.

Lastly, I must thank Jay and Jeanie Schottenstein, the Joseph Kanter Foundation, Jay and Jean Kislak, Harvey and Connie Krueger, the M. I. Homes Foundation, Bruce and Joy Soll, Norm and Carol Sue Traeger, and Fred and Kay Zeidman—all of whom helped fund the Leadership Caravan book tour.

And thank you to anyone and everyone whom I may have neglected to mention.

If the book proves helpful in developing pro-American, pro-democracy, pro-human rights, and pro-Israel leadership in the United States, all of the above share in the credit. If there are errors or mistakes in this book, they are mine alone.

Index